EASY GUIDE TO
SHAKESPEARE

EASY GUIDE TO
SHAKESPEARE

FALL RIVER PRESS

New York

FALL RIVER PRESS

New York

An Imprint of Sterling Publishing
387 Park Avenue South
New York, NY 10016

© 2007 by Spark Publishing

Published in 2014 by Fall River Press.

Illustrations by Daniel O. Williams/textile.net

ISBN 978-1-4351-5427-8

For information about custom editions, special sales, and premium and
corporate purchases, please contact Sterling Special Sales at 800-805-5489
or specialsales@sterlingpublishing.com.

Manufactured in the United States of America

2 4 6 8 10 9 7 5 3 1

www.sterlingpublishing.com

CONTENTS

PART I:
SHAKESPEARE THE MAN: Everything you really need to know about his life, career, and world

PART II:
SHAKESPEARE'S PLAYS: Everything you really need to know about each of Shakespeare's plays

The Top Ten: Ten plays that everyone should know

Plays That Show You're Really Well-Read

Plays with Which to Seriously Impress Your Teacher

Plays for Hardcore Shakespeareans

Bonus: Poetry!

EASY GUIDE TO
SHAKESPEARE

PART I

SHAKESPEARE THE MAN

Everything you really need to know about his life, career, and world

ONE

WHAT'S SO GREAT ABOUT SHAKESPEARE?

Does the Emperor Have Clothes?

Let's face it. Hearing people talk about Shakespeare can be pretty annoying. Particularly if you feel like you don't understand him. When people talk about which of Shakespeare's plays they like best, or what they thought of so-and-so's performance, they often treat Shakespeare like membership in some exclusive club. If you don't "get" him, if you don't go to see his plays, you're not truly educated or literate. You might be tempted to ask whether the millions of people who say they love Shakespeare actually know what they're talking about, or are they just sheep?

The Two Things That Make Shakespeare Worth Reading

The greatness of Shakespeare basically boils down to two things:

- the emotional impact of the stories he tells
- his use of language to convey character

SHAKESPEARE'S STORIES

For the most part, Shakespeare did not create his own stories. Of his thirty-eight plays, only *Love's Labor's Lost* and *The Tempest* seem to have been invented by him. Shakespeare mainly rewrote stories that had been told elsewhere. He adapted stories from history books about English kings, tragedies by the Roman playwright Seneca, biographies of ancient Romans written by Plutarch, and sometimes stories and characters from older romances (a romance is a long narrative in poetry or prose).

One thing that most of these stories have in common is that they deal with the extremes of human experience. People in these stories commit the worst possible crimes—murder, obviously, but also treason, regicide, patricide, maiming, dismemberment, and torture. Even in the comedies, people suffer the worst kinds of experiences, such as the loss of siblings (sometimes twins), parents, and children; the loss of money, status, and identity; public shaming; and so on. Another thing that many of these stories have in common is that in the original sources, the point of the story is not to show characters with complex motivations and rich, contradictory psychological profiles. (There are some exceptions, such as Plutarch's biographies or Chaucer's *Troilus and Cressida*.)

One of the chief differences between Shakespeare's plays and the stories they are based on is that Shakespeare is interested in the complexities of character and motivation and is able to make the emotions of these characters seem real. To understand why people find his plays so compelling, it helps to think of these two things at once: how extreme the stories are and how real he makes them feel. Most writers wouldn't touch the stories Shakespeare was attracted to because they're almost impossible not to turn into melodrama—overwrought, implausible nonsense. (Many modern adaptations of Shakespeare plays, such as *Othello* reset in a high school basketball team, seem interesting to us because we know

they're adapting Shakespeare—if they weren't adaptations they'd just be laughable.) But by taking these stories and pulling it off, Shakespeare creates plays that are unique in their emotional impact.

People who don't like Shakespeare often complain that the stories are in fact implausible and unrealistic. Why would Lear be so stupid as to give his kingdom to daughters who hate him? How could Othello become so jealous that he actually falls down in an epileptic fit? People who ask these questions are seeing something that's actually there (the extremeness and implausibility of the stories), but they're only seeing part of what's there. To see the other half, the emotional realism, you have to look at Shakespeare's use of language to convey character.

SHAKESPEARE'S USE OF LANGUAGE TO CONVEY CHARACTER

The two most basic facts about the language of Shakespeare's plays are (1) that it's virtually all dialogue (just a few stage directions here and there) and (2) that most of it is poetry. The fact that it's all dialogue means that characters are saying all of these words. When a character speaks in any piece of writing that we would consider literature, what the words tell us indirectly about the character is at least as important as what the words are actually saying. A character's speech *shows* us who he or she is at the same time that it conveys a message.

Shakespeare is not the first person to use poetry to write his dialogue. Poems have always had dialogue, and plays have always been written in verse (just think of *The Odyssey* and *Oedipus Rex*). But Shakespeare used poetry to create effective dialogue in a very new and innovative way. Poetry, together with rhetoric (the art of persuasive speaking or argumentation), features an entire arsenal of techniques that enable a writer to convey a message with both clarity and emotional force. Shakespeare mastered all of these techniques, such as metaphor, simile, repetition, rhythm, meter—the list would fill a book, and every student in Shakespeare's time *did* have a book that listed them.

But instead of using these techniques in the way they were intended to be used, to communicate a message or tell a story with emotional impact, he bent these techniques to show us something indirectly about the characters who were speaking these bits of poetry.

TWO

FAMOUS SHAKESPEARE LOVERS

It's not difficult to find people who are ready and willing to praise Shakespeare to the skies. Shakespeare has been praised to the point that he enjoys an almost mythical status in our society. However, the following five writers usually knew what they were talking about, and here's what they had to say about Shakespeare.

Ben Jonson (1572–1637)

Ben Jonson, a playwright and contemporary of Shakespeare, was one of the first (and most famous) people to grant Shakespeare the status that he holds without question today. Jonson wrote a dedicatory poem printed near the front of the first published collection of Shakespeare's plays, the 1623 First Folio. This poem includes the famous adage, "He was not of an age, but for all time," a sentiment that has been echoed by Shakespeare adulators in the centuries following. Jonson also praises Shakespeare's tragedies as equal to those of the best classical dramatists and claims that Shakespeare's comedic ability is unmatched by anyone else. Jonson mythicizes Shakespeare by likening him to the Roman gods Apollo and Mercury and envisioning him as a star in the sky with the power to judge the theater, which became desolate in his absence.

Alexander Pope (1688–1744)

Alexander Pope, the famous eighteenth-century English poet best known for *The Rape of the Lock*, was well known in his own time as the editor of a complete works of Shakespeare. In the preface to his edition, Pope praises Shakespeare's originality and the uniqueness of his characters.

> [E]very single character in Shakespeare is as much an Individual as those in Life itself; it is as impossible to find any two alike; . . . had all the Speeches been printed without the very names of the persons I believe one might have apply'd them with certainty to every speaker.

Though some have questioned the plausibility of Pope's assertion, his admiration for the diversity and naturalness of Shakespeare's characters has often been quoted.

Samuel Johnson (1709–1784)

Samuel Johnson, an early editor of Shakespeare's works, praises Shakespeare as a natural writer, one who writes about the desires and values common to all mankind. "Shakespeare is above all writers, at least above all modern writers, the poet of nature; the poet that holds up to his readers a faithful mirror of manners and of life." For Johnson, Shakespeare's power lies in his ability to accurately depict life, both its laughter and sorrow. However, Johnson criticizes Shakespeare for neglecting to provide moral instruction in his plays and claims that writers should not simply create the world as they see it but attempt to improve their world by creating a better one.

Thomas Carlyle (1795–1881)

Thomas Carlyle, the Scottish historian and satirist, furthered the Shakespeare myth by writing in his book *On Heroes, Hero-Worship, and the Heroic in History* (1841) that Shakespeare is a symbol to unite English men and women from around the world. That he "shine[s], in crowned sovereignty, over us all, as the noblest, gentlest, yet strongest of rallying-signs; indestructible." For Carlyle, Shakespeare's genius lies in revealing the "inmost heart" of a matter and that he portrays a varied range of characters with equal care and fullness. Carlyle believed that for years to come people would continue to relate to the astute characterizations of Shakespeare and claim him for their own. "Yes, this Shakespeare is ours; we produced him, we speak and think by him; we are of one blood and kind with him."

Ralph Waldo Emerson (1803–1882)

Ralph Waldo Emerson, the American poet and philosopher, claimed that Shakespeare "was the poet of the human race." Emerson praised Shakespeare's ability to express human experience and emotion beyond all other authors and noted that Shakespeare has "fulfilled the famous prophecy of Socrates, that the poet most excellent in tragedy would be most excellent in comedy." Emerson lectured publicly of the genius of Shakespeare and wrote about him in a book of essays called *Representative Men*. Emerson argued that the genius of Shakespeare lies in his wisdom, his humanity, and his language. "[H]e wrote the text of modern life; . . . he drew the man, and described the day, and what is done in it: he read the hearts of men and women." For Emerson, Shakespeare succeeded in documenting life to the point of expanding our understanding of our own existence.

THREE

HOW DID SHAKESPEARE GET SO SMART?

Good Timing

Shakespeare could not have become the author we know if he had lived in a different era. If he'd been born fifty years earlier, he would have died before England's first theater was built. Fifty years later, and the theaters would have been closed for the eighteen years during which he wrote his major plays. Genius depends in part upon luck and timing, and Shakespeare was truly a man of his day. While Ben Jonson, as noted earlier, famously said that his competitor "was not of an age but for all time," Shakespeare is immortal because he was the greatest writer of an excellent age.

When we ask what made Shakespeare so great, the answer must come in two parts: the materials that Shakespeare's society gave him to mold, and the inner genius that Shakespeare brought to the task of shaping them. For better or worse, we know a lot more about the society he lived in than we will ever know about his inner life.

A School Curriculum Focused Exclusively on Writing

Growing up in Stratford-upon-Avon, Shakespeare benefited from an excellent public education. He would have first learned to read and write in English, progressing from the alphabet to basic religious texts such as the Psalms and the Lord's Prayer. At about the age of seven, Shakespeare would have been sent to grammar school, as we still call it. The name, however, was more literal for Shakespeare than it is for us. Our grammar schools teach everything from science to social studies. At the King's New School in Stratford, and throughout England, Latin grammar was the chief subject. Without the modern-day variety of topics, Shakespeare and his fellow students received a Latin education whose rigor is almost unimaginable today. Shakespeare would have learned to read and write Latin through the repetition of model sentences and maxims. As he mastered those basics, he would have moved on to decomposing and reassembling arguments, and finally graduating to writing orations. All of this would have been done in a constant dialogue between English and Latin, translating from the one to the other and back again until the Latin both captured the English thought completely and conformed to the stylistic example of the classical masters.

Availability of World Classics in Translation

Shakespeare's education gave him greater command of languages than all but the brightest students today. Even so, he benefited along with the rest of English society from the outpouring of excellent translations in the sixteenth and early seventeenth centuries. Classics of Greek, Latin, French, Italian, and more gradually became available in editions which themselves helped to form the still-evolving

English language. Many of these versions became classics in their own right. Two centuries after Shakespeare's death, the poet John Keats still turned to George Chapman's 1598 translation of Homer to experience the Greek classic. The new wave of translations gave Shakespeare and the rest of England ready access to more great literature than had ever been possible before. These broad new horizons appear again and again in Shakespeare's plays.

Racy Stories Cheaply Available

Shakespeare's influences include mundane works as well as classics. Though he benefited from access to great books, he seems to have gained nearly as much from the culture of cheap print that London had to offer. Lurid ballads, scandalous broadsides, and murder pamphlets—the pulp fiction and gossip sheets of their day—were sold in book stalls alongside printed plays. These salacious tales offered Shakespeare a completely alternate set of plots and preoccupations from those available in great books. Shakespeare visited this world again and again as he prepared his plays. And like so much in his rapidly changing society, the world of cheap print would not have been available in any recognizable form even fifty years earlier.

Immersion in the Many Speech Patterns of London

Finally, Shakespeare was influenced not only by books but by the spoken word. Much of the greatness of Shakespeare's plays flows from their author's keen ear for the evolving language spoken around him. Over the years, people have argued that Shakespeare must have spent time as everything from a sailor to a lawyer to a falconer, all because he had mastered the dialect of those hobbies and professions and could reproduce convincingly the way such people spoke. Shakespeare's London was the sort of place where an attentive ear could hear innumerable professional and regional variants of English spoken, and the playwright seems to have listened more attentively than most anyone else.

FOUR

WHAT DID SHAKESPEARE CARE ABOUT?

No one has been more exhaustively researched than Shakespeare, yet what kind of person he actually was remains an enigma. Given the lifetimes that have been spent pursuing traces of him in archives, it's not likely that we're going to find out much more about his life than we already know. And it's remarkable just how little that is. There is so much that we would like to know about Shakespeare. Who were his friends, and who were his enemies? Did he tell a good joke? What did he like to do with his free time? (Well, that one's easy: He went home and wrote.) Above all, what *mattered* to him?

Money

Though we will never know as much as we want to about Shakespeare, we can begin to answer this basic question. To begin with, Shakespeare cared about what we all do: money. He achieved a great deal of financial success as a playwright, a profession not known for producing wealth, and that success did not come by accident. Actors reigned over writers on the Elizabethan stage much as they do in present-day Hollywood, and the proceeds were divided accordingly. Leading actors were shareholders in their companies, entitled to a cut of the profits, whereas playwrights generally worked for a flat fee. Shakespeare, in contrast, was both an actor and a writer for his company and a shareholder in it as well. When the Globe Theatre was built in the late 1590s, Shakespeare invested, buying an additional slice of revenue for himself. When the company began performing in the indoor Blackfriars Theater in 1608, Shakespeare again put money into the venture. The great playwright owned a substantial part of the major entertainment conglomerate of his day.

No starving artist, Shakespeare knew how to build a fortune for himself, how to keep it, and how to pass it along. Having watched his father fall from a position of affluence and status within their small village, he invested his money wisely and did not lose track of even small sums. In 1597, Shakespeare bought a large house in Stratford, permanently establishing his place in the community. By then he was known to be a man of some means; a letter from the following year records a rumor that he was looking to buy more property in the area. Several years on, he did just that, acquiring a substantial plot of good farming land just north of town. Shakespeare owned more than just property, however. Like any sensible investor, he diversified. He purchased a lease on a portion of the "corn, grain, blade and hay" produced in and around Stratford; it produced a steady, sizeable income for the rest of his life. He bought commodities directly, acquiring malt and selling it to his neighbors. When one neighbor failed to pay up, Shakespeare sued—not the only time that he would pursue a small debt in court. And when the time came to leave it all behind, Shakespeare wrote a will that protected his younger daughter from her suspect husband while providing richly for his older daughter and the descendants he hoped to, but would not, have.

Social Status

Shakespeare clearly cared about social status too. Shakespeare's father, John, had risen from being a glover to hold a series of public offices in Stratford, culminating in a term as bailiff—a very powerful version of a mayor—and many years as an alderman. At some point during these years, John Shakespeare applied for a coat of arms, which allowed a man to call himself a gentleman, in those days a formal title and not a vague description of manners. In theory, such an honor could only be inherited; in practice, it could be bought with enough money and social standing.

That description, however, did not apply to John Shakespeare for long enough to gain him the privilege. He seems to have fallen into financial straits in the late 1570s, and his application was never completed. Not, that is, until it was revived in 1596. Though we have no direct evidence that William Shakespeare renewed the request, by that year he was financially successful in the theater. No one else would have had both motive and means to pursue the matter. This time, the application went through. The Shakespeares were granted a coat of arms, complete with a motto translating as "Not Without Merit." Five years before his death, John Shakespeare was a gentleman, and so were his heirs. Shakespeare would sign his last will with that title. But his dedicated social climbing had drawn notice. In the sequel to *Every Man in His Humor*, a play in which Shakespeare performed, Ben Jonson includes a character who purchases a foolish coat of arms at great cost. A friend suggests a motto: "Not Without Mustard."

His Place in History . . . Well, Actually Not

We know what Shakespeare didn't care about: preserving his work. Though it is hard for us to imagine, the greatest English playwright seems to have made no effort to ensure that his achievements would survive him. At his death, only eighteen of Shakespeare's plays had been printed. All of these works appeared as quartos: small, single-play editions similar to a pamphlet in size and appearance. Perhaps the modern-day equivalent would be a paperback—not a volume meant to survive the ages. Moreover, it seems that Shakespeare played no role—aside from the obvious one—in making these books. His in-attention shows. *Hamlet,* for example, appeared in two substantially different quarto editions in Shakespeare's lifetime. One may have been produced by supporting actors recalling their lines as best they could, a process that produced such odd-sounding readings as "To be or not to be? Aye, there's the point." The second, much longer quarto may have been printed from a playhouse promptbook, or even from Shakespeare's manuscript. But there is no evidence that Shakespeare took the slightest interest in any of these matters.

Shakespeare did have other options and *could* have taken an interest in publication if he had so chosen. Ben Jonson saw his plays into print with impeccable attention. *Sejanus,* a drama set in Ancient Rome, was printed with scholarly notes citing classical authorities to justify the descriptions and the action of the play. The printer even employed a font resembling the inscriptions on Roman monuments to identify the act and scene divisions. Without question, Jonson was involved with every aspect of the printing. He even ensured that his masques—court entertainments that were even more ephemeral than plays, typically receiving only one production—were brought into print with much of the same care that was given to *Sejanus.* Jonson wrote a description of the costumes used in his *Hymenaei,* an entertainment performed for a noble wedding, that was four pages by itself.

When Shakespeare died in 1616, more than half of the plays we now have of his had never been printed. In that same year, Jonson published his *Works.* A large folio volume the size of a modern reference book, this edition was a landmark of English printing. For the first time, someone was claiming for modern plays an importance and a lasting value that had only been assigned to classical playwrights such as Plautus and Terence.

Jonson's book served as the model for the Shakespeare Folio, which was assembled by two of Shakespeare's friends after his death. Had it not been for John Heminges and Henry Condell, who edited that volume with such care, fully half of Shakespeare's plays would have been lost. What his literary reputation would have been we can only guess. Of all the mysteries about what mattered to Shakespeare, it is this gap that remains the most puzzling. The man who was sure to see that his life's fortune would survive him, passing from one generation of heirs to the next, paid no such attention to his life's work. If there is one thing that we can be sure Shakespeare cared about, it was his plays. Yet he didn't care to save them for us.

FIVE MYSTERIES OF SHAKESPEARE'S LIFE—AND WHY THEY MATTER

Was Shakespeare Gay?

Show this book to your Shakespeare professor, and he or she will laugh and tell you how misguided we are for even asking the question. In college, they'll tell you that first of all, no one was "gay" back then. Yes, sometimes men slept with men

(and women with women), and some men *only* liked to sleep with men,[1] but back then they didn't have these categories for talking about people as gay or straight or bisexual. And then they'll tell you that in Shakespeare's time, it was perfectly okay for men to praise each other's beauty and talk about loving each other—as we see some of Shakespeare's characters do, most notably the speaker of his sonnets—because it was customary to

---

[1] Shakespeare's great predecessor, the playwright Christopher Marlowe, was overheard in a tavern saying that "all they that love not tobacco and boys are fools."

flatter aristocrats in flowery rhetoric, or because male friendship was more idealized back then, or for a number of other reasons. And then they'll tell you that you're naïve for trying to infer things about an author's life based on his works.

There are some memorable gay characters in the plays, of course—Antonio, the merchant in *The Merchant of Venice,* is love-sick for Bassanio, and then there's another Antonio, in *Twelfth Night,* who's in love with Sebastian. Shakespeare even makes the mighty hero Achilles gay. But memorable minor characters obviously don't tell us anything about the author.

The sonnets, on the other hand, seem to offer something more personal. It would be foolish to assume that they're autobiographical, or that they're based on reality, but they do seem to tell a story about a man *like* Shakespeare, whose name is Will and who is an actor and a poet. In this story, that man, the speaker of the sonnets, first tries to persuade a young man to marry so that his beauty will be preserved, but then after the first seventeen sonnets, he gives up on that and writes love poetry to this man. Lots of love poetry. And not just praising him, but displaying jealousy and despair, creating guilt trips, bargaining with the loved one, and a range of other things that people do in love poetry. Toward the end of the sequence, he introduces a new character, his own mistress, who has gone behind his back and cheated on him with the young man he loves. This betrayal is a source of agony to the speaker, and the mistress is often a source of disgust, but generally the speaker says he still prefers the young man and values his friendship above the mistress's. That's pretty much it. You have to connect a lot of dots to even claim it's a coherent story, and it might be fiction, but despite what your professor will tell you about other sonnet sequences and conventions, no one else wrote anything remotely like this in Shakespeare's time.

Did Shakespeare Hate His Wife?

Notwithstanding Shakespeare's being gay or not gay, as the case may be, he certainly had a wife, Anne Hathaway, and is credited with having three children by her. We don't know much of anything about their relationship, since no letters between them survive and no one who knew them left a record describing what they were like as a couple. But the few facts that we do know have led many people to speculate that he must have hated his wife. The reason it matters is that Shakespeare made a very unusual life choice in deciding to leave his family behind in Stratford while he lived most of his professional life in London, supporting them from afar and occasionally visiting. If he hadn't gone to London, it seems most unlikely that he would have become who he became, so wanting to get away from his wife might have played a part in how Shakespeare became Shakespeare. Whether that's true or not, here are the facts.

THE SHOTGUN WEDDING

The marriage was hastily arranged, and the reason for that seems clear: Anne gave birth to a child six months later. She was twenty-six, which was old for a bride then, while he was only eighteen, ten years younger than the typical groom in those days. He also lacked a job and means to support them, so they moved into his father's house. Somewhere, someone may have had a happy marriage in similar circumstances, but the conventional wisdom is that all of this is a recipe for disaster.

THE LONG CAREER AWAY FROM HOME

This by itself might be evidence that he wanted to be away from her.

THE SECOND BEST BED

In his will, the only mention of his wife is "Item, I give unto my wife my second best bed with the furniture." This item comes after he be-queaths most of his fortune to his oldest daughter, Susanna, and gives a substantial gift of money to his daughter Judith. Not only do the goods go to the daughters, but their bequests are much longer and more detailed, in part because he takes elaborate precautions to ensure that Judith's husband won't get his hands on any of Shakespeare's principal.

Scholars have debated endlessly whether to interpret the "second best bed" as a pointed slight against Anne. Some say that the best bed was the one for guests, and that this was their marriage bed, perhaps with sentimental connotations. Others point out that the widow inherited a third of the estate automatically, so there was less need to spell things out.

THE TOMB

Shakespeare is buried inside Holy Trinity Church in Stratford-upon-Avon. He's not buried inside the church to honor him because he's a famous author. He's buried there because he paid a big sum to the church. So he knew he was going to be there and chose to be there. And his wife is not there with him. The epitaph on his tomb, which he is believed to have written, includes the lines "blessed be the man that spares these stones, / And cursed be he that moves my bones." In other words, don't put my wife here, and don't you *dare* move me out into the graveyard with her. Do you still want to argue that the second best bed had sentimental attachment?

Where Was Shakespeare During His Twenties?

Shakespeare married Anne Hathaway when he was eighteen, then had his daughter Susanna six months later, and then when he was twenty had twins, Hamnet and Judith. The next record that refers to him appeared when he was twenty-eight, and it makes clear that by that time he was in London acting and writing plays. Because we don't know what he was doing during those eight years, they're referred to as his "lost years." It would be nice to know, because these years hold the story of how and why he decided to leave his family in Stratford while he went to London and, more important, how he became an actor and writer. The following are some of the most common guesses.

HE WAS POACHING DEER

Kind of like Robin Hood. This story is about three hundred years old. Richard Davies, the same guy who first said Shakespeare was Catholic (see below), wrote that Shakespeare frequently stole venison and rabbits from the park of a rich man named Sir Thomas Lucy, who often had him whipped and imprisoned, and who finally drove him out of the area, forcing him to flee to London, which, as we know, worked out rather well for him. Another early biographer claims that Lucy forced Shakespeare to flee because Shakespeare wrote an especially nasty ballad attacking him—Shakespeare's first attempt at poetry. These stories probably aren't true, though. For one thing, Lucy didn't even keep a game park in that part of the country.

DOING THE CATHOLIC THING

As described in the next section, "Was Shakespeare Catholic?," he *might* have been working as an actor for the Catholic aristocrat Alexander Hoghton—if the reference to a "William Shakeshafte" in

Hoghton's will actually means Shakespeare. He could have gone to Hoghton's house as a tutor and then maybe gotten involved with the performers who worked for Hoghton. Or he could have made a living as a tutor in some other rich person's house.

HE WAS WORKING

He had to support his family somehow, and poaching deer and rabbits wouldn't have gotten the job done. Some people say he must have worked for a lawyer—his plays are crammed with legal knowledge and terminology. (They're also crammed with technical jargon and knowledge from many other professions.) He might have been a schoolmaster. How he found his way into the theater remains a mystery.

Was Shakespeare Catholic?

A lot of people would *really* like to know the answer to this one, and the answer feels so close we can almost touch it. The reason it matters whether Shakespeare was a Catholic is that it was illegal to be a Catholic in England during Shakespeare's lifetime. Queen Elizabeth had officially separated the Church of England from the Catholic Church five years before Shakespeare was born, and over the course of his lifetime, the state's attempts to stamp out Catholicism gradually intensified. People who remained loyal to the Catholic faith risked a great deal, as those who refused to attend Protestant services were subject to fines, while those suspected of actively conspiring against the government on behalf of the Catholic Church were tortured and killed. So if we knew that Shakespeare were secretly Catholic, we'd be discovering a BIG secret, almost amounting to a double life. If we knew that he was Catholic, we might even speculate that he was an enemy of his own government. After all, the pope *had* excommunicated Elizabeth and called on Catholics to overthrow her.

There is no direct evidence that Shakespeare was Catholic. The oldest record in which someone claims that he was is in some notations on his birth and death records made by the clergyman Richard Davies at the end of the seventeenth century. Davies writes that "Shakespeare died a papist" (i.e., a Catholic). But Davies doesn't give any proof for this claim, and he seems to have been wrong about other things. Beyond that, all of the evidence is about the people around Shakespeare—his family, his teachers, and those he may have associated with. His father reportedly wrote a testament to his own Catholicism and hid it in the rafters of the house where Shakespeare was born (the document is now lost). His mother came from a staunchly Catholic family that resisted conversion. Simon Hunt, who was probably his teacher in grammar school, later became a Jesuit—a capital crime in Elizabethan England.

Finally, the proponents of Shakespeare's Catholicism have put together a story about his "lost years" that, while mostly conjecture, is certainly provocative and compelling. Another of Shakespeare's schoolmasters, John Cottam, was also Catholic and even had a brother who was executed for his Catholicism. Cottam was involved in recruiting talented young men to serve as tutors in the houses of aristocratic Catholics of his acquaintance. One of these Catholic aristocrats was Alexander Hoghton of Lancashire, who in 1581 signed a will in which he left all of his musical instruments and costumes to his brother, or in the event that his brother didn't want to support a troop of players, to a friend named Sir Thomas Hesketh, whom he asks "to be friendly unto Fulk Gyllome and William Shakeshafte now dwelling with me." If "Shakeshafte" is actually "Shakespeare," then it seems possible that Cottam arranged for Shakespeare to work in Hoghton's household, which at one stroke would support the idea that Shakespeare was Catholic, *and* tell us where he spent his lost years, *and* give us a sense of where he might have begun his career as a professional performer.

However, the problem with Shakespeare's Catholicism isn't only that all of this evidence falls short of proving anything conclusively. Another problem is that even though his Catholicism *seems* like a big secret with big consequences, there's no hint that this was the case for Shakespeare. While some English Catholics did lead double lives, conspiring against the government, secretly harboring priests, prose-lytizing, and so on, there's no evidence that Shakespeare did anything of the sort. Everything we know about him shows that he focused all of his time and attention on professional matters, so even if he were Catholic, his faith might have been a completely private matter, or religion may simply not have been of central importance to him.

The same point applies to the plays. Scholars have already combed through the plays trying to find traces of Catholicism, and there are a few things here and there that suggest Catholic leanings. Hamlet's father implies that he's in Purgatory, for example, some-thing that Protestants didn't believe in. Catholic religious vocations (priests, friars, nuns) are generally treated with reverence rather than scorn in his plays. But it just doesn't seem to matter as much as we think it would. If, instead of reading the plays for evidence that he was Catholic, we actually *knew* he was Catholic, that fact wouldn't unlock any secret meanings or major new dimensions to the plays. At least, none that anyone has found.

Did Shakespeare Have a Sexually Transmitted Disease?

Yes, gross, we know. But there are a *lot* of references to these nasty and painful infections in Shakespeare's works, and they're pretty vivid. We don't actually know whether he suffered from one, and it doesn't really matter, but here's the dirt for those who want to know.

The big sexually transmitted disease in Europe at the time was syphilis. Scientists disagree on where it came from, but many believe that the disease was brought back to Europe from the New World by

Christopher Columbus. By Shakespeare's lifetime, it was very widespread and often fatal. Syphilis was not well understood in those days, but the way it works is that after exposure through sexual contact, the bacterium that causes syphilis incubates for about twenty-one days before primary syphilis presents itself, characterized by chancres or ulcerated sores on the skin and/or genitals. That goes away, and then one to six months later, secondary syphilis develops, characterized by a red rash on the trunk or limbs and broad white lesions on the skin and mucous membranes. One to ten (sometimes up to fifty) years after *that* goes away, tertiary or advanced syphilis develops, in which soft, tumorlike growths appear throughout the body, including the skin and skeleton, and a host of internal problems may occur, generally resulting in madness and/or death. In Shakespeare's time, people sometimes wore copper prosthetic noses after losing their own noses to tertiary syphilis. The treatment in those days was exposure to mercury, which caused brittle bones.

In Shakespeare's plays, syphilis is the subject of a host of references ranging from subtle jokes and innuendoes to brazen insults and accusations. In *Measure for Measure*, for example, Lucio and two gentlemen joke about the infections they have earned. As a bawd (madam) approaches, Lucio admits that he has "purchased . . . many diseases under her roof" and tells his companion that "thy bones are hollow," a reference to the brittle bones associated with syphilis that were probably actually caused by the mercury used to treat it. In *Timon of Athens*, the title character tells a prostitute to exact her revenge on men and "Make use of thy salt hours; season the slaves / For tubs and baths; bring down rose-cheeked youth / to the tub-fast and the diet," referring to two common treatments for syphilis: hot baths and starvation. He then goes on to describe in great detail the symptoms of advanced syphilis, from pain and baldness to a weak voice and a collapsed nose.

Shakespeare's sonnets end on a disquieting note invoking the syphilis motif. The last two of Shakespeare's sonnets tell a story in which Cupid, having fallen asleep, has his torch of love stolen by nymphs who try to extinguish it in a cool lake. But Cupid's flame is so powerful that, instead of the lake cooling the fire, the fire warms the lake. In treating this theme, Shakespeare alludes explicitly to the "seething bath which yet men prove / Against strange maladies a sovereign cure"—that is, the hot baths that were used as a cure for syphilis. The "cool well" may also be read as the woman's vagina, which is warmed even as it cools male passion—and which may both absorb and transmit additional heat if it develops a burning sore—or as the warm place that, paradoxically, a man hot with desire craves.

SIX

DID SOMEONE ELSE WRITE SHAKESPEARE'S PLAYS?

No.

Alternative authorship theories are for suckers. It's true that we don't have a full and rich record of Shakespeare's inner life, and in that sense his biography is a bit scanty, but there's no shortage of records that factually document that he lived and wrote those plays—at least most of them. Bear in mind that most of the plays were published as books not that long after they were performed, with Shakespeare named as the author on the title page. People who saw the plays on stage also knew that he wrote them, so presumably he was named as the author on playbills. Business records show that he was a shareholder in the company that performed his plays and that he profited from them—and when he died, he left behind the cash to prove it. So there definitely was a Shakespeare, and to believe that someone else was the author, you not only have to come up with a candidate who seems like they could have done it, you also have to believe that there was an elaborate hoax to perpetrate the idea that Shakespeare was an author. And there's no evidence for the existence of such a hoax at all.

It's not that it couldn't possibly have happened. Stranger things have. But to believe in an elaborate conspiracy theory with no evidence to support it, just because you want to, is a little, well . . . crazy. You might well ask why people came up with these theories in the first place. One of the main reasons is that many people have refused to believe that a commoner—a country boy, the son of a tradesman, someone who never went to a university—could have written with such excellence. It must have been an aristocrat, just as all the great poets and playwrights of the Renaissance were university-educated aristocrats. Um, except Marlowe, Jonson, Donne, Spenser, Daniel, Middleton, Heywood, and Dekker. But never mind—no one said this argument was based on facts.

Anyway, here are the candidates that people usually propose. If you see anyone in real life making these arguments, do not try to argue with them. Back away, slowly.

Sir Francis Bacon (1561–1626)

The first person to be proposed as Shakespeare's ghostwriter was Sir Francis Bacon, England's premier Renaissance man. Bacon, an important member of the royal court and a prolific writer, made major contributions to philosophy, politics, and numerous other fields, but he won most fame as the "father of modern science"—devising the basic methods of experimentation and observation used by scientists to this day.

Bacon certainly possessed a breadth of knowledge equal to the task of writing Shakespeare's plays. Based on the wealth of detailed references and allusions in his plays, critics have credited Shakespeare with a thorough knowledge of everything from seamanship and ancient Greek to court affairs and English constitutional law. Anti-Stratfordians (the name for people who reject Shakespeare's authorship) argue that such diversity of intellect seems unlikely in William Shakespeare, a man who never attended university and whose parents and children were, most experts agree, illiterate.

The strongest argument against the Baconian theory, apart from the total lack of direct evidence for it, is that Bacon's own work fills so many volumes that it hardly seems possible he could also have written the entire Shakespearean canon.

The Baconian theory was first espoused in 1785 by Rev. James Wilmot, though he did not dare to publish an account of it during his lifetime. Baconian scholars are, in general, the most eccentric of the anti-Stratfordians. One class of Baconians, seizing on Bacon's penchant for cryptology, scours the writings of Shakespeare in search of elaborately encoded messages revealing Bacon as the true author. Perhaps the most famous Baconian is Mark Twain, whose essay, *Is Shakespeare Dead?*, is the most amusing (if not the most even-handed) argument against Shakespeare of Stratford-on-Avon.

Edward de Vere, Earl of Oxford (1550–1604)

De Vere, the seventeenth Earl of Oxford, is one of the more popular candidates to have secretly written Shakespeare's plays, due to his education, intimate knowledge of the upper echelons of Elizabeth's court, and because he actually was a writer. When de Vere was twelve, his father died, leaving him the title of Lord Great Chamberlain of England. As a young member of the queen's court, de Vere would have received a first-class education in matters both military and academic, and as one of England's highest officers of state, he would have known intimately the customs and politics of courtly life.

In addition to having an educational background commensurate to Shakespeare's works, de Vere was well known during his lifetime as a poet. Although no independent samples of de Vere's dramatic work remain, one contemporary author ranked de Vere as the "best for comedy" (several places above Shakespeare, who is given a separate entry in the same text). As first set out in 1920 by the aptly named J. Thomas Looney, the Oxfordian case rests also on extensive similarities between Oxford's life and the plots of some of Shakespeare's best plays.

Though the arguments in favor of de Vere are somewhat richer than those in favor of Bacon, there are also more daunting obstacles to proving his authorship. De Vere died in 1604, and while strident Oxfordians are eager to throw out accepted chronologies of Shakespeare's plays, there is solid evidence that *The Tempest* was inspired by a shipwreck in 1609, and *Henry VIII* is on record as a "new" play in 1613.

Sigmund Freud was one of the earliest converts to the Oxfordian cause, but the Oxfordian theory finds its greatest recent support among theater practitioners, including famous Shakespearean actors Sir Derek Jacobi, Sir John Gielgud, Kenneth Branagh, and Mark Rylance.

Christopher Marlowe (1564–1593?)

Of all the leading anti-Stratfordian contenders, Christopher Marlowe represents the only literary professional. Marlowe, like Shakespeare, belonged to a family of provincial tradesmen, but unlike Shakespeare he gained a thorough local education and went on to receive a university degree from Cambridge. Although born in the same year as

Shakespeare, Marlowe began writing at an earlier age and was already one of England's leading literary luminaries by the time Shakespeare first came to London in the early 1590s.

In May of 1593, Marlowe was charged with heresy, a crime punishable by death. The courts certainly would have found him guilty since his atheistic beliefs were a matter of common knowledge, but they never had a chance to hear the case. A few days after the charges were levied, Marlowe was murdered. Marlovians believe that his murder was staged in order to avoid certain death at the hands of the English judiciary, and the circumstances of his death exude just enough mystery to make this story compelling. For instance, we know that Marlowe served as a spy for the British government, and all three of the men present at his death (including the murderer, who was later acquitted on grounds of self-defense) had strong ties to British intelligence.

Marlovians argue that Marlowe continued writing in secret under the name of Shakespeare, and they claim to have found scientific evidence to support their hypothesis: although the testing methods are a matter of some controversy, computerized analysis has shown Shakespeare's and Marlowe's literary fingerprint to be nearly identical. Stratfordians counter that there should be nothing surprising in Marlowe's linguistic influence on Shakespeare and that stark differences in style and content outweigh any computerized "proof."

The Underdogs

Other candidates (ones that have not been met with the same seriousness in academia) include Sir Walter Raleigh and even Queen Elizabeth. Raleigh, a famous explorer, poet, philosopher, statesman, and courtier, lived until 1618, which aligns well with the chronology of Shakespeare's works. He was a celebrated court poet, but he was never known to write a play, and very few believe his talent equal to Shakespeare's writing.

The candidacy of Queen Elizabeth is the most fanciful of the anti-Stratfordian suggestions, based mainly on comparisons between portraits of the queen and the engraving of Shakespeare in the First Folio of 1623, the first collected edition of Shakespeare's plays. We'll say it again: back away, slowly.

Group Theories

Recently, a number of people have proposed the theory that a group of collaborators could have written Shakespeare's works. Most group theories pair one or more aristocrats (e.g., the Countess of Pembroke or the Earls of Rutland and Stanley) with one of Shakespeare's rival playwrights (e.g., Ben Jonson or Thomas Middleton). Group theories are attractive since they allow the theorist to mix and match writers to account for every aspect of Shakespeare's extraordinary imagination and intellect. However, most of the academic world views group theories of Shakespearean authorship as the scholarly equivalent of a Rube Goldberg Machine. (A fanciful invention that goes through a number of convoluted steps to accomplish a simple task.)

SEVEN

FAMOUS SHAKESPEARE HATERS

The critical response to Shakespeare has not been limited to praise and rapture. The following are some of the most famous and/or vitriolic of the Bard's detractors from the past four centuries.

Robert Greene (1558–1592)

Robert Greene was a famous playwright and an infamous ruffian. In fact, many critics assert that Greene provided the inspiration for "Sir John Falstaff," the philosopher-debaucher, gentleman-cheat in Shakespeare's *Henry IV*. Greene looked down on actors generally, but he absolutely despised the actor who would dare to start writing plays— i.e., Shakespeare:

> "Yes trust them not: for there is an upstart Crow, beautified with our feathers, that with his *Tiger's heart wrapped in a Player's hide*, supposes he is as well able to bombast out a blank verse as the best of you: and being an absolute *Johannes Factotum* [i.e., a jack-of-all-trades, a know-it-all], is in his own conceit the only Shake-scene in a country."

As an indication of how much Greene hated Shakespeare, the passage references a line from Shakespeare's *Henry VI* ("O tiger's heart wrapped in a woman's hide!") describing Margaret, who has just offered the weeping York a handkerchief drenched in his own son's blood.

John Dryden (1631–1700)

John Dryden, the preeminent playwright and critic of the Restoration, wavered between respect and repulsion when it came to Shakespeare:

> He is the very Janus of poets; he wears, almost everywhere, two faces: and you have scarce begun to admire the one e'er you despise the other.

However, one thing he hated unequivocally was Shakespeare's use of language.

> [The English language] is so much refin'd since Shakespeare's time, that many of his words, and more of his Phrases, are scarce intelligible ... and his whole style is so pester'd with Figurative expressions, that it is as affected as it is obscure.

... and Dryden composed these lines mere decades after Shakespeare's death.

Thomas Rymer (1641–1713)

Nowadays, Thomas Rymer, a Restoration translator and critic, is most famous for his vicious condemnation of *Othello*. He spends an entire chapter of his book *A Short View of Tragedy* picking it apart

scene by scene, but his outrage at what he calls a frivolous and improbable play can be summed up in one line:

> So much ado, so much stress, so much passion and repetition
> about a handkerchief! Why was not this called the *Tragedy of
> the Handkerchief*?

In the end, all Rymer can hope is that people who see Shakespeare

> ... go to the playhouse as they do to church: to sit still, look on
> one another, make no reflection, nor mind the play more than
> they would a sermon.

Voltaire (1694–1778)

Voltaire, the French Enlightenment philosopher and writer, once
called Shakespeare's works an "enormous dunghill" that contained
"a few pearls." Neoclassicists like Vol-
taire had extremely strict views of what
made a good play, and Shakespeare did
not fit the mold. They believed that
the action of drama should be limited
to what can happen in one location on
one day. Shakespeare's plays, in contrast, span years and continents. They
also believed that tragedy and comedy
should not mix, but Shakespeare paid

no heed to such a distinction. For these reasons and more, Voltaire
could say (with as much disdain for the British generally as for
Shakespeare), "Shakespeare is a drunken savage with some imagination whose plays please only in London and Canada."

Lord Byron (1788–1824)

As a rule, Shakespeare found some of his most ardent devotees among the English Romantic poets of the early nineteenth century, but Byron proved an exception to the rule. He was an outspoken critic of the Bard, and not (as one might expect of the ever-eccentric Byron) a flippant one. He did not argue that Shakespeare was worthless, but rather that

> Shakespeare's name, you may depend on it, stands absurdly too high and will go down.

Above all, he accuses Shakespeare of a lack of imagination, saying,

> He has no invention as to stories, none whatever. He took all his plots from old novels, and threw their stories into a dramatic shape, at as little expense of thought as you or I could turn his plays back again into prose tales.

Byron, like many of Shakespeare's detractors, depicts the Bard as a man more ruled by the desire to churn out crowd-pleasers than by any real artistic genius.

Leo Tolstoy (1828–1910)

Tolstoy, the preeminent Russian novelist, spent most of his life masking his poor opinion of Shakespeare. He read and reread the plays, hoping to see in them the 'genius' that his contemporaries saw, but, as he writes in *Shakespeare and the Drama*, he "invariably experienced the same feelings—repulsion, weariness, and bewilderment."

Tolstoy directs much of his disgust toward Shakespeare's use of language:

> In love, preparing for death, fighting, or dying, they all talk at
> great length and unexpectedly about quite irrelevant matters,
> guided more by the sounds of the words and by puns than by
> the thoughts.

Tolstoy was most persistent, though, in condemning the moral outlook of Shakespeare's plays—one that propagates "the irreligious and immoral attitude of the upper classes of our world" to the extent that the audience "loses the capacity to distinguish between good and evil."

For these reasons and more, Tolstoy declares that Shakespeare "was not an artist and . . . his works are not artistic productions."

George Bernard Shaw (1856–1950)

Many scholars will argue that Shaw is the second-greatest playwright in the English language—second, that is, to Shakespeare. In any case, he is unarguably the most fervent loather of Shakespeare, whom he accuses of having a nihilistic worldview.

> Shakespeare wrote for the theatre because, with extraordinary
> artistic powers, he understood nothing and believed nothing.
> Thirty-six big plays in five blank verse acts, and … not a single
> hero!

Shaw also finds Shakespeare's stabs at "philosophy" cheap and flimsy, speaking of his

> incapacity for getting out of the depth of even the most ignorant
> audience except when he solemnly says something so transcen-
> dently platitudinous that his more humble-minded hearers

cannot bring themselves to believe that so great a man really meant to talk like their grandmothers.

So why, in Shaw's opinion, is Shakespeare so popular? In the end, he can only chalk it up to seductive jingle-jangle of Shakespeare's language, declaring, "In a deaf nation these plays would have died long ago."

WHERE DID SHAKESPEARE GET HIS IDEAS?

Shakespeare's Library

If we were able to look at Shakespeare while he was working on a play, we might very well see these books stacked up by his elbow. Though we could list quite a long number of books that he must have read at one point or another, these are the ones he went back to again and again.

HOLINSHED

Raphael Holinshed's *Chronicles of England, Scotland, and Ireland* (1587) provided source material for thirteen of

Shakespeare's plays, including his history plays as well as *Macbeth*, *King Lear*, and *Cymbeline*. Holinshed attempted to record the entire history of the British Isles from antiquity, beginning with how Noah divided the world after the flood, to his present, including the reign of Elizabeth I. The histories of England, Scotland, and Ireland are presented separately and in chronological order. Though the *Chronicles* were published as a historical account of Britain's history, the early stories are based on famous fables, such as those of King Arthur and Merlin. As Holinshed approaches his own time, the narratives become more grounded in historical fact, but they also become more controversial. Holinshed's treatment of political events during the reign of Elizabeth I sparked some controversy, which resulted in a number of passages being censored prior to publication.

The *Chronicles* is a massive tome comprising three volumes and approximately three and a half million words. Holinshed appropriated the work of other writers when compiling the *Chronicles*, a practice that today we would call plagiarism but that was common and accepted in the Renaissance. In turn, Shakespeare drew plot elements, character names, and descriptions from Holinshed. However, Shakespeare reshaped the history presented in the *Chronicles* to suit his own dramatic purpose. For example, Shakespeare altered depictions of historical figures (like Joan of Arc), added characters (like Falstaff), and compressed time (the reign of Macbeth).

HALL

Edward Hall's chronicle history, *The Union of the Two Noble and Illustre Families of Lancaster and York* (1548) criticizes the strife and civil wars that plagued England prior to the reign of Henry VII. Shakespeare turned to Hall when writing *Richard II*, both parts of *Henry IV*, and *Henry V*. Hall's account of the power struggle between the house of Lancaster and the house of York, two branches of the royal family that vied for the throne of England, helped shape the three parts of *Henry VI* and *Richard III*. Shakespeare's plays seem at many points to share Hall's point of view about who was good and who was to blame throughout these episodes of history.

Hall's writing is distinctly moralistic. Hall condemns the years of unrest and portrays Henry VII (a descendent of the house of Lancaster) as England's savior for uniting the two sides by marrying Elizabeth of York. The *Union* is written as an apology for the Tudors that glorifies the reigns of Henry VII and Henry VIII. Like many chroniclers, Hall draws on his predecessors and modifies their work with his own embellishments and language. From the accession of Henry VIII onward, however, Hall differs from other writers of his time in that he ceases to rely on existing stories and instead provides his own eyewitness account of historical events.

PLUTARCH

Lives of the Noble Grecians and Romans by the Greek writer Plutarch (circa 45–125 a.d.) provided Shakespeare with a source for his Roman plays: *Julius Caesar, Timon of Athens, Antony and Cleopatra,* and *Coriolanus.* Plutarch's *Lives* is not another chronicle in the vein of Holinshed or Hall but is instead a series of in-depth biographies of important individuals. Plutarch, like Shakespeare, was concerned with developing a dramatic narrative and exploring personal tragedy, frequently at the expense of historical accuracy. The biographies are arranged in pairs (twenty-three extant), with one Greek and one Roman, in order to show the similarities between the two cultures. Thomas North's 1579 English translation of *Lives* is of particular importance to Shakespeare. In both *Antony and Cleopatra* and *Coriolanus* Shakespeare changed North's poetic prose into verse without significant alteration. This direct appropriation of North's text attests to both the dramatic nature of Plutarch's work and the quality of North's translation.

OVID

Shakespeare makes refererence to the Roman poet Ovid (43 B.C.–17 A.D.) more than any other classical writer. Ovid's influence on Shakespeare's plots can be seen in *Venus and Adonis, The Rape of Lucrece, Titus Andronicus, The Winter's Tale, The Tempest*, and *A Midsummer Night's Dream*. On a broader scale, Shakespeare's works contain innumerable verbal allusions to Ovid's *Metamorphoses. Metamorphoses* is a collection of myths that explore the origin of things, beginning with the creation of the world and ending with a goddess transforming the soul of Julius Caesar into a star. Each of the stories stands alone, yet they also progress from one to the next, developing the overarching theme of change. In *Metamorphoses*, people are transformed into trees, flowers, birds, reptiles, constellations, and other natural phenomena. The gods often transform humans as a punishment for their actions, but sometimes the changes occur in order to save the mortals from harm or death.

SENECA

Seneca (4 B.C.–65 A.D.), a Roman dramatist and philosopher, wrote tragedies about deception and revenge that were far more gruesome and violent than those of his contemporaries. His plays frequently include a murder, the appearance of the ghost of the murdered, escalating hostility and plotting between two factions (the murderer and avenger), and a violent climax that destroys most of the characters, including the avenger and his nemesis. Revenge tragedies, based on Seneca's model, became widely popular among Renaissance playwrights starting in the late 1580s. Seneca's depiction of violence and passion in his most famous work, *Thyestes*, can be seen in Shakespeare's early tragedy *Titus Andronicus*. The gory finale of *Titus*, in which Titus serves Tamora food made from the flesh of her own sons, is taken directly from Seneca. Shakespeare continued to use tragic elements from Seneca in *Macbeth, Hamlet, Othello, Richard III*, and *King Lear*. In these later tragedies, Shakespeare moves beyond Seneca by focusing on the psychological complexity of his characters.

PLAUTUS

Shakespeare developed as a comedy writer in part by borrowing judiciously from the comedies of the Roman dramatist Plautus (254–184 B.C.). Based on Greek plays, Plautus's comedies were widely popular for their broad humor, quick action, bawdy puns, and satire. A large portion of each play was originally set to music, much like modern musical theater. Plautus was particularly adept at portraying clever lower-class characters who outwit their upper-class counterparts. *The Comedy of Errors*, one of Shakespeare's early works, combines two comedies by Plautus: *Menaechmi* and *Amphitruo.* Some comedic devices borrowed from Plautus—mistaken identity caused by twins and the bed trick—appear again in *Twelfth Night, Measure for Measure,* and *All's Well That Ends Well.*

BOCCACCIO

Giovanni Boccaccio's *The Decameron* (1353), or "ten days," is a collection of one hundred short stories told by a group of ten people who have fled to the country to escape the plague that is devastating Florence. The speakers of the tales declare that the tales are love stories aimed to console women afflicted by unrequited love. In reality, the stories are full of sexual innuendoes that provide a means of flirtation between the men and women of the group. We can easily understand why Shakespeare would have been drawn to the bawdy tales in *The Decameron.* Unfortunately, Shakespeare's only access to Boccaccio was in a highly censored edition by William Painter called *Palace of Pleasure* (1566). Sixteen of *The Decameron*'s more conservative tales are included in Painter's anthology of novellas. Shakespeare referred to Painter's edition when writing *All's Well That Ends Well* and *Cymbeline.* The influence of Boccaccio's writings can also be seen in *The Merry Wives of Windsor, Two Gentlemen of Verona, Timon of Athens,* and *The Rape of Lucrece.*

NINE

SHAKESPEARE'S WORLD

Though admirers have often touted Shakespeare's treatment of universal and timeless themes, a little knowledge about the actual religious, cultural, and political climate of Shakespeare's England can go a long way toward helping us understand the plays. The following are the five most important things to know about Shakespeare's England.

Religion Was a Touchy Subject

During the decades before Shakespeare's birth in 1564, England experienced enormous changes in the way religion was practiced. King Henry VIII split with the Catholic Church in the late 1530s when the pope would not annul his first marriage. He seized the church's lands and wealth, destroyed England's many monasteries, and proclaimed the foundation of a new Anglican Church under his own leadership. England reverted to Catholicism for a brief while under the reign of Henry VIII's daughter, Queen Mary. She earned her famous nickname, "Bloody Mary," by viciously persecuting non-Catholics, burning over three hundred "heretics" at the stake during her five-year reign. Upon Mary's death in 1558, however, the crown fell to Elizabeth, who finally succeeded in striking a compromise of sorts.

While Queen Elizabeth avoided the religious violence of her predecessors, her compromise was still far from what we would consider "tolerant" today. The Anglican Church was the official state church, and anyone openly practicing another religion could be prosecuted. In fact, she enacted a law that made it treasonous for any Catholic priest of the Jesuit order to set foot in England. However, she expected only an outward show of conformity in her subjects. As long as they showed up to official Anglican services every Sunday, English citizens could privately believe whatever they liked. She was plagued by extremists on both sides. A particular sect of Protestants, pejoratively dubbed "Puritans," pushed for a more complete Reformation. At the same time, multiple Englishmen plotted to assassinate Elizabeth in the name of the Catholic Church. However, Elizabeth managed to fend off extremists and secure a middle road for the Church of England.

In the face of all of these rapid changes, amidst all of these sectarian tensions, the common people of Shakespeare's day were left to wrestle with their consciences over what to truly believe. Most writers of Shakespeare's time, keenly aware of the political implications, made sure to portray characters of non-Protestant religions in a negative light. Catholics, in particular, were often an object of mockery in English Renaissance drama. Shakespeare, on the other hand, is notable for his compassionate portrayal of characters of all religious denominations. His pagan (pre-Christian) characters speak movingly of and to their gods. Shylock, the famous Jewish character in *The Merchant of Venice*, delivers a stirring speech on the essential humanity of Jews, saying,

> Hath not a Jew eyes? Hath not a Jew hands, organs, dimensions, senses, affections, passions; fed with the same food, hurt with the same weapons, subject to the same diseases, heal'd by the same means, warm'd and cool'd by the same winter and summer, as a Christian is?

Even Shakespeare's Catholics are compassionately rendered, though certain of his audience members would probably have insisted on seeing them as villains. For instance, though Friar Lawrence, in *Romeo and Juliet*, bungles his plan to help the young lovers, Shakespeare portrays him as an intelligent man with good intentions. Shakespeare's refusal to patriotically tow the party line of Anglicanism has led many historians to believe that Shakespeare may have been a secret Catholic himself. However, most people see, in Shakespeare's wide-ranging religious tolerance, what Samuel Coleridge famously called a "wonderful philosophical impartiality."

Shakespeare Was a Humanist

Shakespeare was born into an age of rapidly expanding knowledge and extraordinary artistic production. It has since been termed the "English Renaissance" in order to compare it to the similar flourishing of culture earlier in continental Europe, particularly in late-fifteenth-century Italy. Like the Renaissance in Italy, the English Renaissance saw the rise of "humanism" as both an artistic and a moral movement.

Humanism, first and foremost, consisted of a resurgent interest in the arts, sciences, and history of ancient Greek and Roman civilizations. Several of Shakespeare's plays take their plots straight from the chronicles of classical antiquity. For example, Shakespeare's *Julius Caesar* depicts the historical assassination of the Roman emperor Julius Caesar by his friend and ally, Brutus. Regardless of what time period a Shakespeare play inhabits, though, the revival of Greek and Roman cultures is apparent in the constant use of ancient gods, heroes, and villains as a source of comparison and metaphor.

Shakespeare's plays and poems also perfectly embody the moral philosophy of humanism. Humanism, as a philosophical system, forcefully asserts the value of each individual human life. In this way, Shakespeare's humanism is readily apparent in his compassionate approach to all of his characters. Most of the time, Shakespeare shows even his villains as recognizably human beings with a full range of emotions and logical, if immoral, motives for their villainies. A notable exception is Iago, in *Othello*, who seems to have no reasonable motive for tempting Othello into murderous jealousy. For this reason, Iago has become one of the most hotly debated of all Shakespearean characters. But Iago is the exception that proves the rule. His motiveless evil, common in non-Shakespearean villains of the English Renaissance, makes the rich humanity of other Shakespearean characters stand out even more starkly.

Shakespeare also adopted another important aspect of philosophical humanism: namely, the belief that only through exploring the human experience can man come to know himself, nature, or God. Shakespeare's poems and plays eschew simplistic moral or theological narratives, exploring instead the emotions and moral choices faced by secular men in extreme circumstances. Before the English Renaissance and the rise of humanism, *Hamlet* would have been a morality play pitting the temptation of revenge against the restrictions of Christian dogma. Instead, Shakespeare's great tragedy explores Hamlet's situation as a human, not a divine, dilemma. On one level, Hamlet desperately wants to obey the demand for revenge issued by his father's ghost, but he is paralyzed by such practical considerations as his need to know Claudius's guilt for certain.

Elizabeth Was a Cultural Icon

Elizabeth reigned as Queen of England for most of Shakespeare's life, and her influence looms large in Shakespeare's plays. During her entire forty-five-year reign (longer than that of any previous English monarch), she consistently refused to marry, devoting herself instead to single life and to virginity. Her unmarried status allowed her much political power. For instance, she secured alliances with foreign monarchs by constantly holding out the possibility that she would marry from among their royal relatives. It was also, however, a source of much political anxiety. If Elizabeth were to remain unmarried, then she would never produce an heir to the throne. The English people knew only too well the kind of bloodshed and civil unrest that could result from the scramble for the throne should Elizabeth die without an heir.

A devoted patron of the theater, Elizabeth frequently invited Shakespeare's theater company, the Lord Chamberlain's Men, to

perform for her in court. Whether explicitly because of these royal performances or because of a more general patriotic pride in the queen, Shakespeare inserted thinly veiled flatteries to Elizabeth in multiple plays, focusing on the virtue of her virginity. For instance, in *A Midsummer Night's Dream*, Oberon, the fairy king, speaks admiringly of "a fair vestal throned by the west," or a beautiful virgin ruling a Western country. Shakespeare clearly means Elizabeth.

Besides such blatant references to Elizabeth, her personality may be behind the many strong and witty heroines in Shakespeare's plays. So many female characters in Shakespeare set out on their own to attain their goals. Often, they dress as men, not only to disguise their identities but to gain access and credibility that they could never have as a woman. This state of affairs calls to mind Elizabeth's famous speech rallying troops to fight an invading Spanish force, where she proclaimed,

> I know I have the body but of a weak and feeble woman; but I have the heart and stomach of a king, and of a king of England too, and think foul scorn that Parma or Spain, or any prince of Europe, should dare to invade the borders of my realm.

Shakespeare has been called an early feminist, but it is also possible that he was simply being patriotic in extolling the virtues of strong women.

Unlike the comedies and tragedies that celebrate the virtues of virginity, Shakespeare's history plays explore the darker side of Elizabeth's virginity: the lack of a clear heir to the throne. As the history plays trace the bloody civil wars of the previous few centuries in England, Shakespeare is clearly aware of the ambition and strife that plague any uncertain succession.

Shakespeare's Late Plays Reflect King James I's Interests

In 1603, when Shakespeare was thirty-nine years old and a well-established playwright, Queen Elizabeth died without an heir. Contrary to the fears of many Englishmen, civil war did not erupt over the succession. King James VI of Scotland, Elizabeth's distant cousin, became King James I of England, thus uniting Scotland and England into what James called "Great Britain." The racist assumption in much of England was that Scotsmen were dirty, barbarous, and uncultured. James could not have been further from this stereotype. He was a cultivated intellectual who continued to produce scholarly treatises even after ascending the throne.

James was also even more devoted a supporter of the theater than Elizabeth had been. One of his first acts as King of England was to delegate the patronage of London's major theater companies to members of his royal family. Shakespeare's own company changed from the Lord Chamberlain's Men to the King's Men, which effectively promoted all of the members of the company to gentlemen. It also gave Shakespeare much incentive to follow the king's interests in choosing the topics for his plays.

One of James I's major interests was magic and the occult. He had written a scholarly book on the history and practice of witchcraft and genuinely feared that witches might try to assassinate him or ruin his family's health with black magic. *Macbeth*, a play that features three witches who tempt a Scottish nobleman into stealing the Scottish throne, was clearly calculated to please James. Not only did it cover his interests (Scottish history, witchcraft), but it actually portrays a relative of his, Banquo, as a diamond in the rough. In the play, the witches reveal to Macbeth that Banquo's ancestors will be rightful kings, parading seven such monarchs in front of Macbeth and promising many more. The eighth in the succession need not appear on stage, because he was probably sitting in the audience: James himself. James's interest in magic can probably also account for the proliferation of mystical characters in Shakespeare's late plays, from men who can raise tempests to women who can bring statues to life.

James, as a learned monarch, also took an interest in political philosophy and theories of good government. No wonder, then, that so many of Shakespeare's later plays explore the problems of human law and the proper conduct of leaders. Whereas the history plays that Shakespeare wrote under Elizabeth focused mainly on problems of war and succession, the political plays that Shakespeare wrote under James explore more complex issues of the relation of morality to law, the proper delegation of power, and so on.

Shakespeare's Plays Contrasted Starkly with the Surrounding City

When Shakespeare arrived in London in the late sixteenth century, it was a burgeoning metropolis, with a population of over 200,000. That figure seems small to a modern reader, but keep in mind that this made it fifteen times more populous than any other city in the country. Mortality rates in the city were high due to crime, unsanitary water, and the quick spread of disease in the filthy, crowded city streets. The population kept growing, nonetheless, thanks to a constant influx of young people, mostly young men, from the countryside.

Rural commoners came to earn their fortune, and country gentlemen came to participate in London's lucrative commerce. In fact, so many country gentlemen relocated to the city that rural towns often complained of being unable to locate suitable people to serve as magistrates and town officials. Shakespeare, a country boy himself, must have appealed greatly to this transplanted population. Even if they did not know that Shakespeare himself was born, raised, and educated in the countryside, they would have seen it in the deft way that his characters refer to rural flowers and trees, to livestock and birds, and to the English landscape. They would have appreciated his insertion of authentic country dances and festivals into his plays. Part of the reality of city life, for many Londoners, then, was a longing for the country.

The respectable areas of town bustled with commerce. Goods arrived and were sold. Gentlemen brushed shoulders with commoners. Pickpockets preyed on both. The increasing international trade brought more and more foreign fashions to London, but most merely met with the mockery of nationalistic Englishmen. It was a place of collision for different cultures, different values, different tastes. In other parts of the town, called "liberties," located on lands formerly owned by the church and therefore under no secular jurisdiction, lawlessness of all sorts thrived.

The location of Shakespeare's theater, across the Thames from London proper, more closely resembled this latter sort. Around the theater were prostitutes and thieves, beggars and cheats. Theater companies vied for business with bearbaiting, cockfighting, and "houses of resort" (i.e., whorehouses). When Shakespeare, in a rare instance, shows us on stage the city of London beyond the royal court, he shows us the kind of London he encounters every day around the theater. He shows us the seedy taverns of Eastcheap, where Prince Hal (later Henry V) mingles with thieves and drunkards. This was the London where most of his audience spent their days, and, except in the case of special performances in the royal court, even noble members of his audiences would have had to slog through this part of London before seeing his plays. You can imagine, then, how marvelously escapist it would be, to see rural shepherds or courtly kings take the stage; to see the performance of brave deeds and the exchange of intimate vows.

SHAKESPEARE'S THEATER

Shakespeare's professional career spanned the golden age of English drama. When Shakespeare first came to London, presumably in the late 1580s, the earliest permanent theater companies were just becoming established in the city. Until that time, English drama consisted mainly of religiously themed morality plays and ad hoc performances by troupes of traveling players. As theatrical activity began to coalesce in

London—drawn to the intense energy of the growing metropolis—the theater took root as one of the most important and characteristic art forms of the English Renaissance.

Because companies now found themselves in thrall to a novelty-hungry, increasingly sophisticated audience, they needed a larger repertory of plays to meet the growing demand. Playwrights were in hot demand, and the period saw the development of more varied, complex plots as well as the growth of different dramatic genres. (In *Hamlet*, the doddering councilor Polonius praises a troupe's facility in "tragedy, comedy, history, pastoral, pastoral-comical, historical-pastoral, tragical-historical, tragical-comical-historical-pastoral.") Permanent playing venues also allowed companies to invest in larger stocks of properties and costumes as well as experiment with new staging devices and features, such as trapdoors that allowed actors to drop below the stage and machines that allowed actors to be lowered from the rafters.

The theater of Shakespeare's period helped give birth to the modern art form as we know it, yet it looked, felt, and sounded very different from the theater we're used to seeing today. While you can definitely enjoy Shakespeare's plays without knowing anything about the way they were originally performed, knowing a little bit about the original productions will help you enjoy them even more. Here are six important facts you should know about Shakespeare's theater.

Plays Were Lively, Daylight Events

The most famous theaters of the period were the amphitheaters, which were large, open-air structures with tiered seating on three sides. Shakespeare's company, the Lord Chamberlain's Men (later known as the King's Men when James I became their patron), performed in an amphitheater called the Globe, which was located along the south bank of the river Thames. The amphitheaters used natural sunlight to illuminate their stages so performances took place during the working day at around 2 P.M. and played rain or shine.

The atmosphere at these daytime performances could be downright rowdy and unruly. A sizable portion of the audience stood in the large yard directly in front of the stage, where they enjoyed a uniquely interactive theatergoing experience that involved heckling and cheering in equal measures. As a yardling, your attention could be pulled away from the stage at any moment: by the jostling of customers on their way to buy refreshments or proposition local prostitutes (many of whom plied their trade amidst the commotion of the theaters), the cracking of nuts as they were crushed underfoot, or the hissing of beer bottles as they were opened—a sound that, according to a popular joke, many nervous playwrights sitting offstage confused with the hisses of a displeased audience.

Not all performances took place in the outdoor amphitheaters, however. Around 1609, after Shakespeare had been producing plays for over twenty years, theater companies began using smaller, indoor playhouses as well. In 1609, the King's Men began performing at the Blackfriars Theatre, which they used to mount plays during the winter seasons when the Globe was closed. These smaller, more intimate venues more closely resembled modern theaters, with the entire audience seated in rows before the stage, and charged higher admission fees, which meant that poorer audience members—the kind of people who filled the yard at the Globe— were excluded from the performances. The indoor playhouses also led to another modern theatrical convention: the intermission. Indoor theaters used candles to light their stages, and a brief interval after the first half allowed stagehands an opportunity to trim the candlewicks, lest the hall become too smoky. The rise of the indoor theater, with its tightly controlled, upper-class audiences, helped usher in a new era of respectability and acceptance for the English theater.

Everyone Went to the Theater . . .

In today's culture, theatergoing has become an elite and often expensive activity. But in Shakespeare's day, the theater provided common entertainment, competing for audiences with such popular spectator sports as fencing, bearbaiting, and cockfighting.

The amphitheaters served as a microcosm of London itself and were among the few venues where various social classes could mix relatively freely. These large, outdoor theaters provided seats for every budget. Generally speaking, the higher up you sat, the more you paid. Standing in the yard cost a penny, roughly equivalent to the better part of a laborer's daily wages. This made playgoing affordable (if not exactly cheap) for London's poorer citizens, their "apple-wives," and idle apprentices. The most expensive seats, known as the Lord's Rooms, were located on an upper level behind or next to the stage. Aristocrats sat here to be seen and admired in their expensive finery, even though the rush of being on display meant they enjoyed relatively poor visibility of the stage itself.

Even the queen loved plays, and famously so. Popular legend has it that Elizabeth commissioned Shakespeare to write *The Merry Wives of Windsor* because she was so charmed by the gluttonous, rascally Falstaff in the *Henry IV* plays. However, despite what you may have seen in the 1998 film *Shakespeare in Love*, Queen Elizabeth never went to the theater—instead, the theater came to her. Companies brought their plays to court every year, and in 1583 Queen Elizabeth patented her own royal company. For nine uninterrupted years, the new Royal Servants played three or four plays before her each year. Companies such as the Lord Chamberlain's Men brought their most popular plays to the palace at Whitehall to celebrate weddings, holiday festivities, and political events, as well as for private command performances. In fact, the theater companies' very existence was legally justified as a kind of laboratory and feeding ground for the queen's private repertory. Officially speaking, plays were honed in the public arena in order to make them ready for royal consumption, not to entertain the masses or earn profit for the producing companies.

Keen audiences spurred an astonishing outpouring of work in the period. Companies could perform up to fifteen different plays in a month, cycling through a new one every day, and dramatists worked feverishly to meet the public's appetite. Scholars estimate that several thousand plays were written and performed during the three decades of Shakespeare's career.

. . . But Not Everyone Approved of It

In his 1584 screed (lengthy discourse) *An Anatomy of Abuses*, the Puritan preacher Phillip Stubbes claimed that:

> The shameless gestures of players serve to nothing so much as to move the flesh to lust and uncleanness. And therefore . . . no Christian man or woman should resort to plays and interludes, where is nothing but blasphemy, scurrility, and whoredom maintained.

In Shakespeare's day, even when playgoing had become a fashionable, well-established activity, the theater was often linked with depravity. Plays took place during the workday, which implied that spectators were either shirking their responsibilities or else worthlessly unemployed. Pickpockets, prostitutes, and other petty criminals attended the theater, where they could mingle freely with—and sinfully influence—law-abiding citizens. The Red Bull Theatre in North London, for example, had a special reputation for violence and riotous behavior, and in 1628 the "magician" Dr. Lamb, physician to the unpopular Duke of Buckingham, was mobbed and brutally murdered by a crowd on his way back from the Fortune Theatre.

Stubbes and other critics, particularly the strictly moralist Puritans, believed that the plays themselves caused moral corruption. They argued that the vulgar, wicked behaviors depicted onstage (sexual indiscretion, political revolution, and drunken debauchery among them) encouraged these susceptible audience members to imitate such conduct in their own lives. They also argued that acting was, at its core, a kind of institutionalized lying. In a society as rigidly hierarchical as early modern London, where even a person's wardrobe was dictated by law according to his or her social class, the sight of commoners openly pretending to be kings and deities smacked of subversion.

The theater implied other dangers, as well. During the Elizabethan period, Londoners lived under constant threat from the plague, which decimated between a quarter and a third of the city's population. Playhouses were seen as prime breeding grounds for the disease, and whenever the number of plague deaths in a week rose above thirty the government ordered their closure. During especially long stretches of such plague outbreaks, such as occurred in 1593, 1603, and 1608, companies were forced to earn revenue by undertaking arduous tours throughout the country. Historians have suggested that authorities also feared that the yards might foster another kind of contagion: civil unrest. Amphitheaters offered an opportunity for large numbers of people from across the social spectrum to gather together and watch politically inflammatory plays, a potentially combustible situation in an otherwise highly regulated society.

In this atmosphere of distrust, theater companies could only gain an official license to assemble and perform (known as a *patent*) if sponsored by an aristocratic or royal patron. According to a government act of 1572, players not affiliated with such a patron were to be considered "rogues, vagabonds, and sturdy beggars." Even if a company did manage to secure patronage, the city authorities were a constant source of interference. As a result, theaters clustered around the suburbs of London, a sort of Renaissance red-light district that lay largely outside the jurisdiction of city authorities. Still, all plays performed in London had to be approved by the Master of Revels, a royally appointed official charged with overseeing entertainments in both the court and the city at large. The Master of Revels censored plays for both political and moral reasons, and many playwrights preemptively avoided such external tampering by skillfully disguising the contemporary resonances in their work, especially in regards to politically sensitive topics.

Plays Were Performed on a Bare Stage

Theater companies in Shakespeare's time kept dozens of plays in active repertory, often performing a different play every day of the week for up to six days at a stretch. Because of this prodigious output, complicated, immobile theatrical sets would have been impractical. Instead, companies performed on large, relatively simple stages whose structure recalled the inns and banquet halls of early English performance.

The Globe, which opened in 1599, had a wide, possibly square stage that thrust out into the yard, allowing standing patrons to gather on all three sides. Three doors along the stage's back wall led to the tiring house, a backstage area where actors got dressed and prepared for their entrances. A balcony above the large middle door could accommodate musicians, expensive spectator seats, or the occasional bit of staging, such as the balcony scene in *Romeo and Juliet*. A roof (commonly referred to as *the heavens*) hung over the stage, supported by pillars that could stand in for trees or other architectural elements during a performance. Certain key set pieces, such as beds, benches, and tables, were brought on when needed and painted tapestries may have been hung on the stage wall, but by and large companies didn't rely on elaborate, play-specific visuals.

Instead, productions of the time relied on language and the audience's imagination to conjure the world of the play. The usual functions of a set—efficiently conveying to the audience where the action is taking place, in what season, and in what time period—were instead accomplished through evocative dialogue. *Hamlet*, for example, opens on a cold winter night on the ramparts of Denmark's Elsinore Castle. The actors, though, would have been standing on an undressed stage in the light of an English summer afternoon. Within the play's first minute, Shakespeare not only communicates where and when the action takes place but also establishes the wary, melancholy mood that will permeate the play:

[*Francisco at his post. Enter to him Bernardo.*]

BERNARDO
Who's there?
FRANCISCO
Nay, answer me: stand, and unfold yourself.
BERNARDO
Long live the king!
FRANCISCO
Bernardo?
BERNARDO
He.
FRANCISCO
You come most carefully upon your hour.
BERNARDO
'Tis now struck twelve. Get thee to bed, Francisco.
FRANCISCO
For this relief much thanks: 'tis bitter cold,
And I am sick at heart.
BERNARDO
Have you had quiet guard?
FRANCISCO
Not a mouse stirring.
BERNARDO
Well, good night.
If you do meet Horatio and Marcellus,
The rivals of my watch, bid them make haste.

In addition to dense, poetic language, audience members were also treated to music and numerous sound effects, including thunder (cannonballs rolled along metal sheets), battlefield explosions (fireworks), and ghosts (flutes or other wind instruments played in the space below the stage, colloquially referred to as *hell*). At the Globe, the attic above the heavens housed a cannon, which was fired to herald the entrance of significant royal characters. In 1613, during a performance of Shakespeare's *Henry VIII*, an errant spray of sparks lit the Globe's thatched roof on fire, causing the entire structure to burn to the ground in a matter of hours. Miraculously, no one was killed in the incident. One man's breeches did catch on fire, but happily a fellow patron was standing by with a bottle of ale to extinguish the offending garment. (The Globe itself was rebuilt in 1614 before being shuttered for good in 1642.)

All this emphasis on the aural experience doesn't mean that the Globe offered its patrons nothing to look at, however. The interior of the Globe itself was beautifully gilded and painted, and the heavens above the stage bore elaborate mythological and astrological illustrations. (When Prospero speaks of "the great globe itself" in *The Tempest*, with its "cloud-capped towers," "gorgeous palaces," and "solemn temples," he is ostensibly speaking about Earth, but Shakespeare's audience may have caught a passing reference to the theater they sat in.)

The onstage action offered numerous other spectacles. Trapdoors in the floor and descent mechanisms from the heavens provided numerous opportunities for spectacular entrances and exits, often by actors playing ghosts or deities. Thrilling sword fights featured prominently in many plays, and most performances—comedies, romances, and tragedies alike—ended with the entire cast performing a jig, or lively dance, that was often the most popular element of the afternoon. In sharp counterpoint to the bare, neutral stage, theater companies owned extraordinarily lavish costumes, which were often real, aristocratic castoffs and which usually constituted the company's most valuable holdings.

All the Roles Were Played by Males

Throughout Shakespeare's lifetime, women were forbidden from performing on the public stages of London. The reasons for this provision are unclear. Though the acting profession was deemed an unsuitably lewd and immoral pastime for women, in other, equally patriarchal societies across Europe such as Italy and Spain female actresses freely participated in the theater. Some historians believe the all-male companies reflect the all-male institutions that gave rise to the public theaters: the church and the university. Although aristocratic women did perform in masques, the elaborate courtly spectacles staged in private homes and banquet halls, women were not seen on the public English stage until after Charles II reinstated the London theaters in 1660. The first known appearance by an actress took place the same year, when Margaret Hughes performed the role of Desdemona in *Othello*.

Until that time, though, female characters—with the possible exception of older, comic female roles, such as Juliet's Nurse and Mistress Quickly of the *Henry IV* plays—were played by boy actors whose voices had not yet broken. Puberty seems to have set in later during the Renaissance, so a young actor might play female roles long into his teens. Boy actors were generally apprenticed to an older member of the company, who trained him and, in exchange for the boy's wages, gave him room, board, and a small personal allowance. Many boys eventually graduated to male roles when they reached maturity. Scholars often note that Shakespeare must have had access to a particularly skilled boy actor in the very early 1600s, when he wrote some of his greatest female roles: Lady Macbeth, Cleopatra, and Volumnia of *Coriolanus*.

Modern audiences often wonder if their Elizabethan counterparts "bought" the fiction of men playing women. Elizabethan audiences weren't foolish or stupid: They understood the convention as exactly that—a convention. Spectators embraced the illusion just as contemporary playgoers accept the notion that a kind of invisible one-way mirror separates the stage from the audience, through which we may spy on another world that never suspects our presence.

That isn't to say, though, that they thought nothing of it. Shakespeare, for example, often called attention to the cross-dressing nature of his theater with plots that called for female characters to dress as men. In the most dizzying example, Rosalind, the feisty young heroine of *As You Like It*, goes into exile disguised as a boy named Ganymede. While in the forest of Arden, Rosalind/Ganymede meets Orlando, who is in love with Rosalind, and offers to cure his lovesickness by "pretending" to be Rosalind and weaning him off his obsession. Rosalind—who is in love with Orlando herself—then seizes the opportunity to covertly woo and test her beloved. Shakespeare's audience would have definitely recognized the comic potential of having a boy play a woman playing a boy playing a woman.

Still, some members of the audience may have found the practice deeply unsettling. In Shakespeare's day, people who engaged in same-sex relations weren't thought of as homosexuals, since the concept itself had yet to emerge. Sexual behavior in the period was considered just that—behavior, and not a fundamental element of human identity. Sodomy, however, was violently condemned, and many audience members may have felt fear or distaste at the sight of two men playing lovers onstage. Puritans denounced the practice of using boy actors, arguing that it encouraged a dangerous blurring of the sexes and a kind of freewheeling lust in both men and women. William Pryne called such actors "beastly male monsters," and the ever-cranky Philip Stubbes fulminated that the "wanton gestures" and "bawdy speeches" caused playgoers to go home "very friendly" with one another to "play the sodomites, or worse."

Shakespeare Did More Than Just Write the Plays

Shakespeare began his theatrical career in the mid-1580s, when he was about twenty years old. Although little concrete evidence exists about his early years in London, we know that he was performing regularly in addition to writing. Some playwrights felt offended by his eventual switch to the literary side: In 1592, the dramatist Robert Greene called Shakespeare an "upstart crow" for presuming, as an actor, to write plays. Greene warned his fellow playwrights not to trust a "tiger's heart wrapped in a player's hide," who "supposes he is as well able to bombast out a blank verse as the best of you." Even as Shakespeare's dramatic reputation rose over the following decades, he continued to act, and some evidence suggests that he may have played such small, pivotal roles in his own plays as the Ghost in *Hamlet* as well as faithful old Adam in *As You Like It*.

Shakespeare never achieved the same fame for his performances as he did for his plays, which made him a bona fide celebrity in early modern England. But despite becoming the greatest dramatist of the age, Shakespeare would never have become rich from his writing. Companies paid about two pounds per script, after which they owned the play outright. (Copyright and the notion of intellectual property as we know it did not exist at the time.) The premiere of a play on a public stage was the most important "publication"; more than half of Shakespeare's plays didn't appear in print form until many years after he died. Shakespeare was much more concerned about the publication of his verse, which was considered the proper way to establish a truly literary reputation.

Of course, in the end it was his plays and not his verse that cemented Shakespeare's eternal legacy. But it was his business investments, not his plays, that eventually made him his fortune—a sizeable income that allowed him to return to Stratford-upon-Avon and purchase the second-most-expensive home in town. Theater companies of the period were set up as shared partnerships, with a few core members pooling their resources and splitting the majority of the revenue. Companies normally had around ten sharers, and these men did everything from commission plays to run rehearsals to perform the lead roles. Shakespeare thus wrote plays for a company of men and boys he knew intimately and which he had a strong hand in shaping.

Shakespeare joined the newly formed Lord Chamberlain's Men in 1594 and stayed with the company for the rest of his professional life. He became a major shareholder five years later, when James Burbage, the famed theatrical impresario, needed funds to build the Globe Theatre. By the time the Lord Chamberlain's Men became the King's Men in 1603, they were the most popular company in London, and their steady stream of star performers and celebrated playwright ensured full audiences and tidy profits. By some estimates, Shakespeare may have netted up to 150 pounds a year, roughly thirty times as much as a laborer, or fifteen times as much as a university-educated schoolteacher.

ELEVEN

SHAKESPEARE'S LANGUAGE

Shortly before he murders her, Desdemona pleads with her husband, Othello, to explain his agitated and suspicious behavior. "I understand a fury in your words," she says, "but not the words."

For modern audiences, seeing or reading Shakespeare for the first time can make us feel a bit like the bewildered Desdemona. Even if we know something about the characters and have a general sense of the plot, individual lines can sound like impenetrable riddles. But Shakespeare's plays were massive hits in their time, not just arcane texts to be puzzled over in your freshman English class. Were Shakespeare's original audiences just smarter than we are today?

As Shakespeare's contemporaries, Globe attendees did have the advantage of a shared culture. Even the most uneducated spectators were familiar with the Bible and classical mythology, which Shakespeare often alludes to in his plays. Local references would have been more obvious too. When Hamlet tells Ophelia "Get thee to a nunnery," we easily recognize *nunnery* to mean "convent," but in the period it was also slang for "brothel," a pun that would have reminded Londoners of the infamous whorehouses of the neighboring Southwark district. Recognizing the many dialects used by Shakespearean characters—high class, low class, French, Welsh, Scottish—would also have come naturally to his audience, since the urban streets of London featured a mix of people from different backgrounds, nationalities, and social classes.

In the sixteenth and seventeenth centuries, the English language was also much more flexible than it is today. In Shakespeare's England there was still no formal dictionary of the language, and English grammar and syntax had yet to be codified. Word order and spelling was variable and could be highly random. Shakespeare didn't even have a set way of spelling his own name: sometimes it was *Shakespeare*, and sometimes it was *Shakespear, Shackspeare,* or even *Shaxpere.* A sentence like "To thine own self be true" sounds backward to us because we expect the more modern subject-verb-object formula ("[You] be true to yourself.") Shakespeare's audience, however, was accustomed to fluctuations in meaning and pronunciation, so they would have had a much easier time processing his constant wordplay.

But even though Shakespeare's audience shared his Elizabethan idiom, none of them spoke in iambic pentameter, or habitually used one word to mean three different things, or went around delivering  philosophical soliloquies whenever life became complicated. If his first audiences found certain elements of Shakespeare's language easier to understand, they had their own linguistic issues to deal with. Taken together, the plays, sonnets, and poems contain over 25,000 different words. Estimates put the average vocabulary of a likely Shakespearean theatergoer at only 800 words. The average adult in the year 2000, by contrast, had a vocabulary of 7,000 to 10,000 words, many of which Shakespeare himself made current. *Weird, swagger, radiance, lament, invitation, frugal, bedazzle,* and *accuse* are just a few of the words for which the *Oxford English Dictionary* cites Shakespeare as the first known use. There is no way of knowing which of these he truly invented and which simply benefited from his publicity. But at least some of the words we understand easily today would have sounded newfangled or even nonsensical to his own audiences.

But no matter how big your vocabulary is, Shakespeare's language can be tough. Daunting, even. Send-you-screaming-for-the-hills hard. But the density and beauty of his language is precisely what's made his work stand the test of time. Shakespeare uses language to create a rich experience for his audience, rather than simply conveying a story. Working your way through his words will help you understand his genius.

Language and Character

Even if you don't understand every word they speak, you can start to get a feel for Shakespearean characters if you pay attention to the *way* they speak. The language characters use reveals details about their social class, personality, mood, and current situation. When characters experience a change, their language changes as well. For example, we're first introduced to the character who will become King Henry V in *Henry IV, Parts One* and *Two*, where he is known as Prince Hal. Prince Hal's evolution from a wild mischief-maker into a heroic king in *Henry V* is probably the most famous conversion in Shakespeare. In *Henry VI, Part One*, the young prince's tavern talk is vulgar and riddled with slang:

> Wilt thou rob this leathern jerkin, crystal-button,
> not-pated, agate-ring, puke-stocking, caddis-garter,
> smooth-tongue, Spanish-pouch,—

However, when he banishes Falstaff, his longtime partner in crime, after being crowned King of England, Henry's speech becomes correspondingly stately in order to distance himself from the unruly boy he was:

> I know thee not, old man: fall to thy prayers;
> How ill white hairs become a fool and jester!
> I have long dream'd of such a kind of man,
> So surfeit-swell'd, so old and so profane;
> But, being awaked, I do despise my dream.

The first set of lines sounds raucous and wild—a lot like Prince Hal himself. The second set sounds staid and high-handed, appropriate for the king that Henry has become. If you can describe the words a character uses, you begin to understand the character.

Shakespeare regularly uses a handful of speech patterns in his characters' dialogue. If you can recognize the following tactics, you can see how words sometimes speak louder than actions.

DOES THE CHARACTER SPEAK IN PROSE OR VERSE?

This can be a clue to the character's class standing or emotional situation. Poetry (whether rhymed or unrhymed) is more formal and highbrow than prose, so gentlemen and kings tend to use it more than commoners. Comic characters generally speak in prose. Formal speeches and announcements tend to be written in verse, and characters often fall into it when they're in heightened emotional states, whether in love, enraged, or in lamentation. One of the most famous examples of how Shakespeare uses poetry to convey extreme emotion is when Romeo and Juliet first meet at the Capulets' ball: their first exchange forms a perfect, fourteen-line love sonnet.

HOW LONG ARE THE CHARACTER'S LINES?

Sometimes the key isn't what characters say but how long they take to say it. Long-winded characters tend to have extreme personalities. Falstaff of *Henry IV, Parts One* and *Two* and *Henry V*, and *Hamlet*'s Polonius are two comical examples: both wise old windbags, but the first a little wiser and the second a little more of a windbag.

HOW MANY LINES DOES THE CHARACTER HAVE?

Characters with a lot of lines tend to be very smart, though they may use that intelligence in diverse ways. King Richard III has the second most lines of any character in Shakespeare, and is arguably the most evil. More than his wicked deeds, though, it's Richard's ability to use good words for bad purposes that makes him so terrifying. The #1 most talkative character in Shakespeare (with 1,422 lines in a single play) is in many ways the opposite of Richard III. "Words, words, words," Hamlet babbles at one point. But while Richard uses words to manipulate the world around him, Hamlet uses his words to figure out what's going on inside his own head and the heads of others. Hamlet is king of the monologue, or long uninterrupted passage of dialogue, as well as the soliloquy, or a monologue a character speaks to him- or herself (or the audience). Soliloquies are usually moments of unguarded self-revelation, such as when Hamlet's devious uncle Claudius confesses to feeling guilt over his brother's murder. Characters who frequently use this method of speech tend, like Hamlet, to be deep, contemplative thinkers.

DOES THE CHARACTER SPEAK IN RIDDLES OR RHYMES?

Characters who are somehow out of the ordinary—whether sick, insane, or magical—communicate in ways that are also out of the ordinary. Instead of speaking they may sing, rhyme, or jabber nonsensically. Some characters use language as a source of power: Prospero, the wizard from *The Tempest*, and Puck, the fairy from *A Midsummer Night's Dream*, speak in rhymes and contradictions when conjuring their supernatural powers. The three witches of *Macbeth* also tend to speak in riddling incantations, and in the first scene they speak in perfectly rhymed couplets. On the flip side, when characters begin to lose their mental faculties their language abilities go with it. When King Lear and *Hamlet*'s Ophelia go mad, for example, they begin to rave and sing enigmatic songs.

Metaphors and Figurative Language

Shakespeare's plays and poems are full of figurative language. There are many types of figurative language, but they all do basically the same thing: equate or compare two seemingly unrelated things. Many of Shakespeare's similes and metaphors are famous all on their own: "Life is but a walking shadow" and "Brevity is the soul of wit." Others are so short and apt that they've become common phrases in everyday English: "the mind's eye," "salad days," and "jaws of death" are just a few.

Shakespeare's metaphors are often rich and complicated. When Romeo says, "Juliet is the sun," he obviously doesn't mean it literally. (That could be painful.) But Juliet makes Romeo think of the sun, because of her brightness, her warmth, the fact that his whole world revolves around her, and his feeling that his life depends on her. However, like many of Shakespeare's metaphors, Romeo's worshipful declaration has additional implications that Romeo may not be aware of. Shakespeare's audiences would have been very familiar with the classical myth of Icarus, the boy who flew too close to the sun while wearing wings made of wax. As Romeo looks up to his beloved's balcony, the audience might start to get a sense of the couple's impending doom.

Another of Shakespeare's favorite figurative techniques is personification, which gives human qualities to animals, objects, or even ideas. Shakespeare frequently uses personification to describe emotions or events that have taken on a life of their own. When Lady Macbeth considers the evil deeds that she and Macbeth must undertake to get the crown, she cries:

> Come, black night! Come, thick night
> And pall thee in the dunnest smoke of hell,
> That my keen knife see not the wound it makes,
> Nor heaven peep through the blanket of the dark,
> To cry, "Hold, hold!"

In these lines, the night smears itself in smoke, the knife's vision grows cloudy, and heaven holds its tongue. By making it seem as if these inanimate objects have wills of their own, Lady Macbeth tries to deny any control over the escalating situation.

Shakespeare uses metaphors and other kinds of figurative language to pack his lines with extra meaning, which is why reading his plays can be such a confounding but ultimately rich experience. Unfortunately, there's no single method for interpreting them. Sometimes Shakespeare helps us out by making a metaphor extended and obvious, as in Jaques's soliloquy from *As You Like It*, which starts with the famous line "All the world's a stage" and goes on to compare the stages of a human being's life to the acts in a play and human beings to actors. Other metaphors recur in bits and pieces throughout a play and help to establish the major themes. *Hamlet*, for example, is full of metaphors of the human body, comparing aspects of life to individual body parts, diseases of the body, and sexuality. *King Lear* is replete with animal metaphors, appropriate for a play that dwells on the theme of man's inner beast. *Romeo and Juliet* relies on metaphors of the sun, the stars, and the seasons in repeated motifs about love and fate.

Puns

Shakespeare just adored puns, or plays on words. The guy couldn't get enough of them. Like metaphors and similes, Shakespeare uses puns to pack his dialogue with layers of meaning. Some of his puns are quick and easy, such as when the joker Mercutio, dying of a stab wound, tells his friends, "Ask for me tomorrow, and you shall find me a grave man." Many Shakespearean puns, however, are longer and more intricate and may play on meanings of words that aren't common in today's English. For example, when Romeo asks Juliet for assurances of her love, he says:

> [I]f the measure of thy joy
> Be heaped like mine and that thy skill be more

> To blazon it, then sweeten with thy breath
> This neighbor air and let rich music's tongue
> Unfold the imagined happiness that both
> Receive in either by this dear encounter.

In other words, "Juliet, if our loves are equal in measure, and since you are better at expressing yourself, let me hear the wonderful sound of your voice describing all the happiness of our having found each other." Although the word *measure* here primarily means "amount," it also has the secondary meaning of "musical phrase." Romeo plays on this alternate definition by telling Juliet that he anticipates the "rich music" of her response. *Measure* is one of Shakespeare's favorite pun words, and whenever it pops up you can expect there to be multiple images attached to it.

The word *dear* is another one of Shakespeare's heavy hitters. In Elizabethan English, the word meant both "cherished" and "expensive." Romeo means it in the first sense, but he may not be fully aware of the additional implication. Audience members who know the doom that lies ahead for Romeo and Juliet would agree with the poor boy: the love that he holds dear will come at a very dear cost, indeed.

A character's use (or misuse) of puns can also help us understand that character's level of intelligence. Bumbling comic characters often pun unintentionally. The foolish constable Dogberry in *Much Ado About Nothing*, for example, tends to mix up his fancy words when trying to sound cultured. He tells the governor Leonato, "Our watch, sir, have indeed comprehended two auspicious persons"—meaning that the rustic policemen have *apprehended* two *suspicious* persons. Intelligent characters, on the other hand, are in full control of their wordplay. Hamlet, for example, speaks in double, triple, and opposite meanings and doesn't particularly care who understands him. This carelessness lets us know that Hamlet, for all his reputation as a sensitive mama's boy, has a nasty little arrogant streak.

Most plays have a character who excels at verbal roughhousing and who constantly entertains or mocks those around him by manipulating language. *The Taming of the Shrew* has two of them: the warring spouses Katherine and Petruccio. Their repartee, such as this typical exchange, gives the play its dynamic comic quality:

KATHERINE
Asses are made to bear, and so are you.
PETRUCCIO
Women are made to bear, and so are you.
KATHERINE
No such jade as you, if me you mean.

Sexual puns are everywhere in Shakespeare (and we really do mean *everywhere*—don't let your teachers hide the good stuff from you), but they're rarely so bawdy, overt, and unrelenting as Kate and Petruccio's banter. *Bear*, another frequent Shakespeare pun, has four meanings in this case: to carry, to expose, to give birth, and to put up with. Kate's first line means both "Donkeys are made to carry things, and you are a donkey" and "Buttocks are made to be exposed; you're an ass." Petruccio's reply means all of the following: "Women are made to give birth," "Women are made to take off their clothes," and "Women are made to bear the weight of a man." Kate then retorts that she's not a tired old horse who will bear (put up with, lie underneath) a jerk like him.

Puns are so ubiquitous in the plays that many critics begin to see them in places that Shakespeare himself may not have intended, and arguments about the different meanings of a particular word have filled books themselves. The important thing is to be as playful in listening to Shakespeare's words as he was in composing them. Once you're open to multiple meanings, you'll start noticing them everywhere too. Besides *measure*, *dear*, and *bear*, some of the words that pop up most frequently in Shakespearean puns are *heart-hart* (a male deer), *grace*, *will*, *son-sun*, *lie*, *light*, *crown*, *color*, *use*, *state*, *kind*, and *arms*.

Syntax

One of the things that makes Shakespeare most complicated for modern readers is the variability of his syntax. English sentence structure today follows a fairly predictable subject-verb-object (SVO) pattern, with very few exceptions (e.g. "Romeo went to the ball," "Macbeth killed Duncan"). Elizabethan grammar was much more flexible, swapping subjects, objects, and verbs around seemingly willy-nilly.

Shakespeare took special advantage of this flexibility, aggressively bending sentence structure to serve the meaning and rhythm of his compositions. Sometimes, reading Shakespeare can feel a bit like listening to *Star Wars'* Yoda. (Really, is there that much difference between "Do or do not, there is no try" and "To be or not to be, that is the question"?) But as unique and strange as Shakespeare's language is, it's precisely that poetic quality that has made such lines as "to thine own self be true," "let slip the dogs of war," and "we are such stuff as dreams are made on" ring in people's ears for the past four centuries.

Shakespeare makes frequent use of some sentence structures we're not used to seeing today:

SUBJECT-OBJECT-VERB (SOV)

In this exchange from *Hamlet*, Queen Gertrude upbraids her wayward son:

GERTRUDE
Hamlet, thou hast thy father much offended.
HAMLET
Mother, you have my father much offended.

Both Gertrude's admonishment and Hamlet's retort place the accusatory word *offended* at the end, lending their exchange an extra punch and severity. If Shakespeare had used the SVO construction we're more used to hearing ("Mother, you have much offended my father") the sentences would have ended on *father*, a much softer word with more pleasant associations. Also, in this context, the SOV word order makes Gertrude's reproach sound more rhythmic: *thou HAST thy FA-ther MUCH of-FEND-ed.*

SOV word order also makes pronouncements sound more formal. This is no ordinary moment of parent–child bickering: this is the showdown in which Hamlet finally confronts his mother and accuses her of being a wicked, sinful adulterer. Because of its heightened formality, Shakespeare often uses the SOV word order in courtly speech or for situations of high drama, such as the moments before battle ("Remember, lords, your oaths to Henry sworn," from *Henry VI, Part One*) or expressions of grief ("but his flawed heart, / Alack, too weak the conflict to support!" from *King Lear*).

Some other examples of Shakespearean SOV structure include:

- "A glooming peace this morning with it brings." (*Romeo and Juliet*)
- "That handkerchief did an Egyptian to my mother give." (*Othello*)
- " . . . thou among the wastes of time must go . . . " (Sonnet 12)

OBJECT-VERB-SUBJECT (OVS)

One of Shakespeare's most famous lines, "What a piece of work is a man!" uses another unfamiliar sentence structure: object-verb-subject. Shakespeare uses this OVS word order when he wants to emphasize to the person, place, or thing being described. In *Richard III*, for example, a citizen exclaims, "Oh, full of danger is the Duke of Gloucester!" By arranging a sentence this way, Shakespeare creates a sense of suspense: the reader or audience member must wait for the source of this danger to be revealed.

Even in Elizabethan London, object-verb-subject word order was almost entirely literary, rarely occurring in everyday colloquial speech, and its use in the plays is often highly poetic. In *The Winter's Tale*, a scene opens with a character announcing, "Nine changes of the wat'ry star hath been / The shepherd's note," meaning, "Nine changes of the moon have been observed by the shepherd," or even more simply, "Nine months have passed." This kind of syntax is often used by characters making introductions and conclusions, magical incantations, or emotional exclamations.

Other examples of OVS phrases from Shakespeare include:

*   "Away from light steals home my heavy son . . . " (*Romeo and Juliet*)
*   "As thick as hail / Came post with post . . . " (*Macbeth*)

OBJECT-SUBJECT-VERB (OSV)

When Banquo and Macbeth, two Scottish lords, meet three witches in the forest, and the old crones prophesy that Macbeth will soon receive glorious new titles, Banquo says:

> *My noble partner*
> *You greet with present grace and great prediction*
> Of noble having and of royal hope,
> That he seems rapt withal: *to me you speak not.*

In the italicized portions of the passage, Banquo uses the formal-sounding object-subject-verb structure. In this case, though Banquo addresses the witches (therefore making the plural "you" the subject), he's more concerned about Macbeth and himself. By placing the objects at the beginning of these italicized phrases, a sulky Banquo emphasizes the comparison between him and his friend and the disparity in the gifts they have received.

These OSV phrases similarly draw attention to the object in the beginning:

*   "Me they shall feel" (*Romeo and Juliet*)
*   "His soul thou canst not have" (*Richard III*)
*   "two-and-twenty knights / Balked in their own blood, did Sir Walter see" (*Henry IV, Part One*)

TWELVE

THE FIVE GREATEST SHAKESPEARE CHARACTERS

Hamlet

Hamlet, the anti-hero of Shakespeare's most famous tragedy, embodies the inertia and bewilderment of an introverted young man in an operatic world of passion, violence, and betrayal. Claudius has murdered Hamlet's father and married his mother, Gertrude, yet when his father's ghost demands that Hamlet seek revenge, the prince cannot act. While Hamlet admires people like the Player King, an actor who can conjure passions from thin air, ultimately, not even the vicious murder of his father can stir sufficient rage in him. Why not? Despite centuries of performances and whole libraries of criticism, Hamlet's reasons remain essentially a mystery. It is as if there is a black hole at the center of this character—an unseeable, unknowable chasm, as attractive to us as it is destructive to him. This explains why actors approach the role with such awe and trepidation and why audiences return again and again, hoping for another glimpse past Hamlet and into the void.

Falstaff

Falstaff may be a lecherous old fool, but his frank amorality and infectious joie de vivre have consistently captivated theatergoers, especially Queen Elizabeth I. In fact, legend has it that *The Merry Wives of Windsor* was Shakespeare's response to a specific request from the queen that he show "Falstaff in love." Although Falstaff appears in three history plays (*Henry IV, Parts One* and *Two,* and *Henry V*), he is purely a creation of Shakespeare's imagination: both an embodiment of Prince Hal's notoriously loose youth and a witty, expansive counterpart to the grave and exact proceedings of state. If he is dishonorable, at least he is honest with us about it, famously retorting, "What is honor? A word." In the *Henry IV* plays, where the "honorable" nobility slowly hack each other to death, Falstaff's philosophical cowardice satisfies not only as comic relief but as a protest against the ruthless honor of those around him.

Richard III

Cunning and brutal in equal measure, Richard, the hunchbacked Duke of Gloucester in *Richard III,* has elicited the cheers and jeers of four centuries' worth of audiences. He mercilessly quells all opposition to his swift and unjust rise to the throne; but he accomplishes his most horrifying feats through charisma, not violence. In the most famous scene from *Richard III,* Richard seduces Lady Anne, whose husband he has killed. Historically, this courtship happened long after Anne's bereavement, but Shakespeare has Richard, in a spine-tingling feat of rhetoric, seduce her in the middle of the funeral procession, even as she mourns over her husband's corpse. The most enduring source of Richard's popularity as a character, though, is the string of monologues throughout the play in which he confides his schemes to the audience. Simultaneously heartless and alluring, vile and giddy, these speeches allow the audience an illicit view into the revolting pleasures of villainy.

Lady Macbeth

"Unsex me here," pleads Lady Macbeth in her first appearance in *Macbeth*, "And fill me from the crown to the toe top full of direst cruelty!" With this early invocation, Lady Macbeth transforms herself, but in doing so, she calls attention to a dangerous rift in her character—between who she truly is and who she has chosen to become. Having decided to give her ambition full rein, she masterminds a bloody plot for her husband's enthronement. Audiences thrill at her strength and nerve, which stand out starkly against the background of her husband's ambivalence; but if her audacity

is greater, so too is her guilt. As her husband ascends from indecisiveness to royal power, she descends into madness, trying—in her sleep—to scour the invisible bloodstains from her hands, and ultimately committing suicide. Shakespeare never explicitly reveals the cause of Lady Macbeth's instability, but he tantalizes audiences with the possibilities.

Mercutio

Sparkling with wit and imagination, Mercutio is the soul of *Romeo and Juliet* and its most innocent victim. In defiance of the heavy metaphors and naïve sincerity of his good friend, the love-struck Romeo, Mercutio peppers his language with wordplay and sexual innuendo. As a relentless satirist, Mercutio mocks Benvolio as much for his hotheaded pride as he teases Romeo for his exasperating notions of love, but like all satirists, he harbors a serious purpose. His critique of the Montague family's bombastic feud with the Capulets is genuine, and if his wit sugarcoats his criticisms a little too carefully, he himself suffers the consequences. In a duel intended to involve only Romeo and Tybalt (Juliet's cousin), Mercutio receives a fatal wound. Even with his final gasping lines, the indomitable Mercutio manages to crack a few jokes, though, saying, "Ask for me tomorrow, and you shall find me a grave man."

PART II

SHAKESPEARE'S PLAYS

Everything you really need to know about each of Shakespeare's plays

THE TOP TEN

TEN PLAYS
THAT EVERYONE
SHOULD KNOW

ONE

HAMLET

Prince Hamlet seeks to avenge his father's murder by bringing his uncle Claudius, the new king, to justice.

Brief Synopsis

Prince Hamlet of Denmark is visited by the ghost of **King Hamlet,** his recently deceased father. The ghost reveals that his own brother **Claudius** killed him. Claudius has married **Queen Gertrude** and taken the throne. Hamlet vows to revenge his father's murder, but he wants more proof that what the ghost says is true. To keep Claudius from detecting his plans, he decides to behave as if he is insane, which concerns Claudius and Gertrude. **Polonius,** the lord chamberlain, suggests that Hamlet is lovesick for Polonius's daughter, **Ophelia,** but when they test this suggestion, Hamlet spurns Ophelia.

To test whether Claudius is guilty, Hamlet arranges for some actors to perform a play in which a king is murdered in a manner similar to that of King Hamlet. Claudius leaps to his feet and leaves the room when the murder is enacted, which Hamlet interprets as a proof of his guilt. Hamlet goes to kill Claudius, but when he sees Claudius praying, he decides not to kill him. Hamlet angrily confronts his mother, Gertrude, in her bedroom, and when he hears the noise of someone hiding behind a curtain he stabs the person, who turns out to be Polonius. Claudius orders that Hamlet be sent to England, and he entrusts the courtiers **Rosencrantz** and **Guildenstern** to deliver a letter asking the King of England to put Hamlet to death at once.

Ophelia goes mad after her father's death and drowns in a river. Her brother **Laertes** returns from France to avenge Polonius's and Ophelia's deaths, which Claudius blames on Hamlet. Hamlet returns to Denmark after pirates attack his ship, and Claudius arranges a fencing match between Laertes and Hamlet in which he poisons Laertes's sword and a cup that he intends to give Hamlet. Laertes wounds Hamlet, but then is poisoned by his own sword, Gertrude drinks out of the poisoned cup, Hamlet kills Claudius, and then Hamlet dies from his poisoned wound.

What to Remember About *Hamlet*

HAMLET IS A UNIQUELY COMPELLING CHARACTER.

For most of the past 400 years, Shakespeare's readers have pointed to Hamlet himself as the interesting thing about the play. The role of Hamlet is one of the most coveted among actors, and critics and scholars have written more about Hamlet than about any other character—and possibly any other topic in Shakespeare. Today, many Shakespeare experts would argue that this obsession with the title character is excessive and that it prevents us from seeing everything else that's going on in the play. But if you want to understand what all the fuss regarding this play is about, it makes sense to start with why people think Hamlet is such a special character.

HAMLET IS DIMENSIONAL.

Robert McKee, the author of *Story*, defines *dimension* as "a contradiction consistently maintained" by a character. For example, if a character always acts helpful or friendly but always cheats the people he's helping, that character has a dimension. If we see a character behaving all different ways at different times, we would say that the character was erratic or inconsistent, and we wouldn't be able to make sense of him. But when we see characters *consistently* display two contradictory attitudes, behaviors, or traits, we enjoy it because we feel like we're figuring out the characters, seeing something about them that isn't on the surface.

Hamlet, as McKee notes, displays many contradictory pairs of traits, meaning that he's multidimensional. For example, many readers have characterized Hamlet as contemplative and hesitant, a man of thought rather than action, but he's actually not so one-sided. Many of his speeches reveal that he prizes resolute and decisive action when he sees it in other people, and at times he acts very impulsively and decisively (as when he stabs Polonius, or when he sends Rosencrantz and Guildenstern to their deaths). His moments of hesitation are interesting because they consistently contradict his own stated values. At times he seems very careful, worried about the consequences of taking action and anxious to know as much as possible, and at other times he acts blindly and recklessly.

Hamlet's madness reflects this contradiction between carefulness and recklessness. Right after he speaks with the ghost, he tells his friends that he's going to deliberately pretend he's mad, which makes us think that pretending to be mad must be part of his plan to get revenge. This strategy is familiar from history and literature—by acting crazy (or stupid) you make your enemies think you're harmless and you keep them from seeing what you're really up to. But when Hamlet actually does start acting crazy, he does it in a way that makes no sense at all strategically. He draws attention to himself and makes everyone, particularly his enemy Claudius, worry about what he's doing. Claudius quickly concludes that he's dangerous and should be sent away, even put to death. Hamlet's "madness" is so pointless and counterproductive that many people conclude that Hamlet actually *must* be at least partly insane, notwithstanding the fact that he warns us that he's going to pretend to be insane.

Hamlet's other consistent inconsistencies include the following:

- Sometimes he acts like he loves Ophelia, at other times like he hates and mistrusts her.
- Sometimes he acts as though his primary concern is avenging his father's murder by Claudius, but he often seems more upset that his mother has chosen to sleep with Claudius.
- He claims that he hates the world and desires to be back at the university, but at other times he claims that he hoped to be king.

If you hate the play, you might argue that Hamlet is so inconsistent that the play simply makes no sense and that there is no answer to questions like whether he loves Ophelia or whether he ever goes mad. But if you see these inconsistencies as dimensions, it helps to explain the enormous popularity of the play and the character. When you catch him in the act of being inconsistent, you feel like you've seen past his façade and glimpsed who he really is, which means that his contradictions foster the illusion that he's real.

THERE'S MORE TO HAMLET THAN MEETS THE EYE.

Actually, that's one of the first things we hear Hamlet say about himself—he has "that within which passeth show," meaning there's something inside him that you can't tell just by looking at him. But it's true that at many points in the play we get the sense that there's something going on inside Hamlet beyond what he's actually saying. In fact, our feeling that there's more than meets the eye goes much deeper than this. We actually get the sense that there are things going on inside Hamlet that even he isn't aware of. It's an illusion, of course—there is no real person underneath the words—but the illusion that we're seeing a real human being is very effective. Much of it is created by the inconsistencies between the things he says, or between what he says and what he does, so that it seems to us that he doesn't even really know what's motivating him to act the way he does but is justifying his actions with whatever rationale comes to his mind. But this impression only makes us feel more strongly that he has a *real* motivation that's just out of our reach.

Another important way in which Hamlet conveys an illusion of depth is by delivering soliloquies that seem to only hint indirectly at what's on his mind. Most people think of the "To be, or not to be" soliloquy as a particularly soul-baring moment, but in that soliloquy he never says the word "I," never discusses himself or his feelings directly, and never comes out and says that he wants to kill himself. He doesn't deal in concrete specifics about himself. Instead, the whole soliloquy is framed as a question of abstractions—to do this, to do that, this is a "consummation . . . to be wished" for—as if it were a debate he might be arguing in school. The fact that we have to infer why he's giving voice to these abstractions makes him seem powerfully realistic, as if there's something he can't say directly, and he's saying this instead. The same is true of his speech to Rosencrantz and Guildenstern in Act 2, scene 2:

> What piece of work is a man, how noble in reason, how infinite
> in faculties, in form and moving how express and admirable,
> in action how like an angel, in apprehension how like a god: the
> beauty of the world, the paragon of animals . . .

He's not speaking about himself or the other characters but instead discussing man in the abstract and drawing on a passage from a famous Renaissance writer, Pico della Mirandola. But by doing so he gives the impression that he has feelings that he's unable to state directly.

TWO

ROMEO
AND
JULIET

Despite their families' mutual hatred, Romeo and Juliet fall in love and marry, only to die because of a misunderstanding.

Brief Synopsis

In the city of Verona, the houses of the lords **Montague** and **Capulet** are engaged in a violent, seemingly endless feud. After a fight breaks out in the public square, the **Prince of Verona** threatens death to anyone who further dares to break the peace. That night, **Romeo,** the son of Montague, goes to a masked ball at the Capulet house and falls desperately in love with Capulet's only daughter, **Juliet.** Juliet falls for Romeo just as quickly. Soon they are married secretly by Romeo's confessor, **Friar Lawrence,** who hopes the marriage will bring an end to their families' longstanding feud.

The day after the wedding, Juliet's hot-headed cousin **Tybalt,** who had recognized Romeo as an intruder at the ball, challenges Romeo to a duel. At first Romeo refuses to fight his new kinsman, but when Tybalt kills Romeo's friend **Mercutio,** Romeo flies into a rage and kills him. The prince banishes

Romeo from Verona, but Romeo lingers one night to consummate his marriage to Juliet.

Juliet's father tries to force her to marry a nobleman named **Paris.** She seeks Friar Lawrence's help, and he tells her to take a potion that will make her appear to be dead—after her family leaves her for dead in the family tomb, she can be with Romeo freely. She takes the potion, fools her family, and is placed next to her ancestors in the tomb. A plague quarantine prevents Friar Lawrence's message from reaching Romeo, however, who hears only that Juliet has died. A despondent Romeo visits Juliet's grave at night, where he meets and kills Paris when Paris challenges him. Romeo swallows a poison and dies by Juliet's side. Juliet wakes and, finding her beloved dead, kills herself with his dagger. Friar Lawrence reveals the whole story to the crowd that gathers at the scene, and the sorrowful Capulet and Montague families pledge to end their feud.

What to Remember About
Romeo and Juliet

THE ADULTS ARE TO BLAME FOR THEIR CHILDREN'S TRAGEDY.

Romeo and Juliet is Shakespeare's only play to focus primarily on very young characters. The adult figures in the play mostly serve as obstacles (Capulet, the prince) or facilitators (Friar Lawrence, the Nurse) to the teenagers' passions. For this reason, *Romeo and Juliet* is usually considered a youthful romantic tragedy. However, the play also concerns the cynical world of adult experience, and the play's terrible ending can be blamed in large part on the adults who attempt to use the young lovers as pawns in a grown-up game of political strategy.

Against his better judgment, Friar Lawrence facilitates a speedy marriage for Romeo and Juliet in the hopes that it will bring a swift and sudden end to the feud between the Capulet and Montague families. As his confessor, Friar Lawrence listened as Romeo pined—as recently as the day before the ball—about another girl, Rosaline, making him skeptical of Romeo's seriousness. Nonetheless, he proceeds with plot after covert plot, each more intricate and dangerous than the last, in order to secure the dubious marriage. If he had recommended to Romeo the same course of moderation that he did regarding Rosaline, maybe the tragic ending could have been avoided. Instead, applying a double-standard in the service of political goals, he hastens a rash marriage, one that he has good reason to suspect is more founded on naïve, sexual infatuation than true love.

Juliet's father, Lord Capulet, also proves guilty of political maneuvering at his daughter's expense. Initially, Lord Capulet encourages Paris to court Juliet but strongly asserts two conditions. First, he will not allow Juliet to marry for another two years, as he knows that early marriage and young pregnancy can be dangerous for the mother's health. He also urges patience because he respects his daughter's opinion: He warns Paris that the final choice of husband will belong to Juliet alone. This fatherly concern contrasts sharply with his extreme change of heart a few days later, when, without consulting his daughter, he suddenly exclaims that he will wed her to Paris immediately. The only plausible answer for his anxious rush is that Capulet, frightened by the fact that his kinsman Tybalt has just killed Mercutio, a relative of the powerful Prince of Verona, wants to reassure the prince of his family's loyalty by marrying his daughter—his most potent and precious bargaining chip—to Paris, another of the prince's relatives. By joining the Capulets to the royal family in matrimony, he can gain a degree of immunity, not to mention a lasting upper hand in the feud against the Montagues. While Capulet cannot foresee the dire consequences his political schemes will have, his rash tactics lead directly to the play's high body count.

THE MONTAGUE-CAPULET FEUD HOLDS NEW MEANING FOR EACH GENERATION OF AUDIENCES.

No one seems to know why the Capulets and Montagues have been fighting for as long as they have—perhaps not even the feuding families themselves. The hostility simply functions as an accepted precondition of the play's events, yet the lack of a reason for the families' rank hatred forms an intriguing void at the heart of *Romeo and Juliet*. Perhaps Shakespeare avoids providing a reason because he doesn't want to give his audiences an opportunity to rationalize or justify the feud. Plus, by leaving the backstory so unspecific, Shakespeare also invites the audience to fill in the gaps for him. Modern productions have used the play to comment on sectarian violence of all kinds, from racial divisions in the United States to political hostility in Ireland to religious differences in India. If two groups have fought, chances are there's been a production of *Romeo and Juliet* somewhere that used that violence as a framework.

Audiences in Shakespeare's day would have probably seen contemporary parallels of their own in *Romeo and Juliet*. Under the reign of Elizabeth I, England experienced a golden age of achievement and prosperity, but it was certainly not a time of peace. Abroad, an undeclared war raged with Spain, and at home, religious strife spurred frequent assassination attempts on the queen. To Shakespeare's audiences, the cyclical violence between the Capulets and the Montagues might have called to mind the ongoing feud between Catholics and Protestants. Since King Henry VIII split with the Catholic Church and established a new Church of England, English Catholics had been viciously persecuted. When Queen Mary I, a staunch Catholic, inherited the crown from her father, she retaliated by torturing and killing several hundred Protestant leaders—earning her the eternal nickname of Bloody Mary. When Queen Elizabeth ascended the throne in 1558, she tried to set the country on a more even keel by refusing to strictly enforce the laws persecuting Catholics, but religious violence erupted nevertheless. In 1570, John Felton, a wealthy

English Catholic, nailed to the Bishop of London's door an official papal command excommunicating Elizabeth. This led to a renewed cycle of violence that persisted throughout Elizabeth's reign.

Shakespeare doesn't set out to create a rigid system of symbols in which the families and their actions represent specific historical events. Instead, he channels all the hostility and paranoia of the times into a story of young love thwarted by a nameless but pervasive source of brutality. This indirect approach allows successive generations of audiences to see in Verona's "new mutiny" a representation of their own era's tensions.

MERCUTIO STEMS THE TIDE OF TRAGEDY.

According to a legend that circulated after his death, Shakespeare once said that he had to kill off the character Mercutio before Mercutio killed him. Whether or not Shakespeare actually said this, it does point to something strange about the play—namely, that Mercutio doesn't seem to belong in it. Mercutio's name derives from that of the Roman god Mercury. According to Renaissance astrological beliefs, someone born under the influence of Mercury would be energetic, quick-witted, and, above all, volatile. Mercutio fits this description perfectly. He forcefully inserts himself into the action, stealing scenes left and right. While he is an undeniably theatrical character, he seems almost anti-theatrical in the way that he rebels against all of the forces that push the play to its conclusion: He is too crass for the adults' smooth political maneuverings, too glib for the easy sentimentalism of the young lovers, and too willfully erratic to be believably ruled by fate.

Mercutio is first and foremost a satirist, and like most satirists, he occupies a privileged position, simultaneously insider and outsider. As a good friend of Romeo's, Mercutio is close to the action, but as one of the few people not related to the feud through kinship ties he maintains a sense of detachment. From this location, Mercutio can both diagnose and mock the excessive passions the feud engenders. His barbs are equal opportunity insults: He ridicules Benvolio for his hot-headedness and Tybalt for his bombast. He challenges the play's romantic notions with lewd rants about sex and the female anatomy. Even his very language is rebellious: Against Benvolio's blunt talk of honor and Romeo's earnest, metaphor-heavy verse, Mercutio offers eccentric, sophisticated dialogue laced with puns and innuendo. Mercutio, the most consistently funny character in *Romeo and Juliet* apart from the Nurse (though infinitely more insightful than that jolly old woman), cuts against the grain in every fashion.

Verona is sick with turbulence, but Mercutio provides an antidote to all the deathly seriousness. While he lives, Mercutio's insightful repartee keeps the play's mounting passions—both love and hatred—from boiling over. When he dies, any hope for balance in Verona dies with him. Though he continues to crack jokes as he lays dying (telling his friends to ask after him tomorrow, when they will find him a "grave" man), his final words carry a bitter curse against the feuding households. In this way, Mercutio's satire is like Romeo and Juliet's love. Both represent forces that might heal this rank, infested society, so in order for the play to reach its tragic conclusion, both of these forces must be snuffed out. Mercutio's death represents the turning point where *Romeo and Juliet* shifts undeniably from a potential comedy to a certain tragedy.

ROMEO AND JULIET IS THE SISTER PLAY TO *A MIDSUMMER NIGHT'S DREAM.*

In *A Midsummer Night's Dream*, the young nobles Hermia and Lysander elope into the forests surrounding Athens. They are followed by Hermia's other suitor, Demetrius, and Helena, the woman Demetrius has spurned. As the comedy unfolds, the sprites and fairies of the forest use their powers to disentangle this knotty love quadrangle.

At first glance, *Romeo and Juliet* and *A Midsummer Night's Dream* could not seem more different. One is an epic tragedy, pitting naïve love against the unstoppable forces of divine fate and human violence; the other, a silly fantasy about fairies and trysts. However, there is much historical evidence to suggest that the two plays were written in sequence (if not simultaneously) between 1595 and 1596. With this chronological link in mind, a deeper look reveals many plot similarities and thematic connections.

Plot-wise, both stories emerge from the same problem: Two youths fall into a forbidden love and must pursue a secret scheme in order to secure their future together. The thematic similarities, though, are less obvious and rely mainly on a single, shared image. In Act 1, scene 4 of *Romeo*, Mercutio mocks Romeo's ominous dreams with an elaborate description of Queen Mab, the fairy who brings dreams. This famous speech shows the strongest trace of *A Midsummer Night's Dream* in *Romeo and Juliet*. At first, the creature that Mercutio describes seems to belong more to the beneficent dreamworld of *Midsummer* than the violent world of *Romeo*. Tiny as a ring and riding in a chariot made of grasshoppers' wings and spiders' webs, Queen Mab appears charming and winsome. As the speech continues, though, Queen Mab earns her place in the grimmer world of *Romeo and Juliet*. The dreams that Queen Mab brings, it seems, show only what the dreamer wants to see, aggravating rather than resolving conflicts. After all, the same fairy that brings visions of kisses to the young maid also brings gruesome, drunken dreams to the soldier. *Romeo and Juliet*, it turns out, is the dark complement to its sister comedy. Whereas *A Midsummer Night's Dream* disproves Lysander's fear that, in love, "quick bright things come to confusion," *Romeo and Juliet* affirms this pessimistic view.

THREE

KING LEAR

King Lear attempts to divide Britain among his three daughters, which brings ruin to the kingdom.

Brief Synopsis

In *King Lear*, Shakespeare offers a searing portrayal of the complex family relations that exist between aging parents and their adult children.

Lear, the elderly King of Britain, decides to step down and divide his kingdom among his three daughters. In a public ceremony, Lear tests each of his daughters by asking them to describe how much they love him. Because his youngest daughter, **Cordelia,** refuses to flatter him in her turn, he disowns her and gives the kingdom to his older daughters, **Goneril** and **Regan.** When Goneril and Regan subsequently abuse Lear, he slowly begins to lose his grip on reality. During a terrible thunderstorm, he wanders out onto the heath, or field, cursing nature and raging at his fate.

Meanwhile, an elderly nobleman named **Gloucester** also experiences family problems. His illegitimate son, **Edmund,** tricks him into believing that his legitimate son, **Edgar,** is trying to kill him. Fleeing the manhunt that his father has set for him, Edgar disguises himself as a mad beggar and calls himself Poor Tom. Like Lear, Edgar heads out onto the heath. When the loyal Gloucester realizes that Lear's daughters have turned against their father, he decides to help Lear in spite of the danger.

Regan and her husband, **Cornwall,** discover Gloucester helping Lear, accuse him of treason, blind him, and turn him out to wander the countryside. His son Edgar—still in his Poor Tom disguise—leads him to the city of Dover, where Lear has been taken.

In Dover, a French army lands as part of an invasion led by Cordelia to save her father. Edmund, who has become romantically entangled with both Goneril and her sister Regan, conspires with Goneril to kill Goneril's husband, **Albany.**

The blind, despairing Gloucester tries to commit suicide, but Edgar saves his father by tricking him into thinking that a gentle slope in the ground is actually a high cliff.

The English troops reach Dover where, led by Edmund, they defeat Cordelia's army. Lear and Cordelia are captured. Edgar duels with Edmund and kills him. Gloucester's heart breaks upon his reconciliation with Edgar, and he dies. Goneril poisons Regan out of jealousy over Edmund and then kills herself. Cordelia is executed on Edmund's earlier orders, and Lear dies of grief.

What to Remember About *King Lear*

THREE WORDS HOLD THE KEY TO UNDERSTANDING *KING LEAR.*

King Lear is a vast and disorderly play, but three words echo repeatedly throughout the text: *fortune, fool,* and *nature.* Each word meant many different things in Shakespeare's day, and many of those distinctions are lost on today's audiences. Understanding the significance of these three words, however, is half the battle of understanding *King Lear.*

FORTUNE: **THE CHARACTERS OF** *KING LEAR* **WONDER WHY BAD THINGS HAPPEN TO GOOD PEOPLE.**

The characters in Shakespeare's tragedies usually meet with incalculable grief and suffering. In their anguish, these injured parties repeatedly debate whether people are ultimately responsible for their own torment or whether mortal lives are ruled by some power beyond humanity's grasp. This debate reaches a fever pitch in *King Lear*, mostly because the suffering is so intense and its distribution seems so manifestly unfair. In one of the most famous lines from the play, King Lear declares "I am a man / More sinn'd against than sinning," but Cordelia, Gloucester, Kent, Edgar, and perhaps even the Duke of Albany could assert this same claim. In fact, in no other Shakespearean play do characters experience a greater imbalance between their flaws and the extreme suffering those flaws incur.

Because their actions are so often met with such wildly excessive punishment, the characters in *King Lear* tend to blame their tragedies on external, cosmic forces. They don't want to believe that they have genuinely earned such suffering, nor that any human being could orchestrate such violent and degrading events. Gloucester is typical of most characters in *King Lear*, alternately blaming the stars and the gods for his situation.

Gloucester's bastard son, Edmund, who confidently manipulates everyone around him, tends to take the opposite view. As a villain who deliberately and methodically causes the suffering of others, Edmund believes that humans are completely in charge of their own destinies. He ridicules his father's belief in astrology, scoffing that it is an "excellent foppery," or great foolishness, that when humans experience a downturn in their fortunes, they tend to blame those disasters on "the sun, the moon, and stars," even though such events are often the result of their own excessive behavior. For Edmund, free will and human failings can explain all of the world's supposed injustices.

However, despite all the play's talk of divine versus human will, most of the characters blame their situations on random, impersonal fortune. From the Middle Ages onward, fortune was thought of as a continuously rolling wheel that crushes some as it carries others aloft. In a single revolution, those at the height of their destinies could suddenly find themselves in the dust. Even the ever-confident Edmund, felled by his brother, Edgar, in a hand-to-hand duel, finally accepts this notion of fortune, saying, "The wheel is come full circle, I am here" (here in the dust, that is). We may read *King Lear* as a pessimistic play that claims there is no such thing as true justice, merely the inevitable rise and fall of fortune. At the same time, the play invites us to seek moral meaning in its random chaos—just as human beings must do in their daily lives.

FOOL: IN *KING LEAR*, NOT ALL FOOLS ARE FOOLISH.

When Shakespearean characters use the term *fool*, they sometimes mean what we understand the word to mean today: a stupid or gullible person. Kent intends this meaning when he asks, "Smile you my speeches, as I were a fool?" Lear and Gloucester are both fools in this sense, in that they harm themselves by acting ignorantly. Lear rewards Goneril's and Regan's insincere flatteries and punishes Cordelia's plainspoken duty, allowing himself to be willfully misled as to his daughters' intentions. Similarly, Gloucester allows himself to be duped by Edmund into believing the worst of his rightful heir, Edgar.

Lear's Fool, on the other hand, embodies a different meaning of the term. In this sense, the word *fool* contrasts with the word *clown*. Clowns are characters who remain comically naïve, immersed so fully in the present moment that they seem to have no memory or sense of perspective. They fall for the same tricks over and over again, or else they frustrate other characters with their inability to understand simple facts or instructions. Fools, by contrast, often possess precocious wisdom and always maintain at least the appearance of detachment. If they sometimes use clownish tactics—uttering nonsense or feigning ignorance—they do so in order to mask their otherwise impertinent behavior. Using humor as a sort of smokescreen, a fool may criticize anyone at court, even the monarch if he dares, with relative impunity. Lear's Fool is the only character wise enough (or brazen enough) to openly disparage Lear for thinking that he could retain his authority after relinquishing his lands.

When Lear carries Cordelia's dead body onstage, he cries, "[M]y poor fool is hang'd! No, no, no life!" Here, Lear uses the word *fool* in a third way, this time as a common term of endearment possibly related to *foal*, or baby animal. However, Lear's wailing also exposes a deeper mystery in Cordelia's character. In the opening scene, two-thirds of Britain had already been distributed when it came time for Cordelia to express her love. Her father had saved her the best third, and all that was required was for her to express some small part of the affection that she clearly felt. Her foolishness sets the play into motion, but in her fateful refusal to pander to her father, it remains unclear precisely what kind of fool Cordelia is: a detached realist who simply missed her punch line or a shortsighted innocent unable to understand the simple instructions being set before her.

NATURE: LEAR LEARNS WHAT IT MEANS TO BE A NATURAL BEING.

In Shakespeare's time, people envisioned the human world as a limited expanse sandwiched between heaven and hell. This mortal space, which hovered between the angelic and the demonic, was further divided into two levels of existence. Human civilization, in its constant attempt to emulate heavenly order and perfection, rose to the top. The lower level was the realm of animals, including everything bestial and mortal in humans. The relationship between these two realms remained ambiguous. One theory maintained that human beings are inherently attracted to the higher levels of being; that is, that human nature is intrinsically moral, noble, and civilized. The other, competing theory held that human beings are naturally drawn to the lower levels of being, with only the forces of civilization separating them from amoral animals. In *King Lear*, the clearest champions for these two extreme worldviews are the play's lead protagonist and its chief villain—that is, Lear and Edmund.

Edmund associates nature with the lower, animal-like levels of human existence. In his eyes, there is nothing natural about the way human beings have chosen to live. Nature to Edmund is an untamed force that opposes the essentially arbitrary customs of civilized interaction. He proclaims this Nature his "goddess," scoffing at the persnickety social rule (which he refers to as "the plague of custom") that makes a son born out of wedlock less valuable than one legitimately born. Nature observes no such manmade niceties, and Edmund invokes its power as a way of justifying his claims. His glorification of the wild and undomesticated allows him to ignore the dictates of morality and social decency in order to pursue personal gain.

Lear, however, begins by exalting the higher level of human existence. Unlike Edmund, Lear does not believe that custom and morality represent superimpositions upon nature. To Lear, these forces of civilization *are* human nature. However, as his hardships mount, Lear's opinions grow increasingly close to Edmund's. When Goneril denies him hospitality, Lear stops appealing to her human nature, calling instead on Edmund's wrathful goddess Nature to punish his daughter. When Regan also rejects him, Lear confronts nature in its rawest form: a violent storm. Over the course of the third act, the storm strips away everything that marks Lear as a well-established member of the civilized world. His entourage abandons him, he loses his sanity, and, in imitation of Poor Tom, he strips off his kingly clothing. He becomes a "natural" man in Edmund's sense of the word.

Lear is humbled as his eyes are opened to the true depths of human character. However, Shakespeare doesn't mean for us to blindly accept Edmund's belief that human nature lacks the potential for grace. Extreme acts of morality, justice, and mercy can elevate nature above the bestial. One of Cordelia's soldiers tells Lear that he has "one daughter / Who redeems nature from the general curse / Which twain [i.e., the other two, Goneril and Regan] have brought her to." While Goneril and Regan's cruelty impressed upon Lear a base view of nature, Cordelia's love and forgiveness raises human nature to a newly sublime level.

FOUR

MACBETH

Macbeth murders his way to the throne of Scotland but remains plagued by his conscience.

Brief Synopsis

Two Scottish lords, **Macbeth** and **Banquo,** return victorious from a battle. On their way home they encounter three **Weird Sisters,** or witches, who predict that Macbeth will be named Thane (or Lord) of Cawdor and eventually King of Scotland as well. They further prophesy that Banquo's heirs will be kings after Macbeth. As the witches disappear, Macbeth and Banquo are greeted by some of **King Duncan**'s men, who announce that Duncan has executed the traitorous former Thane of Cawdor and wishes to bestow his title to the valiant war hero Macbeth.

Macbeth, spurred on by his ambitious wife, **Lady Macbeth,** decides to make the rest of the prophecy come true and murders Duncan while the king visits his home. Macbeth assumes the throne of Scotland. To prevent the prophecy about Banquo's heirs from coming true, he hires murderers to kill Banquo and his children. However, Banquo's son **Fleance** escapes the assassination attempt. Later, at a feast in Dunsinane castle, Banquo's ghost appears to Macbeth, who frightens his guests by raving at the apparition.

Macbeth visits the witches, who tell him to beware a nobleman named **Macduff.** They also tell him he cannot be harmed by any man born of woman, and that he will be safe until Birnam Wood comes to Dunsinane castle. Spurred by the witches' words, Macbeth seizes Macduff's castle, murdering **Lady Macduff** and her young son.

A grieving Macduff, together with King Duncan's son **Malcolm**, invades Scotland with the backing of an English army. Lady Macbeth, already plagued by anxious fits of sleepwalking, dies just before the invasion. Macbeth, emboldened by the witches' divination, is shocked to learn that Birnam Wood is apparently creeping toward the castle: The English army has camouflaged their advances behind branches cut from the trees of Birnam. Macbeth loses his last scrap of hope when Macduff announces that he was not born of woman but delivered from his mother's body by caesarean section. Macduff kills Macbeth, and Malcolm becomes King of Scotland.

What to Remember About *Macbeth*

MACBETH IS AN OPTIMISTIC PLAY.

Despite the gory violence, betrayal, and personal and political turmoil portrayed in *Macbeth*, it proves itself an optimistic play in at least one respect. Not only do Macbeth's crimes meet with their just punishment, but forces in the play also operate to ensure that no sin goes unpunished. Macbeth's downfall isn't simply the result of a personal error or miscalculation; rather, his failure is part of a necessary string of events that follow as steadily and inevitably as a row of falling dominoes. However, Shakespeare does not rely on any Christian notion of judgment or divine intervention. Instead, he relies on two essentially secular ideas: the chain of sins and the notion that "murder will out."

The concept of the chain of sins suggests that one crime inevitably leads to further crimes. The initial offense desensitizes the criminal to vicious acts, thereby making future transgressions easier. In Act 3, Macbeth draws on this notion when he describes his sins as a river. He claims that he has already traveled so far into the river of blood that, even if he turned around immediately, returning to the bank of righteousness would be as difficult as continuing to the other side. At this point, however, Macbeth hasn't yet become a truly hardened criminal—he isn't so cold and calculating as to justify future violence simply by suggesting that the difficulty of stopping his crime spree has outstripped the dangers of continuing. Macbeth is still something of a bungler. In the previous act, he exposed himself to humiliation and suspicion by raving at a ghost that none of his guests could see. For this less masterful sort of criminal, the chain of sins takes on a different meaning: In his desperation to conceal the first act, the criminal must commit many more crimes, not out of cool calculation but from cold terror. Only in the final act, after Macbeth learns of his wife's death, does he become hardened enough to fit the profile of a deliberate serial criminal.

This unstoppable accumulation of misdeeds, each more daring or desperate than the last, supports the proverbial wisdom that "murder will out," or that crimes eventually snowball to the point where they cannot be ignored. However, the phrase also implies that murder will expose itself; that the casual destruction of human life is so vile that it will come to light with no assistance from divine providence or human investigation. After his confrontation with Banquo's ghost, Macbeth worries that his murderous act will literally change the world around him. He recalls legends that tell of gravestones that move and trees that speak when confronted with blood crimes, and soothsayers that used the actions of magpies and crows to reveal murderers' identities. Thanks to these morally positive forces found in nature, the question is never *whether* Macbeth will fall, but merely when.

LADY MACBETH IS THE PLAY'S REAL MISOGYNIST.

The struggle for power between Macbeth and his wife occurs according to rigidly defined gender roles. For example, when Macbeth's resolve falters, Lady Macbeth goads him on by insulting his masculinity, saying, "When you durst do it, then you were a man." When Lady Macbeth feels that she must provide the ambition that her husband lacks, she vividly denies her womanhood in order to rise to the challenge. She calls on the spirits who attend on "mortal" (meaning both "human" and "fatal") thoughts to "unsex" her where she stands, filling her from head to toe with terrible cruelty. This famous speech not only shows Lady Macbeth defiling her own femininity, it also seems to equate her with the three witches, those bearded hags who blend masculine and feminine into a grotesque representation of evil.

However, Lady Macbeth cannot sustain this affected "masculine" identity; as her husband rises to power, she descends into madness. Some readers see a strong strain of misogyny in the play, arguing that Lady Macbeth fails in her quest because Shakespeare never imagines her to be capable of the masculine strength her murderous plans require. Her strange reticence to kill Duncan might support this claim. In a soliloquy, she excuses herself by saying that if Duncan had not resembled her father so closely, she might have done it. The mere image of Lady Macbeth's father has the power to overcome her ambition and drunken boldness, suggesting that he dominates her psyche as a symbol of ultimate masculine authority, reducing her to passive femininity.

It seems just as likely, though, that Lady Macbeth fails because her notion of masculinity as a kind of inflexible, self-serving cruelty is itself an unfounded, sexist notion, unsustainable by man or woman. In contrast to Lady Macbeth's caricature of masculinity, the play's hero, Macduff, embodies a more balanced masculinity, one that includes stereotypical virtues of both men and women. When informed that his wife and children have been murdered, Macduff erupts with grief. Malcolm quickly encourages him to attack the perpetrator, as a man would do. Macduff retorts that he will indeed seek revenge, but that he must also embrace his grief "as a man." He further claims that he could "play the woman"—i.e., weep, with his eyes. Macduff speaks in the sexist vocabulary common in Shakespeare's time, but he uses that language to describe how he will transcend sexist definitions of gender.

THE WITCHES' REAL MAGIC IS THE POWER OF SUGGESTION.

As the witches eagerly await Macbeth's first entrance, one of the witches launches into a lengthy story. She reports that a sailor's wife has insulted her and that she will punish the woman by besetting her husband's ship with troubles. The story seems to be a mere distraction, but toward the end of the story an important piece of information emerges. The witch says, "Though his bark [i.e., ship] cannot be lost, / Yet it shall be tempest-toss'd." The witch admits that, while she can do her best to make the sailor's life unbearable, she cannot do anything so drastic and irrevocable as to sink the ship and kill its crew. In fact, this story outlines an essential limitation of any witch's power, according to common wisdom of the day. While witches can manipulate anything natural or bodily, raising storms and causing disease, they cannot affect the spiritual aspects of human beings. They cannot, in this case, destroy the life that God has bestowed on humanity.

People also believed that, since God had endowed humans with a free will, witches could not force anyone to act in one way or another. Instead, they must work through persuasion and suggestion. In *Macbeth*, the ultimate mark of the witches' success is that at some point, Macbeth can no longer distinguish between the witches' predictions and his own fantasies. Throughout the play, it remains unclear whether the prophecies describe an inevitable course of action or whether they simply offer Macbeth's darkest imaginings the convenient excuse of a foregone conclusion. The prophecy only mentions succession to the throne; it is Macbeth who immediately imagines the need for murder. Even though Macbeth makes a quick about-face, reasoning that if fortune wants to see him as king, then fortune may see to it that he's crowned without any effort on his part, the seed has already been planted, his imagination free to do its worst.

When Macbeth pauses in the hall outside Duncan's bedroom, perched on the brink of his destiny, the ambiguity between Macbeth's predestined fate and his own imagination gains a concrete form. Macbeth sees a dagger floating in the air with its handle pointing toward him—and, presumably, with its deadly point aiming at Duncan. Macbeth reaches out to grab the knife only to see his fingers go right through it. Macbeth calls it a "fatal vision," an ambiguous designation, since *fatal* could mean either "fated" or "lethal." Whether this dagger is a demonic instrument of fate or simply, as Macbeth suggests, "a dagger of the mind," it proves capable of producing real results. As he gazes upon it, Macbeth takes out his own dagger, and when spurts of blood suddenly appear on the illusory dagger, it seems inevitable, to Macbeth's feverish imagination, that his own dagger will soon look the same. "I go, and it is done," he declares, describing the murder as if he has already committed it. Confusing imagination with fate, the avoidable future with the unalterable past: this is Macbeth's tragic flaw.

FIVE

OTHELLO

**Driven to distraction and towering jealousy by Iago's
lies, Othello kills his wife, Desdemona.**

Brief Synopsis

As the play begins, **Othello** and **Desdemona** have just
eloped. Othello is an outsider, a black Moor (North African)
who serves the city of Venice as a general in its wars against
the Turks. Desdemona, the daughter of a Venetian nobleman,
has fallen in love with Othello and runs away from her father's
house to marry him.

Othello doesn't know it, but
he has an enemy who hates him as
passionately as Desdemona loves
him—**Iago.** The cause of Iago's
hatred is unclear, but his plot to destroy Othello is extremely effective.
Iago gets Othello's lieutenant, **Cassio,** drunk and arranges for him to
get into a brawl, all so Cassio will be
dismissed from Othello's service.
Cassio lurks around Othello's house
and asks Desdemona to plead his
case, a circumstance that Iago uses

to suggest to Othello that Cassio and Desdemona are having an affair. As proof, Iago produces the handkerchief Othello gave to Desdemona, claiming that he found it in Cassio's possession. In reality, Desdemona dropped the handkerchief, and Iago's wife, **Emilia,** stole it and gave it to Iago. Enraged, Othello suffocates Desdemona, killing her. After Emilia exposes Iago as the traitor he is, Othello kills himself.

What to Remember About *Othello*

STORIES ARE DANGEROUS.

Much of the plot of this play consists of people telling each other stories. Othello is a consummate storyteller. His stories win him an invitation to the house of Desdemona's father, Brabantio, and stories win him Desdemona's heart. When Brabantio charges Othello with witchcraft, his only defense is to tell the duke his story once again. Though he insists that as a rough, military man all he can deliver is a "round unvarnished tale," in fact Othello is an eloquent, vivid, and affecting speaker. In Othello's stories, suffering, captivity, and struggle give way to escape, success, and victory. They are tales of adventure and romance set in exotic locales. To readers and playgoers of Shakespeare's time, the stories would have been reminiscent of travelers' and explorers' published accounts. Indeed, Shakespeare mined popular travelers' narratives for the details Othello provides about cannibals and men whose heads grow beneath their shoulders.

Iago convinces Othello to see his life as a story of a different kind, but one that was also familiar at the time—that of the old man cuckolded by his unsatisfied younger wife. Iago banks on the fact that this story's familiarity will make it seem plausible to Othello. Getting Othello to change his old stories for new ones is largely a matter of getting him to see himself, Desdemona, and Cassio as characters in a pedestrian narrative. Instead of the unique and improbable hero of outlandish adventures, Iago suggests, Othello is like any man who takes a younger wife: deluded and betrayed. Instead of a rare paragon of virtue, Desdemona is a Venetian woman like any other Venetian woman: attracted to her own countrymen and apt to tire of one partner.

Othello's culture has prepared him to believe Iago's story, but Iago's skill is what sells the tale. A master storyteller, Iago recognizes that indirection can be a more powerful strategy than assertion and that we are always most drawn to the stories we think we have pieced together ourselves. Iago hints at how he would interpret events, but ultimately he gets Othello to tell the story to himself. Both Othello and Iago are skilled storytellers, but in the end, Iago triumphs because his narrative skills trump Othello's.

TIME WORKS STRANGELY IN *OTHELLO*.

This play features a "double time scheme." The main events of the play occur over the course of just a day or two, but a number of minor remarks the characters make suggest that weeks or even months have been passing. The contradiction between the short and the long timelines produces dramatic tension and forces us to share the irrational mindset of the jealous Othello. The short time scheme predominates. The first act takes place during a single night, the second act during a day and a half. Over the course of two days, then, Cassio brawls with Roderigo, Desdemona pleads Cassio's cause, Iago insinuates an affair between Desdemona and Cassio, and Othello smothers his wife and kills himself. It all happens quickly—almost unbelievably so.

The long timeline contradicts the short one. Emilia says Iago has asked her to steal the handkerchief a hundred times—even though Othello and Desdemona have been married for less than a day. Bianca scolds Cassio, saying, "What, keep a week away?"—even though he arrived on the island the day before. The embassy from Venice arrives before word of the Turkish fleet's wreck could possibly have reached their ears; Roderigo complains that he has frittered away money on

Cyprus. These contradictions don't mean that Shakespeare is being sloppy. Rather, he is having it both ways. The short timeline creates a sense of frenzy and urgency, while the long timeline makes the events believable. The medium permits this sleight of hand. In the theater, we get one chance to catch the words as they fly by; it would be easy to see *Othello* without noticing the time warp.

If we miss the discrepancy onstage, and catch it later, we come to the uncomfortable realization that we accepted the irreconcilable contradictions of *Othello*'s plot just as readily as Othello swallows Iago's insinuations. When, in the climactic scene, Othello declares of Desdemona that, "Iago knows / That she with Cassio hath the act of shame / A thousand times committed," it doesn't occur to him that she has barely had time to cuckold him once, let alone a thousand times. (Indeed, it's not even clear that Othello and Desdemona have had time to consummate their marriage.) Nor does this impossibility occur to us. Our experience of watching *Othello* mirrors Othello's experience of living it. We are carried away by his jealousy. Emerging from the spell, we must admit that we kept our wits about us no better than the tragic hero kept his about him.

IN THE ORIGINAL VERSION, OTHELLO AND IAGO BEAT DESDEMONA TO DEATH WITH A BAG OF SAND.

Shakespeare took the story of Othello from a book called the *Hecatommithi*, a series of one hundred interrelated stories about love written in Italian by Giraldi Cinthio. Like many of Shakespeare's sources, this original version of *Othello* is much simpler than the play Shakespeare turned it into. The original story concerns an unnamed Moor who marries the Venetian lady Disdemona against her family's wishes. Unfortunately, the Moor employs an Ensign of "the most scoundrelly nature in the world," whose wife is a good friend of Disdemona's. When the Ensign tries and fails to seduce Disdemona, he blames his strikeout on her love for the Corporal, who is a favorite of Disdemona's because Othello likes him. The Ensign sets out to take revenge on both by accusing them of adultery. The basic plot of *Othello* is there, but Shakespeare makes important changes.

Shakespeare uses Cinthio's plot but turns his opaque characters into deeply complex people. In Cinthio, the Moor and the Ensign beat Disdemona to death with a sand-filled sock, proclaiming that all cuckolding women should be so punished. Though the Moor comes to regret his actions, Cinthio does not show us why. In Shakespeare's murder scene, Othello compares the candle at Desdemona's bedside to her life, noting that an extinguished candle can be lit again, unlike an extinguished life. He kisses his sleeping wife, smells her breath, and tells her that he will still love her after he kills her. Desdemona awakes, and she and Othello talk until, enraged by Desdemona's denials, Othello smothers her to death. This scene is full of love and hate, ambivalence and contradiction, none of which Shakespeare found in Cinthio. Cinthio's Moor and Othello may resemble each other, but no one could ever confuse them.

In the case of Iago, Shakespeare makes the opposite choice, replacing an explanation with an enigma. Cinthio gives the Ensign a clear motivation: He has a bad nature and has been frustrated in his attempt to seduce Disdemona. In contrast, Iago's motivation is murky. He says he hates Othello for promoting Cassio over him, but at first he plots against Cassio, not Othello. Later, he says he suspects Othello of corrupting his wife, Emilia. These explanations are inconsistent and insufficient. Shakespeare transforms Cinthio's explicable villain into a study on the nature of evil. Iago's last lines reinforce his mystery: "What you know, you know. From this time forth I never shall speak word." Iago denies both his captors and the audience the explanation that might lessen the horror of his actions, that might reduce them to something other than what they are: inexplicably evil.

SIX

A MIDSUMMER NIGHT'S DREAM

After a bewildering night in a fairy-haunted forest, two couples are united in marriage.

Brief Synopsis

As **Theseus,** the Duke of Athens, prepares for his wedding celebration, a nobleman named **Egeus** marches in and asks Theseus to compel Egeus's daughter, **Hermia,** to marry a young man named **Demetrius.** Hermia loves another young man, **Lysander,** and plans to elope with him. She tells her friend **Helena,** who loves Demetrius but was jilted by him when he fell in love with Hermia. Helena tells Demetrius of Hermia's plan in the hope of regaining his love. That night, Demetrius follows Hermia and Lysander into the woods, and Helena follows Demetrius.

In the woods, the fairy king and queen, **Oberon** and **Titania,** quarrel with each other. Oberon tells his servant **Puck** to sprinkle love juice in Titania's eyes while she sleeps so that she will fall in love with the first creature she sees upon awakening. He also tells Puck to spread some love juice on Demetrius's eyes so that he will love Helena. Mistaking Lysander for Demetrius, Puck makes Lysander fall in love with Helena by accident. When he corrects his mistake, Demetrius and Lysander fight over Helena, who thinks they are mocking her.

Meanwhile, a group of clownish Athenian craftsmen are in the woods rehearsing a play for Theseus's wedding. Puck transforms **Bottom,** one of the laborers, so that he has an ass's head, and causes Titania to fall in love with him. Eventually, Oberon is satisfied with his revenge, and Puck undoes his potions. In the morning, Demetrius realizes he loves Helena, and Hermia realizes that she loves Lysander. The couples are married along with Theseus. Bottom and his group put on a hilarious play at the wedding.

What to Remember About
A Midsummer Night's Dream

A MIDSUMMER NIGHT'S DREAM PORTRAYS LOVE AS AN IRRATIONAL EMOTION.

If you got a bit lost while reading the synopsis of the play, don't worry: You reacted just as Shakespeare intended you to. Although we can make out some differences between the lovers—we know that Helena is much taller than Hermia, for example—they are essentially interchangeable. Shakespeare intentionally blurs the distinctions between his characters in order to suggest that love is arbitrary. *A Midsummer Night's Dream* is not the story of two pairs of unusually irrational lovers. Rather, it is a story about the irrational nature of love.

The forest, where Oberon uses a magical flower to make people arbitrarily fall in love, stands in for the real world, where love is arbitrary even without the deployment of magic potions. In the forest, it doesn't matter whether you fall in love with an Athenian commoner transfigured into a donkey or the best friend of your fiancée. Coincidence is all. Titania, Demetrius, and Lysander offer rationalizations for their love, whether the "sleek smooth head" of Bottom or Helena's "lips, those kissing cherries," but it is obvious that their love causes them to appreciate these qualities, rather than the reverse. In the forest, love is an external force acting on people, not an outgrowth of people's selves. In this way, as in many others, the play's spellbound love resembles real world romance.

Midsummer also trades in the familiar idea that men are inconstant in their affections. Both Demetrius and Lysander begin the play passionately in love with Hermia and spend much of its action enamored of Helena. Demetrius changes his allegiance not once, but twice. Of the lovers, only the men fall under the flower's spell. In contrast, the women of *Midsummer* love consistently. Helena is baffled by Demetrius's rejection of her, just as Hermia is by Lysander's of her. In the forest, love is a passing fancy, rather than a reliable quantity bound up with people's essential characters—a lesson the women happily forget by the play's end. At the play's conclusion, one couple has been restored to true love and the other has been brought together by fairy magic. Shakespeare's refusal to draw a distinction between these brands of affection suggests a merry cynicism about love.

ATHENS PRESENTS THE LAWFUL, ORDERLY PART OF EXISTENCE, WHILE THE FOREST PRESENTS THE UNGOVERNED PART.

A Midsummer Night's Dream contrasts the Athenian world of order with the forest world of love, magic, and whimsy. In Athens, a place of law and power, men are conquerors in war and marriage. Theseus wins his wife, the fierce Amazon Hippolyta, in war. He declares that Hermia must either marry the man chosen by her father, Egeus, or live her life as a nun. Still, though Athens may be governed by law, Theseus has the power to interpret that law, and he is no despot. He worries about the martial way in which he won his wife and is anxious to establish a happier tone for the marriage by having an elaborate wedding celebration. And while Theseus publicly supports Egeus's rights, in private he attempts to persuade him against forcing Hermia into a marriage she abhors and eventually refuses Egeus's demands to punish Lysander.

In the forest, a place of magic and mystery, there is no law. This lawlessness is freeing but also stressful. Because Titania and Oberon have no legal mechanism to settle their dispute, Oberon turns to a magical flower, and madness ensues. In the end, the lovers are paired happily and the king and queen are reconciled, but not before everyone suffers a great deal of confusion and anxiety. The play's structure, which moves from city to forest and back again, reminds us that while our dreams provide an escape from waking life, we can't linger in them forever. We must live in the mundane world. Still, the presence of the fairies at the marriage feast and the lovers' partial memory of their time in the forest suggest that Athens and the forest are not mutually exclusive but rather complementary aspects of the human condition.

SHAKESPEARE USES LANGUAGE TO SHOW THE DIFFERENCE BETWEEN DIFFERENT CLASSES.

Elaborate costumes and sets were not available in Shakespeare's day, but with language alone, he manages to create three distinct worlds in *Midsummer*. Shakespeare gives each of these worlds a characteristic sound, which both deepens our understanding of them and helps us distinguish between them. The lower-class Athenian workmen speak in prose, the plainest of forms. Garbled images and mistaken words fill their lines, as if the language controls them, rather than the other way around. In contrast, upper-class Athenians like Theseus, Hippolyta, and the lovers speak in measured, balanced verse. Until the play-within-a-play, they speak exclusively in iambic pentameter, a stately verse form that suggests status, control, and decorum. Rhyme is used only by the lovers, and then only when they are particularly heated ("One turf shall serve as pillow for us both; / One heart, one bed, two bosoms and one troth."). Even in the throes of passion, the upper-class pairs express themselves in tight couplets.

The fairies also speak in iambic couplets, but of a different sort. Rather than expressing one thought per couplet, the fairies often overflow the structure of the rhyme, which gives the effect of energy and freer thought. The fairies also use short lines in which rhymes occur every seven or eight syllables, rather than every ten ("I do wander everywhere, / Swifter than the moon's sphere; / And I serve the Fairy Queen, / To dew her orbs upon the green."). These frequent rhymes produce a sensation of animation and forward propulsion. When the verse falls into this rhythm, it is always at the instigation of Puck or another minor fairy—or else it is a spell of some sort. In the absence of sound or lighting cues, poetry was the strongest special effect in Shakespeare's repertoire.

SEVEN

JULIUS CAESAR

Brutus helps to murder Caesar to protect Roman liberty, but Mark Antony casts doubt on Brutus's motives, drives him out of Rome, and hunts him down.

Brief Synopsis

Caesar returns to Rome in triumph after defeating his enemy Pompey, and the people of Rome love him. **Cassius,** a Roman nobleman, tries to persuade Caesar's friend **Brutus** that they have let Caesar become too powerful and that Caesar is unfit to rule. Caesar gains even more popularity after **Mark Antony,** Caesar's lieutenant, offers Caesar a crown three times and Caesar refuses it. Brutus fears that Caesar will make himself king and end the Roman republic, so he agrees to conspire with Cassius to kill Caesar.

Despite the misgivings of his wife and the warnings of a soothsayer, Caesar goes to the senate with the conspirators and is stabbed to death. Mark Antony pretends to reconcile with the conspirators but secretly vows revenge. Brutus speaks at Caesar's funeral and tries to calm the crowd by explaining that he killed Caesar to save Roman liberty. Antony speaks afterward. His ironic comments on Brutus's speech and his reading of Caesar's generous will enrage the people against Brutus and the other conspirators, who are driven out of Rome. Caesar's adopted son **Octavius** arrives in Rome and joins forces with Antony to pursue Brutus and Cassius. Defeated, several of the conspirators kill themselves, including Brutus. On finding Brutus's body, Antony declares him the noblest of the conspirators, because he acted out of love for Rome.

What to Remember About *Julius Caesar*

DESPITE HIS FLAWS, JULIUS CAESAR IS A REMARKABLY POWERFUL AND SUCCESSFUL LEADER.

Compared to *Hamlet, Macbeth,* or *Othello, Julius Caesar* does not spend much time with its title character. Indeed, the third act has barely begun when Caesar is stabbed to death. Despite his limited time onstage, however, Shakespeare's Caesar manages to show us both how he achieved such prominence and how his weaknesses left him vulnerable to the conspirators. Much of Caesar's power comes from his rhetoric. In his first appearance, as he processes into Rome in triumph, Caesar speaks in short, decisive sentences full of judgment and command. He dismisses the soothsayer, for example, by saying, "He is a dreamer. Let us leave him. Pass." He demands obedience from the world, and those around him comply immediately and instinctively. Caesar's language is so powerful that it completely overshadows his physical infirmities. He is aging; he is partially deaf; he is epileptic. Yet his strong, confident words manage to blot out his bodily weakness.

Overconfidence and indecision are the chinks in Caesar's armor. To maintain power, Caesar has created a persona of unshakable authority. He is full of certainty when he dismisses the soothsayer's warnings, which turn out to be accurate. He brags that danger itself is less powerful than him. Even when he feels doubt, he publicly exudes confidence. Despite his self-assurance, Caesar can also be indecisive. After promising his wife that he will stay home on the Ides of March, he blusters to Decius that he simply doesn't want to go to the Senate and then changes his mind again and allows Decius to talk him into going. Caesar's weaknesses may leave him open to attack, but his strengths allow him to hold Roman society together for a time. We see just what an impressive accomplishment that is in the play's second half, when chaos breaks out in the great man's absence.

JULIUS CAESAR ANALYZES THE ORATORY AND POLITICS NOT JUST OF REPUBLICAN ROME BUT ALSO OF SHAKESPEARE'S ENGLAND.

Writing a play set in republican Rome, a culture that prized oratory, gives Shakespeare the opportunity to flaunt his rhetorical skill. At the same time, he calls into question the dubious uses to which that skill can be put. At Caesar's funeral, Brutus delivers a carefully wrought but oddly lifeless speech. He does not tell the crowd exactly what happened or explain why Caesar's murder was necessary. Instead, in a series of meticulously balanced sentences, he asserts that his actions were proper. The structure of his sentences reflects his organized thinking: "As Caesar loved me, I weep for him; as he was fortunate, I rejoice at it; as he was valiant, I honor him; but as he was ambitious, I slew him." The four tidy pairs suggest that slaying was the only logical response. The speech feels like a product of the same cold reasoning that led Brutus to murder.

Antony's eulogy, which follows Brutus's, is suppler, more responsive to the audience's mood, and far more effective. His rhetorical pose is subtle: Whereas Brutus openly defends his actions, Antony claims to have no goal at all; whereas Brutus delivers what is clearly a prewritten speech, Antony produces the impression that he is speaking off the cuff. He begins by challenging Brutus's claim that Caesar was ambitious, all the while rushing to praise Brutus as an "honorable man." Then he pauses, supposedly overcome with emotion, and allows the crowd to digest what he has just said. After descending from the podium to display Caesar's corpse and note its many wounds and the men who made them, Antony delivers the final blow: He reveals that Caesar, this supposed tyrant, left a sum of money to every Roman citizen.

The Roman audience's response to the two speeches suggests that oratory has a disquieting effect on a susceptible crowd. When Brutus finishes his speech, the people are ready to build statues in his honor, and even to make him the new Caesar. By the time Antony finishes *his* speech, the people are planning to burn down Brutus's house. This mob violence, which is incited by lofty rhetoric, suggest that republican societies can be dangerous, despite their high ideals. The scene also turns a mirror toward Shakespeare's audience. These members of a monarchical society watched an onstage crowd incited to violence by a high-flown speech—just the sort of danger that English authorities perceived whenever a large crowd gathered in places like the theater. *Julius Caesar* asks its audience to think about the consequences of oratory, both for fictional characters and for themselves.

BRUTUS AND CASSIUS ARE CO-CONSPIRATORS, BUT THEY COULD NOT BE MORE DIFFERENT.

Although Cassius does not have Brutus's gravity or strong moral sense, he respects these praiseworthy qualities of Brutus's. It is that respect that leads to disaster. Brutus's political judgment does not match his moral authority, but again and again, the politically savvier Cassius defers to him. As the conspirators make their final plans, Cassius allows Brutus to overrule him on the swearing of an oath and the decision about approaching Cicero. This knuckling under is a preview of a more significant capitulation. When Brutus argues that Antony should be allowed to deliver a eulogy, Cassius objects but caves in, a submission that turns out to be disastrous.

Cassius and Brutus conspire against Caesar for very different reasons, as the quarrel scene demonstrates. After both men have left Rome and gathered their own armies, they meet to discuss their growing differences. Cassius is hurt that Brutus has denied Cassius's request to be lenient with a corrupt official. Brutus is angered that Cassius would employ their hard-won power for anything but the highest purposes and accuses Cassius himself of corruption and greed. Cassius interprets this recital of his shortcomings as evidence that Brutus does not love him. After Cassius bears his breast and offers Brutus a dagger, the two men reconcile. But their differences remain: Brutus is morally upright, but proud, stubborn, and unperceptive; Cassius is sharp and analytical, but morally sloppy.

EIGHT

THE TAMING
OF THE
SHREW

Petruccio tames his strong-willed wife, Katherine, by subjecting her to a grueling ordeal.

Brief Synopsis

In the English countryside, a lord finds a drunk tinker named **Christopher Sly** asleep in front of a tavern. The lord has Sly carried to his house and treated as a lord by all the servants. A troupe of actors puts on a play for Sly, which constitutes the rest of *The Taming of the Shrew*.

Lucentio, a young nobleman and scholar, arrives in Padua and falls in love with the beautiful **Bianca.** Bianca's father, **Baptista,** refuses to let her wed before her bad-tempered sister, **Katherine.** Lucentio disguises himself as a Latin tutor so he can be with Bianca, while Lucentio's servant **Tranio** disguises himself as Lucentio to negotiate with Baptista for Bianca's hand.

Petruccio, a brash nobleman, arrives in Padua and resolves to marry Katherine for her money, disregarding her reputation as a shrew. After a tremendous duel of words, he obtains Katherine's unstated consent to the marriage. Petruccio tames the wild Katherine by embarassing and abusing her. He makes them leave their wedding before the reception and then forbids her from eating or sleeping. Katherine ultimately satisfies Petruccio by agreeing with everything he says.

Disguised as Lucentio, Tranio persuades Baptista to agree to a marriage between Bianca and Lucentio by promising her a huge sum of money. At the wedding banquet, Katherine's superior loyalty to Petruccio puts the other wives to shame.

What to Remember About
The Taming of the Shrew

THE TAMING OF THE SHREW IS AN ELABORATE PLAY-WITHIN-A-PLAY.

The play-within-a-play device allows Shakespeare to reflect on the means and the ends of his art. In *Hamlet*, the Prince's instructions to the players are often interpreted as Shakespeare's own wish that his plays would be enacted with fidelity to the script and a minimum of exaggerated gesture. In *A Midsummer Night's Dream*, the inept performance of *Pyramus and Thisbe* sends up the failings of Shakespeare's competitors. Usually, Shakespeare's plays-within-plays do not compete with the main play. In *The Taming of the Shrew*, however, the play-within-a-play takes over the entire production. It is ostensibly performed for the amusement of Christopher Sly, a tinker, who has been tricked into thinking he is a lord. But Sly's appearances are so brief, and so isolated from the rest of the play, that editors call them an induction, rather than including them in the numbered acts and scenes.

A play called *The Taming of a Shrew*, published at about the same time that *The Taming of the Shrew* was first performed, bears an uncertain relationship to Shakespeare's play. It may be a source for *The Shrew*, it may be derived from Shakespeare's play, or both it and *The Shrew* may be drawn from a lost earlier play. The plot of *A*

Shrew is substantially similar to Shakespeare's, and in places its dialogue is identical, but its Sly repeatedly comments on the action and draws a moral from it at the end. If someone adapted *A Shrew* from Shakespeare's play, it seems that later author was as troubled by Sly's incomplete role as many readers are today and added lines for Sly to fix the problem.

If, however, *A Shrew* was Shakespeare's source, it seems that he purposefully rejected a more complete version of the Sly framing story. Why? Leaving the silent Sly on stage creates two key effects. First, Sly provides a satirical model of Shakespeare's audience. Just as Sly nods off during the performance, Shakespeare suggests, some Globe patrons are less than attentive. Second, Sly makes it more difficult for the audience members to forget the illusion and artificiality of the production they are watching. With Sly, Shakespeare sets a challenge for himself: Can he make the audience get caught up in his story, even with a constant reminder of that story's theatricality sitting on stage? Sly's presence warns the audience not to be taken in by *The Shrew*; Shakespeare's magic takes us in all the same.

FOR YEARS, KATE'S REFORMATION WAS INTERPRETED AS GENUINE. NOW, SOME PEOPLE THINK SHE'S FAKING IT.

Readers often turn to Shakespeare for timeless wisdom. But *The Taming of the Shrew* reminds us that Shakespeare's age was very different from our own. Elizabethan England's ideas about marriage may seem just as absurd to us as the Elizabethan notions that the earth was the center of the universe, that God ordained monarchs, or that four fluids controlled the human body. But while old ideas about gender and love may strike us as obviously inadequate, we must guard against the assumption that Shakespeare shares our modern sensibilities.

From the first, Petruccio's courtship of Kate conforms to the accepted wisdom about marriage. A woman's dowry (the sum of money she brought to the marriage) was one of her chief attractions; Petruccio chooses Kate for her wealth. A wife's duty was to obey; Petruccio reforms Kate by verbally sparring with her, embarrassing her at their wedding, starving her, and depriving her of sleep. Kate's final speech can be interpreted as evidence of her full submission to Petruccio and therefore as further support for the conventional wisdom of Shakespeare's day. Prompted by her husband to lecture her sister, Bianca, and an obstinate widow about their duties in marriage, Kate replies with an eloquent confirmation that the man, the lord and head of his wife, labors constantly for his spouse and deserves "love, fair looks and true obedience." Kate says that she was once recalcitrant but has been reformed.

Recently, some critics have suggested that Kate's speech is a self-conscious performance rather than an expression of truly changed beliefs. They argue that Kate becomes not a tamed shrew but rather a skilled manipulator who knows that she can master her husband only by seeming to be mastered herself. By telling Petruccio precisely what he wants to hear, these critics argue, Kate sets herself up to be the dominant spouse. This interpretation is attractive to a modern audience troubled by the play's evident sexism. Still, the very appeal of the proposition makes it dangerous. It's just the sort of thing we want badly to believe. While we should consider the possibility that Kate is savvier but unreformed, we must hesitate before we accept it. It is not clear whether such a reading describes the play that Shakespeare wrote or merely the play we wish he had written.

BIANCA PROVES THAT YOU CAN GET YOUR OWN WAY AS LONG AS YOU *APPEAR* TO BE DOCILE.

Bianca appears to be more traditional than her older sister, Kate. Unlike Kate, whose suitor wants her dowry, Bianca attracts men with her personality. Unlike Kate, who does not outwardly resist Petruccio's advances, Bianca toys with her suitors. And unlike Kate, who expresses her will, Bianca acts compliant. But while Bianca often seems to be a model of womanly submission, rebelliousness teems underneath her outward passivity. She responds to her father's doting by playing the dutiful and gracious daughter, declaring herself humbly resigned to his decision that Kate must marry before she does. The next time we see Bianca, Kate has bound her hands. We do not know exactly what happened, but it is clear that Bianca has not been as docile in private with Kate as she was publicly with Baptista. She appears to submit passively to her father and his decisions, but in truth she is furious about the obstructions along her own path to marriage.

Bianca repeatedly submits in public and manipulates in private. To her father, she pretends that Lucentio and Hortensio are what they claim to be: teachers of music and philosophy. In private, though, she is in on the secret that both men are posing as teachers in order to get close to her. Bianca knows all about Lucentio's plots, whereas Kate never knows about Petruccio's. Only Bianca's collusion makes Lucentio's machinations successful. In the end, Kate marries the man her father chooses, and Bianca marries the man she has chosen, a match she brings about through subterfuge. Bianca may appear to be far more docile than her sister is, but it is Bianca who gets her way in the end.

NINE

THE TEMPEST

Prospero, a powerful magician who used to be the Duke of Milan, causes his enemies to wash up on his island and then uses his magic to reconcile with them and regain his dukedom.

Brief Synopsis

A storm strikes a ship carrying a party of Italian princes and noblemen returning from a wedding in Tunis. On board the ship are: **Alonso,** the King of Naples; Alonso's brother **Sebastian** and son **Ferdinand**; **Antonio,** the Duke of Milan; and **Gonzalo,** an elderly courtier of Milan. The storm is the work of the magician **Prospero,** who was the Duke of Milan until his brother Antonio, with Alonso's help, overthrew him and put him out to sea with his daughter **Miranda** twelve years earlier. Prospero and Miranda arrived on an island, and Prospero impressed into service a powerful spirit named **Ariel,** whom he freed from the captivity of a witch, and **Caliban,** the witch's brutish son whom he and Miranda educated and then enslaved.

Prospero causes the ship's passengers to wash up onto his island. He has Ariel lead Ferdinand into Miranda's presence, where Ferdinand and Miranda fall instantly in love. Prospero plans for the two of them to marry eventually, but to test

Ferdinand he first imprisons him and then sets him to work carrying logs. Elsewhere on the island, Antonio bemoans the loss of Ferdinand, whom he believes has died in the shipwreck. Gonzalo tries to comfort him, while Antonio and Sebastian secretly plot to kill their fellow castaways and capture the Neapolitan throne for Sebastian. On another part of the island, Caliban offers himself as a slave to **Trinculo** and **Stefano,** Alonso's drunken jester and butler, and promises to teach them how to kill Prospero. Ariel monitors the entire island, keeping Prospero informed of everything that happens. At one point, Ariel leads Alonso and the other tired, hungry lords to a glorious banquet set by spirits and then causes the banquet to vanish suddenly. Appearing next in the form of a harpy, Ariel chastises Alonso and Antonio for their treachery against Prospero, leaving Alonso to feel remorseful.

Meanwhile, Prospero releases Ferdinand from servitude and gives Ferdinand and Miranda his blessing, ordering spirits to perform a wedding masque for them. Ariel tells Prospero how he used his music to lead Trinculo, Stefano, and Caliban into a filthy pond near Prospero's cell. Prospero and Ariel send spirits in the form of hounds to torment them. Then Prospero brings Antonio, Alonso, and the other lords before him. He confronts Antonio and Alonso with their misdeeds before forgiving them. Alonso apologizes and laments the loss of Ferdinand, whereupon Prospero draws aside a curtain to reveal Ferdinand and Miranda playing chess. The ship's crew, who had been in an enchanted sleep since the storm, appears, as do Trinculo, Stefano, and Caliban. Prospero invites everyone to stay the night and listen to him relate the events of the past twelve years, after which they will return to Italy and Prospero will resume his position as the Duke of Milan.

What to Remember About
The Tempest

THE TEMPEST CAPTURES THE SPIRIT OF THE EXPLORATORY AGE.

Columbus's discovery of the New World in 1492 offered sixteenth-century thinkers all the inspiration of a vast empty canvas. The event provoked radical reimaginings of what civilization could be, as evidenced by Sir Thomas More's famous 1516 book *Utopia* (Greek for "no-place"), which describes in painstaking detail the exotic laws and customs of a fictional New World island. Over a century later, when Shakespeare's *The Tempest* was first performed in 1611, the utopian fervor had reached a new peak: just four years prior, English settlers had rekindled the exploratory spirit by founding Jamestown, the first permanent European colony in the Americas. No wonder, then, that the play abounds with utopian visions. With even more urgency than More had done a century before, Shakespeare's characters ask the question: "If I ruled over an unsettled land, what sort of civilization would I establish there?"

Prospero, the true ruler of the island, constructs the least innovative society, establishing a rigid hierarchy with himself alone at the top. He enslaves all of the island's native inhabitants, natural and supernatural, and treats even his own daughter as a kind of puppet, magically putting her to sleep when he wants to do business with Ariel. For this reason, many readers have thought of Prospero as a negative representative of power-hungry colonizers like the Spaniards, who were notorious even in their own time for enslaving and abusing New World natives. Shakespeare encourages this negative view of Prospero's utopia by mirroring it in the grotesque, drunken antics of Stephano, who takes advantage of Caliban's naïveté and Trinculo's cowardice to act out his own fantasy of complete sovereignty.

Gonzalo gives voice to the opposite kind of utopia, one without any form of sovereignty or social hierarchy whatsoever. Christopher Columbus earnestly believed that he would find the Garden of Eden somewhere on his travels, and Gonzalo seems to believe that he has found something close to it on this island. His vision of utopia not only excludes sovereignty but also denies laws, learning, money, and work. It is a society of innocence and ignorance, where untainted, superabundant nature satisfies all human needs. Surely Shakespeare does not expect his audiences to choose between two such radical extremes. Instead, these polar-opposite visions capture the breathless energy and breathtaking span of the debate surrounding the settlement of the Americas.

PROSPERO IS SHAKESPEARE'S DOUBLE.

Many of Shakespeare's plays involve a domineering figure—whether hero or villain—who tries to script and stage-manage the action around him. These would-be playwrights usually fail miserably. Hamlet, for instance, dies in a tangled conclusion of his own making, and Richard III falls violently from power when people begin to see through his fictions. Prospero, with his supernatural powers, shows far more promise than the other Shakespearean characters in this category. Because of his impressive skill and his majestic command of the play's plot, many readers over the years have seen Prospero as a sort of literary double for Shakespeare himself. Since most scholars agree that *The Tempest* was the last play that Shakespeare wrote by himself, Prospero's epilogue carries a particularly bittersweet resonance, as it seems possible to read Prospero's farewell to magic as an aging Shakespeare's veiled farewell to the theater.

Prospero's failings as a playwright figure can also be read as Shakespeare's personal reflections upon his own artistic shortcomings. Throughout his career, Shakespeare's critics liked to harp on his tendency to mix tragedy with comedy, highbrow with lowbrow. These readers saw Shakespeare's taste for bawdy comedy as a contamination that threatened to taint the greatness of his lofty, noble plays. In this vein, the comic subplot in *The Tempest* involving Trinculo, Stephano, and Caliban might represent a wry joke on Shakespeare's part about how chaos and humor seem to erupt into even his most concerted efforts to remain serious.

Through the cunning manipulation of circumstances, Prospero regains his dukedom, ensures political stability by marrying his daughter into Alonso's family, and draws a heartfelt apology out of Alonso. All in all, he successfully scripts a stately play about greed, transgression, forgiveness, and reintegration into society, yet one aspect of the play remains firmly out of his control. The comic subplot involving Alonso's drunken attendants develops without Prospero's instigation and nearly threatens his life. In fact, the scene in which these three first meet is the only one in the entire play that goes completely unobserved by either Ariel or Prospero. If Ariel had not happened to stumble upon the trio as Caliban was laying out his plan to kill Prospero, the murderous scheme might easily have succeeded. This lends a menacing edge to this otherwise lighthearted portion of the play. Prospero manages, at the last second, to weave this subplot into the fabric of his play by distracting the would-be murderers with gaudy garments and transforming this story into a neat fable against greed and coveting. He must feel more relieved than triumphant, however, that the traitorous plot—which threatens both his life and his artistic control over the play—does not succeed.

PROSPERO'S MAGIC IS BLASPHEMOUS . . .

Prospero is the hero of *The Tempest*, but that doesn't mean that he's entirely free from blame or censure. Many readers have found fault with Prospero's pride and hubris, condemning him for the obstinate way he wields his power over his servants, his enemies, and even his own daughter. Feminist and postcolonial scholars alike have read Prospero as the epitome of European patriarchy, seeking to extend its sovereignty over all it surveys.

In Shakespeare's period, audience members may have shuddered at Prospero for religious reasons as soon as political ones. Prospero is a classic example of the magus figure, a learned sorcerer who traffics in the occult who has powers of conjuration and transformation. The magus both fascinated and frightened people of the time. On one hand, interest in witches, wizards, and other supernatural forces ran high; even James I had, while he was still James VI of Scotland, written a popular treatise on witchcraft called *On Daemonologie*. At the same time, however, the magus aspired to powers that only God could claim by right, and as such practiced a dangerous and potentially wicked art. Faustus, a popular character in European folklore and literature, embodies this line of thinking. Faustus, a deeply learned scholar, yearns for divine knowledge. He trades his soul to the devil for twenty-four years of nefarious power; when his term of enjoyment ends, demons carry him off to hell.

Prospero is another classic magus figure. Back in Milan, he lost the earthly world by steeping himself in books, seeking to expand his knowledge beyond the bounds of humanity's experience. He controls the elements, can make things appear and disappear, and can cause his enemies intense pain without physical action. He also admits to having practiced necromancy, or communicating with spirits of the dead, a deeply abhorrent practice to most people of Shakespeare's day. Prospero claims moral authority over the island because he contrasts his righteousness with the witch Sycorax's wickedness, but audiences of the period might not have accepted these arguments wholeheartedly.

. . . AS IS HIS USE OF MUSIC.

The music of *The Tempest* is often seen as the most charming and delightful element in the play, but it too reveals a dangerous blasphemy on Prospero's part. All but two scenes in *The Tempest* contain some sort of music, ranging in style from Stephano's drinking songs to Ariel's lyrical charms. Unlike the isolated set pieces found in most other Shakespearean plays (i.e., songs that serve as a break from the action of the play), this music often bursts forth spontaneously from the dramatic situation or else drives the plot forward. Ariel's songs, which are the very source of his magical power, fall into this second category. He uses his music to lure Ferdinand into Prospero's grasp, and Ferdinand claims that the music managed to calm both the storm and his own grief with its sweetness. People of Shakespeare's time commonly believed in the power of music to order and balance man's passions, expelling depression and tempering rage, but Ariel's music has a similar power over nature.

From the ancient Greeks onward, music was linked with celestial order. Pythagoras (582–507 B.C.) combined astronomy and musicology, studying common ratios in the movement of stars alongside the mathematical proportions he found in music. Such studies led to the notion of "the music of the spheres," a celestial music produced by the movements of stars and planets, a music that not only represents but indeed creates the order of the universe. Human music, it was believed, derives its power from its imitation (however imperfect) of God's own divine harmonies. Prospero, however, does not use music simply to delight or soothe his listeners. He uses Ariel's music the same way he uses his magic, wielding it as a tool to control the actions of others. Prospero's magical use of music further complicates his moral standing. Perhaps this is why he promises to abandon all his spells during the epilogue: Before he sets off for home, Prospero chooses to begin with a blank slate.

THE TEMPEST COULD EASILY HAVE ENDED IN REVENGE.

Beginning with the wild success of Thomas Kyd's *The Spanish Tragedy* in 1587, a new genre seized the imagination of London theatergoers: revenge tragedy. The category is almost as old as theater itself, but Kyd's play touched off a rebirth. English theaters produced Kyd's play frequently until as late as the 1640s, but more importantly, *The Spanish Tragedy* spawned numerous imitators. The basic elements of the tradition that emerged are as follows:

1. A benign ruler is dispossessed, banished, or killed; often by a non-inheriting relative.
2. That ruler (or his heir) returns either disguised or feigning ignorance in order to carefully exact revenge.

3. The avenger reveals himself and his plot to his enemy just before murdering him.

This last element is crucially important. In a revenge tragedy, mere death will not suffice, as the enemy must not only grasp the meticulous plotting but must also experience some small part of the powerlessness and shame that the avenger felt during the period of banishment or inaction.

The Tempest has nearly all the hallmarks of a classic revenge tragedy. Antonio, with the help of Alonso and Sebastian, has dispossessed Prospero; Prospero, living in banishment, suddenly finds himself unobserved among his enemies. However, unlike the powerless, disadvantaged protagonists of revenge tragedy, Prospero always wields supreme power over the situation. Since *The Tempest*, the most compact play in Shakespeare's entire canon, treats only about four hours of action (from slightly before 2:00 p.m. until slightly after 6:00 p.m.), Shakespeare cannot dedicate more than a string of dense, expository speeches to Prospero's past injuries and the intervening years. With the period of suffering and planning firmly in the past, Prospero can spend the whole play reveling in delicious, empowering retaliation.

By the play's conclusion, though, Prospero has decided not to exact revenge—a sign of his ultimate moral fortitude. Prospero may have never planned on a bloody conclusion, but when Shakespeare devised this story he must have been aware that similarities to the ubiquitous and ever-popular revenge tragedy would create suspense among his audiences. This suspense would be further intensified by the fact that other contemporaneous plays about sorcerers—most notably Christopher Marlowe's *Doctor Faustus*—invariably ended in the magician's death and damnation. When Prospero defies audience expectations by throwing away his chance at revenge, he allows Shakespeare to subvert another set of expectations by letting the magician live and prosper. In other words, Prospero's unusual restraint as an avenger buys him unusual forgiveness for his blasphemous magic.

TEN

THE MERCHANT OF VENICE

Shylock the Jew tries to use the law to butcher the merchant Antonio, but the resourceful Portia disguises herself as a legal scholar and saves Antonio.

Brief Synopsis

Bassanio, a nobleman of Venice, wants to marry **Portia,** a wealthy heiress of Belmont, but he needs money so he can go to Belmont in style. **Antonio,** a wealthy merchant of Venice who loves Bassanio, agrees to guarantee a large loan from **Shylock,** the Jewish moneylender. Shylock hates Antonio because Antonio has abused him, so he makes Antonio guarantee that Shylock can have a pound of his flesh if the money is not paid on time. Bassanio goes to Belmont and wins Portia by successfully passing a test in which he has to select between three caskets. Immediately thereafter, he receives word that Antonio has lost all of his ships at sea and cannot repay the loan.

Bassanio returns to Venice with Portia's money, but Shylock insists on having his pound of flesh. Portia disguises herself as a legal scholar and argues successfully in court that Shylock can have the flesh but must not spill any blood—an impossible task that effectively invalidates the debt. Moreover, as Portia points out to the court, Shylock is guilty of conspiring against the life of a Venetian and therefore must forfeit his land. Shylock is allowed to keep most of his money on the condition that he converts to Christianity and leaves all of his money to his daughter **Jessica** and **Lorenzo,** the Christian man she eloped with.

What to Remember About
The Merchant of Venice

SHYLOCK IS BASED IN PART ON ANTI-SEMITIC STEREOTYPES, BUT HE IS NONETHELESS A COMPLEX AND DEEPLY HUMAN CHARACTER.

Because one its central characters is so clearly drawn from a set of outdated and offensive prejudices, *The Merchant of Venice* can be hard to read today. Yet we should not allow the prejudice so clearly evident in Shakespeare's depiction of Shylock to obscure what his character and the rest of the play have to offer.

Shakespeare had probably never met a Jew. In the thirteenth century, hundreds of years before his time, all Jews were banned from England. The law was not revoked until forty years after Shakespeare's death, and even then conversion to Christianity was required. Like most European countries at the time, England was officially Christian. It was commonly thought that God would reward or punish the nation according to its actions. Peaceably co-existing with people of other faiths could bring down divine punishment—an intolerable risk. While it seems that there were at least a few Jewish traders living in London at the time, Shakespeare learned almost all of what he knew about Jews from books and plays rather than from life.

While Shylock can be an unsympathetic character, other plays treat their Jews far more harshly. *The Jew of Malta* by Christopher Marlowe, acted several years before *The Merchant of Venice*, tells the story of Barabas, the wealthiest inhabitant of an island nation under the control of the Turkish Empire. When the Turks demand a large tribute from Malta, its governors turn to the Jews for the money. When Barabas refuses to either convert to Christianity or yield half his riches, the authorities confiscate them all. Barabas spends the rest of the play scheming to recover his fortune and punish his enemies in ever more evil and outlandish ways, until he finally falls to his death in a booby-trapped pit he had built for others. Although he has some legitimate grievances, Barabas is largely motivated by an evil nature and a hatred of Christians. In one of his most famous speeches, Barabas describes his longstanding and pointless cruelty: "I walk abroad 'a nights / And kill sick people groaning under walls. / Sometimes I go about and poison wells." Marlowe's Jew is a pure villain who does evil for the pleasure of it. Working from the same set of cultural stereotypes, Shakespeare produced a far different figure.

Shylock's cruelty is partially motivated by a long history of mistreatment, especially at the hands of Antonio. When the merchant approaches the moneylender about a loan for Bassanio, Shylock reminds Antonio of all the times that he has berated Shylock for lending money, called him a dog, and spat upon him. Confronted, Antonio replies that he has done just that and will probably do so again. When Shylock plans to "feed fat the ancient grudge" he bears against Antonio, it is a recognizable impulse. Antonio has denied Shylock's common humanity, and Shylock feels the insult deeply. When he asks "Hath not a Jew eyes?... If you prick us do we not bleed? If you tickle us do we not laugh?" we must answer "Yes." Still, Shylock makes this powerful case as a justification for the grotesque cruelty that he intends to inflict. Shylock's point is not that he and Antonio share some inalienable human rights, but rather that he should have the right to behave as inhumanly as the merchant has.

In creating Shylock, Shakespeare modified a long tradition of anti-Semitism just as he did so many other traditions. Shylock is a fuller, more psychologically plausible character than the greedy, Christian-hating Jewish figures that predate him, but he is far from free of their heritage.

PLAYS THAT SHOW YOU'RE REALLY WELL-READ

ELEVEN

TWELFTH NIGHT

Viola's decision to live in disguise in Illyria leads to a messy love triangle and a slew of comic complications.

Brief Synopsis

Viola, a young noblewoman, and her twin brother, **Sebastian,** are shipwrecked and separated. Washing ashore in the kingdom of Illyria, Viola disguises herself as a young man and dubs herself **Cesario.** She finds work in the household of **Count Orsino,** who makes her his page. Orsino sends Viola to deliver love messages to **Lady Olivia,** but Olivia falls in love with Viola—or rather, with Cesario. Viola, meanwhile, falls in love with her master, Orsino.

In Olivia's household, Olivia's drunken uncle **Toby,** her clown **Feste,** and her serving woman **Maria** play a practical joke on the dour steward of the house, **Malvolio,** making him think that Olivia loves him, inspiring him to act strangely to win Olivia's affection. Ultimately, they convince Olivia that Malvolio is mad and have him locked in a dark room for treatment. Meanwhile, Toby's bumbling friend, **Sir Andrew Aguecheek,** tries to woo Olivia, without success. Perceiving that Olivia loves Cesario, Sir Andrew challenges Cesario to a duel.

Sebastian arrives in Illyria accompanied by **Antonio,** a man from a neighboring country who has cared for Sebastian since the shipwreck. Mistaking Sebastian for Cesario, Sir Andrew and Sir Toby attack him. Olivia enters amid the confusion and, also mistaking Sebastian for Cesario, asks him to marry her. A baffled Sebastian sees that Olivia is wealthy and beautiful and is therefore more than willing to go along with her. Meanwhile, Antonio has been arrested by Orsino's officers and begs Cesario for help, mistaking him for Sebastian. Viola denies knowing Antonio, and Antonio is dragged off, crying out that Sebastian has betrayed him. Suddenly, Viola has new-found hope that her brother may be alive. Viola and Sebastian finally encounter one another at Olivia's house, and the misunderstandings are resolved at last. The play ends with three happy couples: Viola and Orsino, Sebastian and Olivia, and Toby and Maria. The bitter Malvolio is released and storms off, leaving the rest of the characters to their celebration.

What to Remember About
Twelfth Night

VIOLA MOURNS HER BROTHER BY BECOMING HER BROTHER.

In *Twelfth Night*, Shakespeare employs one of his favorite plot devices —having a girl disguise herself as a boy—to newly poignant effect. Viola's decision to disguise herself as a man can be difficult to understand, and she never explicitly states why she believes the ruse to be necessary. Shakespeare's other cross-dressing heroines have very clear reasons for their disguises, whether for protection (*As You Like It*), to escape detection (*The Two Gentlemen of Verona*), or to gain entry into a male-dominated world (*The Merchant of Venice*). Viola's decision seems a bit arbitrary: She declares that she will dress as a man in order to serve Orsino, but it seems that if she wanted to, she could simply go to the count and ask for help. Indeed, her femininity would probably move Orsino to greater heights of generosity. So why does she feel the need to lie about who she is?

The simplest answer is that without the identity confusion, the play would be over pretty quickly. But it's also possible that Viola doesn't so much need a disguise as she needs to find a way to cope with emotions that threaten to capsize her. When Shakespeare's female characters disguise themselves as men, they usually invent entirely fictional male identities for themselves. Although Viola adopts a new name, Cesario, in her masculine disguise she becomes the spitting image of her dead brother, Sebastian.

Viola's disguise is her way of memorializing her brother and coping with her loss, just as Olivia decides to memorialize her own brother by cloistering herself away for seven years. Viola, racked with grief and stranded in an unfamiliar place, finds comfort and strength in embracing the spirit of her brother. Pretending to be someone else also allows her some distance from her own grief: By hiding away her true self, Viola can suppress her own pain and focus on the task of surviving. The play builds dramatic tension as Viola realizes that she can't keep a lid on her own feelings indefinitely; when she falls for Orsino, she sees what a complex trap she has laid for herself. Within the play's free-spirited comedy, then, lurk more painful and troubling realities, as Viola struggles to honor and overcome the sorrow that hovers at the play's edges until she is joyfully reunited with the brother she thought she'd be forced to replace.

TWELFTH NIGHT EMBODIES A HOLIDAY SPIRIT.

Twelfth Night, also called the Feast of the Epiphany, is a Christian holiday celebrating the arrival of the Magi to pay homage to the infant Jesus. It is celebrated each January 6. *Twelfth Night*, however, does not mention this holiday at all, nor does it seem to take place during the late Christmas season, although some modern productions of the play have set it during that time. This seems to make the title an odd choice; some scholars speculate that it premiered on Twelfth Night and was simply named after the holiday over which it was first performed. In the seventeenth century, one theatergoer who saw a performance of the play remarked in his diary how stupid he thought it was to call a play *Twelfth Night* when it seemed to bear no relation to the holiday.

The relationship of *Twelfth Night* to Twelfth Night, however, lies not in the holiday itself (though its premiere during Twelfth Night festivities is a possibility) but in the celebratory traditions associated with the holiday in Shakespeare's time. Not only did Twelfth Night feature the riotous drinking, feasting, and merrymaking associated with the entire Christmas season during the period, but it was also a day for inverting Elizabethan society's rigid social hierarchy. For one day, servants could kick back and relax, sometimes even being waited on and served by their masters. Celebrations frequently involved masquerading, bawdy songs, and dances, and anarchy was the rule. A play in which countesses fall in love with servants, stewards aspire to the beds of great ladies, and the most uncouth characters have noble titles is perfectly in keeping with the topsy-turvy spirit of Twelfth Night. It was a day that allowed for liberation from social constraints—which were strictly reinforced the next morning.

OLIVIA'S HOUSEHOLD BOTH USURPS AND REINFORCES SOCIAL ORDER.

Olivia's household is populated by everyone from countesses to servants, and the play delights in subverting the class rules that govern the house's stratified society—before quickly snapping that order back into place. Sir Toby and Sir Andrew, for example, both enjoy high social standing, but Shakespeare makes them buffoonish, putting their status at odds with their behavior. Sir Toby is frequently drunk and disorderly, and Olivia must repeatedly send someone (usually Malvolio) to look after him. Sir Andrew has both wealth and a knighthood but is also dimwitted and short-tempered, never fully aware of what's going on but refusing to let that stop him from speaking his mind or picking a fight. Shakespeare usually reserves this kind of bumbling behavior for lower-class characters, but here he makes his clowns noble knights of the realm. This infuriates Malvolio, who fervently believes in the sanctity of the social order.

At the same time, Malvolio himself frequently oversteps his bounds. As the steward of the household, Malvolio's job is to supervise the male servants and carry out administrative duties on Olivia's behalf. With Olivia consumed with her grief (and later consumed with love for a servant very far beneath her status), Malvolio takes unwarranted liberties with his authority, lording over Maria, who actually holds a status equivalent to his among the female servants, and scolding Sir Toby and Sir Andrew in a manner utterly unacceptable from a servant, no matter how boorish his masters' behavior. Malvolio also dreams secretly of marrying Olivia, an unthinkable deviance given his inferior position. Ironically, the play's most fanatic believer in proper social hierarchy also harbors the most elaborate fantasies about transcending that order. Maria's plot is designed not just to humiliate Malvolio but also to put him in his place.

Olivia's fool Feste, on the other hand, occupies a unique position in the social microcosm of Olivia's household. Technically servants, fools were professional entertainers attached to grand Elizabethan households. Generally exempt from serving duties, fools were instead expected to provide entertainment at a moment's notice. In the interest of a good joke, they were allowed great leeway to say and do outrageous things, and even to (gently) mock their employers, which is why Feste's comments outrage Malvolio but are tolerated by Olivia. In a place where the social order seems to have broken down completely, Feste feels right at home; his own social status practically demands that he subvert order. He is not, though, completely free to do as he likes: Too much insolence might take him out of Olivia's good graces, which is perhaps why he doesn't participate in the trick on Malvolio until he can do so in disguise. Feste most completely embodies the social tensions in Olivia's household: a place where order can be subverted but must also be respected.

TWELVE

MUCH ADO ABOUT NOTHING

Claudio is fooled into abandoning his fiancée, Hero; meanwhile, Beatrice and Benedick fall in love despite their best intentions.

Brief Synopsis

In one of Shakespeare's most beloved romantic comedies, two pairs of lovers follow a complicated path to true romance. In the Italian town of Messina, several noblemen returning from a war stop to visit **Leonato,** the governor of Messina. Among the visitors are a prince named **Don Pedro** and his followers **Claudio** and **Benedick.** Claudio falls in love with Leonato's daughter, **Hero,** and asks Don Pedro to broach the subject with both father and daughter. Don Pedro does, at a masked ball thrown that night by Leonato. The plans are almost derailed by Don Pedro's envious bastard half-brother, **Don John,** who tries to convince Claudio that Don Pedro wishes to marry Hero himself. The misunderstanding is smoothed over, though, and a wedding is happily arranged for a week hence.

Meanwhile, Benedick, a witty joker, continues his longstanding war of words with Leonato's clever niece, **Beatrice.** The two claim to despise one another, but their friends—caught up in the romantic mood of the season—decide to trick them into falling in love. Through a series of staged conversations and faked confessions, Beatrice and Benedick are each led to believe that the other is sick with love for them, and each decides the noble thing to do would be to return the affection.

Before Claudio and Hero's wedding can take place, Don John fools Claudio and his brother into thinking that Hero has committed adultery. Claudio waits until the appointed wedding day and then denounces Hero at the altar, storming out and refusing to marry her. Don Pedro follows Claudio but Benedick stays behind, taking the opportunity to declare his love for Beatrice. A grieving Beatrice returns his profession and begs Benedick to prove his love by killing Claudio. Benedick sadly but resolutely agrees to challenge his friend to a duel. Meanwhile, the rest of the family decides to pull a trick on Claudio and Don Pedro. They will claim that the innocent Hero died of shame and wait till the truth of the betrayal is revealed.

Dogberry, the bumbling town constable, inadvertently manages to bring Don John's treachery to light. Claudio, deeply regretting his rash actions, agrees to make amends with Leonato by marrying Leanato's unnamed niece. On the day of the second wedding, however, the niece is joyously revealed to be none other than Hero herself. Benedick, happily free of the burden of dueling with his friend, publicly asks Beatrice if she loves him. She denies it, but not for long, and soon the entire company is merrily celebrating a double wedding.

What to Remember About
Much Ado About Nothing

THE SECONDARY CHARACTERS' PASSION MAKES THE ROMANTIC LEADS LOOK DULL . . .

At any given moment, whether they are professing their mutual love or swearing their hatred for one another (or doing both simultaneously), Beatrice and Benedick interact with more passion and conviction than Claudio and Hero ever manage to muster. Claudio's approach to wooing Hero can best be described, somewhat distastefully, as responsible. He considers her financial promise as the single heir to Leonato's fortunes, he seeks the approval of his friend and his prince, and he enlists Don Pedro to pave the way by talking to the bride and her father on his behalf. To say the least, this more nearly resembles a considered business transaction than an uncontrollable result of human passion and desire. Hero, likewise, seems motivated more by a sense of propriety or duty than any true feeling. She reacts with equal passivity to the prospect of the prince asking for her hand in marriage as to the reality of Claudio's interest. Claudio and Hero's relationship forms the main plot of the story, but the real dramatic energy belongs to their comic second bananas, Beatrice and Benedick. Indeed, in most productions, the warring jokers are considered the lead roles, with Hero and Claudio relegated to secondary positions of ingénue and straight man.

. . . AND YET, BENEDICK AND BEATRICE ARE SECOND-RATE CITIZENS.

With their quick wits and brazen confidence, Beatrice and Benedick insert themselves casually into any situation. They are first-rate scene stealers, and irreverent ones to boot. While Beatrice and Benedick's ease and assuredness might suggest that they possess a high social standing, putting them above the normal rules of civilized interaction, both are in fact conspicuously second-rate citizens. Beatrice is merely a niece of a local governor. What's more, she's an orphan, which threatens the stability of her social status. As her uncle's ward, Beatrice would have been dependent on Leonato's good graces for her survival. Benedick similarly is a low-ranking gentleman when compared to his constant companions. Whereas Claudio is a count and Don Pedro is a prince, Benedick has no title except "Signior," a generic term for anyone above the level of a common subject.

Beatrice and Benedick's brazenness, then, is more akin to the license enjoyed by court jesters than the privilege of the truly powerful. Their quick minds and their theatrical flair amuse those in power, so Don Pedro and Leonato condescendingly allow them free rein. At times, the two even see themselves as something akin to royal fools. When recalling how Beatrice insulted him by saying that people call him "the prince's jester," Benedick seems wounded by her tone and yet almost ready to concede the point: "The prince's fool! Hah, it may be I go under that title because I am merry." He then goes on to persuade himself that Beatrice was lying, but in a moment of insecurity he does believe that she may be right.

Beatrice doesn't acknowledge her jester-like role quite so explicitly, but her actions speak more clearly than Benedick's words. In one of the play's most unexpected moments, Don Pedro suddenly proposes marriage to Beatrice, as if on a whim. Uncertain of how to react, and probably also knowing herself to be below the prince's station, Beatrice responds in the way she usually interacts with her social superiors: She jests. Don Pedro asks if she will have him for a husband, and Beatrice answers that she will not, unless she might have another husband for working days. "Your Grace is too costly to wear every day," she quips. Beatrice and Benedick both wield their wits like weapons, using them to satirize their superiors. Like many jokers, their humor masks an emotional insecurity, but it also deflects their social vulnerability.

MUCH ADO ABOUT NOTHING LOOKS BACKWARD TO ONE OF SHAKESPEARE'S FIRST COMEDIES AND FORWARD TO HIS FINAL PLAYS.

Shakespeare hardly ever invented his plots from scratch. In fact, when he was not drawing them straight from the annals of history, he usually borrowed them from novellas or plays in the repertories of other London companies. He always made his individual mark on the plots he borrowed, though, adding and subtracting elements in order to transform the story and its meanings. One half of *Much Ado About Nothing*—the plot concerning Claudio and Hero—has numerous precedents in European plays and novellas. Many variations exist on just such a story of a lover deceived into thinking his bride unchaste. Shakespeare usually worked from a single source story, which suggests that the Claudio–Hero plot was Shakespeare's starting point for dreaming up *Much Ado*.

The Claudio–Hero narrative fades into the background, though, when juxtaposed with the explosive and comical scenes between Beatrice and Benedick. Shakespeare's clearest source for this subplot is, in fact, one of his own early comedies. When he sat down to pen the tale of Beatrice and Benedick, Shakespeare had already written a play about two such aggressively witty lovers: *The Taming of the Shrew*. In that play, the wily Petruchio decides that the only way to trick the bitterly clever Katherine into loving him is to horribly mistreat her. In crafting the story of Beatrice and Benedick out of his own raw material, Shakespeare reworks the earlier plot as freely as any other source text, ultimately transforming its significance entirely. He adds faint intimations of a past romance between the two, which color their snide insults with the disconcerting possibility of either true bitterness or lingering love. He also replaces the uneven playing field of *The Taming of the Shrew*, where one lover plays a trick on the other, with a more equitable situation, where both lovers are duped by allied outside forces.

This comic half of the story, however, is nothing more than an oddly dominant subplot. The main plot, structurally speaking, remains the romance between Claudio and Hero. Had Shakespeare given that plot full rein, rather than allowing it to be usurped by the boisterous affair between Beatrice and Benedick, the play might have started to resemble Shakespeare's late romance plays. In two of these final plays, *Cymbeline* and *The Winter's Tale*, he again tells a story of suspected infidelity, the accused woman's real or symbolic death, and her literal or figurative resurrection. In these plays, forgiveness works mysterious, even magical powers. In *Much Ado*, however, the power of forgiveness does not bring about the happy ending. Rather, trickery does, as Leonato and his associates conspire to fool Claudio into believing that Hero has died and into defending her chastity. The real magic in the play lies in its sparkling use of language, not its moral or symbolic truths. This is perhaps the reason that it has become such a beloved piece of literature, but also why Shakespeare may have titled the play *Much Ado About Nothing*—or, "a lot of fuss over nothing."

THIRTEEN

AS YOU LIKE IT

Exiled from a corrupt court, Orlando and Rosalind flee into the forest, where their problems are resolved effortlessly.

Brief Synopsis

Orlando, the younger son of a deceased knight, is deeply frustrated because his spiteful older brother **Oliver** refuses to support him in a manner befitting a gentleman. **Duke Senior** has also been wronged by *his* brother, **Duke Frederick,** who ousted Duke Senior and sent him into exile. Duke Senior now lives with a band of followers in the Forest of Arden, where the former courtiers and gentlemen enjoy a Robin Hood–like existence.

Duke Senior's daughter, **Rosalind,** is allowed to remain at court because of her close friendship with Duke Frederick's daughter, **Celia.** Seeing Orlando defeat a champion in a wrestling match, Rosalind falls in love with him, and Orlando with her. When Orlando flees to the forest to escape Oliver (who has murderous intentions toward his wayward brother), and Duke Frederick experiences a sudden change of heart and exiles his niece, Rosalind and Celia head to the forest as well. Taking along the jester Touchstone, the women adopt disguises for their journey: Rosalind poses as a young man, Ganymede, and Celia as Ganymede's sister, Aliena.

In Arden, the two girls encounter an obsessed Orlando pining away for Rosalind. Taking her to be a young man, Orlando confides in Rosalind that his affections are overpowering him. Rosalind, as Ganymede, claims to be an expert in exorcising such emotions and promises to cure Orlando of his lovesickness if he agrees to pretend that Ganymede is Rosalind and comes to woo her every day. Orlando agrees, and the two engage in a series of love lessons.

Meanwhile, Frederick has sent Oliver on a manhunt to find his brother, whom Frederick assumes has abducted his niece and daughter. While on the way to find Orlando, however, Oliver repents for his misdeeds and reconciles with him, restoring Orlando's inheritance and falling in love with Celia in the process. After a dramatic revelation of her true identity, Rosalind marries Orlando, accompanied by Celia's wedding to Oliver and the weddings of two minor comic couples. Duke Frederick encounters a holy man in the forest and repents, assuming a monastic life and returning the dukedom to Duke Senior.

What to Remember About
As You Like It

THE FOREST OF ARDEN IS A LIBERATING REFUGE FROM THE REAL WORLD—BUT NOT A PERFECT ONE.

Pastorals, a literary form popular in the early seventeenth century, extolled the virtue of simple existences conducted in harmony with nature. Pastorals appealed to city dwellers by suggesting that a happy, uncomplicated world existed in the countryside, far from the squalor, crime, overcrowding, and disease that marred the life of even the wealthiest Londoners. By watching pastoral plays or reading pastoral literature, urbanites could temporarily transport themselves to a more bucolic place. *As You Like It*, a pastoral play, sets up the Forest of Arden as a peaceful, rustic retreat from the city. There, the characters find temporary respite from their problems and enjoy the unsophisticated good cheer of the forest natives.

As the play begins, many of the characters are trapped by the circumstances of their lives: Orlando is being denied his inheritance and an education; Rosalind, Celia, and Touchstone are living under the watchful eye of Duke Frederick; and Duke Senior and his friends have lost their property and been banished. In the forest, where they take refuge, the characters find freedom both from their oppressors and from society's rules. Orlando can indulge his passionate devotion to a woman he just met without worrying about his brother spoiling the fun. Touchstone can fall in love with a goatherd without worrying about the opinion of the others at court. And the lords can dress comfortably, lie in the grass, and pass the time singing. Even Jaques, Duke Senior's perpetually sour follower, is tickled by the people he meets in the forest and the life he finds there.

While *As You Like It* fits comfortably into the pastoral genre, Shakespeare does not make Arden an idyllic paradise. The forest can be cold. Foraging for food there is difficult. And there are snakes and lionesses lurking in it. Perhaps because the joys of simple living are limited, the courtiers eventually leave in order to reclaim their status and property. But despite its dangers, the forest offers undeniable freedom, which the characters must sacrifice in order to return to their sophisticated, complicated lives. The play leaves the question unresolved: Is it better to live a comfortable, courtly life full of intrigue and worldly problems or a simple, less comfortable life full of freedom?

GENDER IS A TRICKY ISSUE.

By disguising herself as a young man named Ganymede (who then "pretends" to be a woman), Rosalind prompts us to question our assumptions about how gender affects our behavior and our attractions. We know that Ganymede is Rosalind in disguise, but Orlando does not. He spends a memorable part of the play wooing Ganymede as a rehearsal for his eventual courtship of Rosalind. The growing attraction between Orlando and Rosalind-as-Ganymede simultaneously suggests two opposite possibilities: that gender is transcendently powerful, and that Orlando is attracted to Rosalind because her femininity shines through her disguise; or that love transcends gender, and that Orlando is attracted to Ganymede because he is compatible with the person he takes to be a young man. By ending with two heterosexual marriages, the play seems to choose the former argument. But by determinedly flirting with homoerotic attraction, Shakespeare raises the possibility that romantic love can exist between two people of the same gender.

The gender confusion doesn't stop with Rosalind's playacting. In Shakespeare's time, it was illegal for women to appear onstage, so all the female roles were performed by men. An audience of Shakespeare's contemporaries would have seen the young actor playing Orlando wooing another young actor playing a young woman, Rosalind, who is playing a young man, Ganymede. These dizzying layers force us to consider that gender—often believed by modern audiences to be an inherent, inextricable part of a person's identity—may be nothing more than a suit of clothes, easily shed and just as easily put on again. Though Rosalind eventually returns to being a young woman and marries Orlando, it would be hard for an audience in Shakespeare's day to forget that after the wedding, the dance, and the epilogue, Rosalind was going to retire to a dressing room, change into street clothes, and go back to being a man.

FOURTEEN

RICHARD III

After resolving to steal the crown from his brother Edward, Richard descends into greater and greater evil as he murders everyone who stands in his way.

Brief Synopsis

After a long civil war between the Houses of York and Lancaster, England enjoys peace under **King Edward IV.** Edward's younger brother, the hunchbacked **Richard,** resents Edward's strong yet peaceful rule. Malicious, power-hungry, and bitter about his physical deformity, Richard plots to seize the throne, resolving to kill anyone in his way.

Richard manipulates a noblewoman, **Lady Anne**—daughter-in-law of his family's enemy, the dead King Henry VI—into marrying him. He has his older brother **Clarence** executed and shifts the guilt onto his sick brother King Edward in order to accelerate Edward's illness and death. After King Edward dies, Richard becomes lord protector of England until Edward's eldest son comes of age.

Richard kills the noblemen loyal to **the princes,** his two nephews, and has their maternal relatives arrested and executed. Richard's allies, led by **Lord Buckingham,** campaign to have Richard crowned king. Richard then imprisons the young princes in the Tower and sends **hired murderers** to kill both children.

By this time, Richard's reign of terror has caused the common people of England to fear and loathe him, and he has alienated nearly all the noblemen. When rumors begin to circulate that the **Earl of Richmond** is gathering forces in France, preparing to invade England, noblemen defect in droves to join his forces.

Richard has his wife, Queen Anne, murdered, so that he can marry **young Elizabeth,** the daughter of the former **Queen Elizabeth** and the dead King Edward. Queen Elizabeth manages to stop him and secretly promises to marry young Elizabeth to Richmond.

Richmond finally invades England. The night before the battle, Richard has a terrible dream in which the ghosts of the people he has murdered appear and curse him. Richard is killed in the battle, and Richmond is crowned King Henry VII. Promising a new era of peace for England, the new king is betrothed to young Elizabeth, thereby uniting the warring houses of Lancaster and York.

What to Remember About *Richard III*

SHAKESPEARE TELESCOPES HISTORY FOR THEATRICAL PURPOSES.

In *Richard III*, Shakespeare compacts events that span more than a decade into what seems to be a few months. Henry VI died in 1471. Richard married Anne in 1472. Clarence died in 1478. Richard ascended the throne in 1483 and died at Richmond's hands in 1485. Shakespeare allows these distant events to mingle and overlap. In doing so, he ignores several historical realities, but this allows him to present highly theatrical scenes where decade-long struggles are collapsed into a single explosive moment.

The most famous of such scenes is Richard's wooing of Lady Anne. In reality, this betrothal happened over a year after the death of Anne's husband, Prince Edward, and Edward's father, Henry VI. Shakespeare, however, combines these events into one scene of mythic proportion. In Shakespeare's version, Richard woos Anne even as she leads Henry VI's funeral procession. Whereas a historian might figuratively say that Richard wooed Anne over the bleeding body of her father-in-law, Shakespeare makes this metaphor literal. According to Renaissance beliefs, a victim's wounds will bleed afresh if the murderer approaches the corpse, and this happens when Richard approaches Henry's coffin. Therefore, Richard *literally* proposes to Anne over Henry's bleeding body, even as the blood makes a new testament to his guilt.

Shakespeare ignores history even more blatantly in his depiction of Queen Margaret. Margaret, the widow of the deposed Henry VI and an enemy of the reigning King Edward IV, inexplicably appears in Edward's court. She lashes out at those in power and bewails the injustices that her family, the Lancasters, have received at the hands of the Yorkists. Although everyone proceeds to denounce and mock her, they oddly tolerate her presence. Not only would Margaret not have been allowed in court, but according to the historical record she was banished from England and dead by the time the events depicted in *Richard III* took place. Yet Shakespeare goes out of his way to insert Margaret into the play nonetheless.

Shakespeare places Margaret on the scene for dramatic reasons. The long, methodical curse that she delivers in Act 1, scene 3, in which she condemns each of the play's major characters, provides the framework for the rest of the play. Every one of her curses ends up being a prophecy that accurately foretells the fate of each character: The young Edward, Prince of Wales, dies in the Tower with his brother; Elizabeth outlives her husband and her children; Rivers, Dorset, and Hastings all meet their mortal ends; Richard himself is plagued by treachery and sleepless nights. As they face their fates, Richard's victims cite this curse, more than Richard's evil, as the cause of their downfall. Whereas historians might see the turmoil of Richard's rise to power as a sort of metaphorical retribution for the Yorkist atrocities against the Lancasters, Shakespeare literally shows Richard's actions as a fulfillment of Margaret's vengeful curses. Richard is, in effect, transformed into an unwitting instrument of Lancastrian revenge.

THE PLAY TURNS TRAGIC WHEN RICHARD TURNS HIS BACK ON THE AUDIENCE.

Richard possesses an extraordinary ability to charm and confuse people into doing things that are, to say the least, against their best interests. Through eloquent persuasion and theatrical flair, he makes a calculated effort to lure his victims away from moral reasoning. For instance, while wooing Lady Anne, Richard bombards her with speech after speech, matching her deflections word for word and pun for pun. When all else fails, he melodramatically offers to kill himself on her behalf. Later, when trying to win the confidence of the Lord Mayor of London, Richard first relies on persuasive words but cements the deal in a later scene with a heavily contrived show of piousness, making a grand entrance between two intoning priests. As a stage artist, Richard's taste may be a little over-the-top, but he certainly gets excellent results.

Richard's showmanship extends to his interactions with the audience. From the very first line of the play, he invites viewers to be his confidantes, sharing with them his frustrations, his joys, and his future plans. Because Richard addresses the audience directly, he has the same demagnetizing effect on the audience's moral compass as he does on the characters around him. Even as his actions remain abhorrent, we cannot help being drawn in by his wit and charisma. As his circle of trusted accomplices grows smaller and smaller, Richard's interactions with the audience nevertheless remain completely frank. For as long as this is true, the play is a sort of comedy of evil, moving at a frenetic, almost joyous pace from one improbable victory to another.

However, as the play progresses, Richard gradually stops speaking even to the audience until, in Act 4, scene 2, we realize that we no longer know what he is scheming. He delivers the charge to Tyrell to kill the two young princes, but then he summons Tyrell nearer and whispers something in his ear. There is no telling what this additional charge is. In the very next scene, we learn that Anne has died. Perhaps Richard has had Tyrell murder her too. Perhaps he has commanded Tyrell to kill Buckingham, who has just rebelled against Richard's judgment. Maybe he has simply reiterated the initial command. Whatever the case, the audience suddenly slips from the empowering position of the villain's confidante to the terrifying status of an uninformed onlooker. From that point on, the illicit joy of watching a villain at work evaporates, and only the grim march toward Richard's bloody doom remains.

FIFTEEN

HENRY V

Despite his wild youth and his suspect claim to the throne, Henry V becomes the greatest king in English history by conquering all of France.

Brief Synopsis

The recently crowned **King Henry V** must convince his unsettled nation that he is a competent and worthy king. He takes advantage of a legal argument that he has a right to the French throne and decides to invade France. The lower-class characters he used to associate with prepare to leave their homes and families to go to war. Three of Henry's noble friends are convicted of treason, and he has them executed to show that he has abandoned his old ways. Against incredible odds, the English conquer the town of Harfleur, after Henry inspires his troops with an impassioned speech. After another powerful speech, Henry's forces rout the French at the Battle of Agincourt, even though the French outnumber them five to one. Henry forces the **King of France** to marry his daughter **Catherine** to Henry and appoint Henry his heir.

What to Remember About *Henry V*

HENRY IS A CONSUMMATE ACTOR.

Shakespeare enjoyed King Henry V so much that he dedicated three whole plays to the heroic English monarch. The bulk of *Henry IV, Parts One* and *Two* detailed Henry's progression from a drunken youth in the seedy taverns of London to a sober prince who nobly assumed the throne on his father's death. In the opening scene of *Henry V*, the Bishop of Canterbury alludes to Henry's reckless youth when he says that the prince's wildness seemed to die at the exact moment the breath left his father's body.

The audience, however, knows that this transformation is partly an illusion. Nearly everyone in Shakespeare's audience would have seen the wildly popular *Henry IV* plays, where the young Prince Hal (Henry's youthful nickname) explains his wildness as a calculated effort to forge his political image. Not only will it make him intimately familiar with the lives and ways of his most common subjects, but also his debauched behavior will make his eventual reformation seem more wondrous and remarkable. His publicity stunt seems to have worked, judging from the bishop's heartfelt wonder and praise.

Shakespeare gives us plenty of reasons to believe that Henry's current role as the epitome of Christian kingship is just as calculated a bit of playacting as was his youthful unruliness. We never see Henry in a casual interaction. He seems to have no close friends. Instead, he is always in the company of policymakers and generals, performing ceremonies of state. In other words, we only see the public king—never the private man. The only time we see Henry in an unguarded moment is when he dedicates an entire soliloquy to debunking the principle that, in the rest of the play, he seems to embody most: ceremony.

Henry's ceremonial tendencies are particularly evident in the stirring yet predictable development of his speeches. All of his longer speeches—of which there are many—exhibit an identical rhetorical buildup. They start with a gesture of personal warmth, putting the listener at ease. Then Henry moves into some sort of self-effacing comment, lowering the listener's expectations and making himself appear vulnerable. Then suddenly, Henry focuses on a forceful idea, after which his rhetoric builds and builds. His sentences get shorter and his vocabulary more clipped. His words become shorter, blunter, and more staccato. Usually, he augments this effect by throwing in the alliteration of sharp consonants. The consistency is too perfect to be merely a quirk of his speech. Instead, it is the polished technique of a studied and self-conscious orator.

SHAKESPEARE UNDERCUTS THE SUNNY PATRIOTISM OF THE CHORUS.

In no other play does Shakespeare rely so heavily on a narrator to comment on and guide the action. The Chorus is a strongly felt presence in *Henry V*, initiating every act with a lengthy speech and capping off the play with an epilogue. The Chorus does help explain the many leaps in time and location that occur between the acts, but Shakespeare wrote many more erratic plays without feeling the need to give his audience a guide. The real function of the Chorus, it seems, is to speak unending praise of Henry. He calls him the "mirror of [i.e., the example for] all Christian kings," the "grace of kings," and the "star of England." He lauds Henry's modesty, courage, and virtue, and in the epilogue he further highlights Henry V's glorious reign by reminding the audience of the domestic strife and international shame that England felt under the next king, Henry VI.

It would be inaccurate, though, to equate the Chorus's raptures with Shakespeare's own political opinions. Shakespeare takes pains to undermine the Chorus's flag-waving tendencies: Though the Chorus charms with his eloquence and captivates with his urgent appeals to the audience's imagination, his assertions seem curiously out of sync with the realities of the situations he introduces. Each of the Chorus's prologues is followed by a scene that blatantly contradicts his nationalistic proclamations. In his first speech, for example, the Chorus prepares the audience to witness "the warlike Harry" displayed in military glory, with "famine, sword, and fire" at his command. Instead, Shakespeare shows us two clergymen planning to pander to the king's military ambitions so that they can win his support in a power struggle between the church and Parliament. In his prologue to the second act, the Chorus depicts the optimism and zeal with which the English prepare for war, claiming that each man in England is preoccupied with thoughts of honor. Immediately afterward, Shakespeare shows us two blundering soldiers engaged in a bitter, petty quarrel over a woman. At the beginning of act 3, the Chorus describes how every able man has thrown himself into the war effort, asserting that England is now "guarded with grandsires, babies, and old women." We know this to be a rhetorical exaggeration, because Henry has resolved in an earlier scene to take only a quarter of the nation's forces to France. The Chorus also lauds England's "choice-drawn cavaliers," but Shakespeare soon shows us Bardolph, Pistol, and Nym cowering behind the back lines at Harfleur, eager to avoid any danger. The Chorus is a sort of cheerleader who speaks bold and powerful praise throughout the play, but Shakespeare consistently shows his wartime rhetoric to be strained or misplaced.

SIXTEEN

HENRY IV, PART ONE

Prince Harry rises above his criminal youth to become a military hero.

Brief Synopsis

King Henry IV has recently seized the throne from **Richard II.** The powerful lords **Worcester, Hotspur (Harry Percy),** and **Northumberland,** who helped King Henry take power, are now turning against him and joining forces with the rebel **Mortimer** and the feared Welsh leader **Owain Glyndwr.** Meanwhile, King Henry's son, **Prince Harry** (often called Hal), spends his time drinking, thieving, and whoring with assorted scoundrels, in particular an obese, debauched knight named **Sir John Falstaff.** Hal's wild ways anger his father and the rest of the kingdom, but Hal's bad behavior is calculated. He wants his eventual reformation to appear spectacularly impressive in contrast with his rowdy youth. When King Henry has to lead his forces against the rebels, Hal reconciles with him and performs heroically in battle, saving his father's life and killing the renowned Hotspur in single combat at the Battle of Shrewsbury. Falstaff abuses the command Harry gives him and behaves like a coward in battle. Nevertheless, he takes credit for killing Hotspur, a lie that Harry backs up.

What to Remember About
Henry IV, Part One

FALSTAFF IS ONE OF SHAKESPEARE'S MOST MEMORABLE CREATIONS.

To create Sir John Falstaff, Shakespeare drew on the medieval mystery plays that were popular in his youth. These transparently allegorical plays, which feature main characters with names like Everyman or Youth, convey unsubtle lessons. In one play, for example, a character named Death denies Everyman additional time on earth. Fellowship tries and fails to cheer up the morose Everyman. Good-Deeds and Knowledge eventually lead Everyman to Confession. Vice, a character who appears under many names in many plays, is an irreverent prankster who dupes the gullible, mocks the pious and powerful, and leads the naïve astray. He is always defeated in the end—a moral tale could hardly allow Vice to triumph—but before the inevitable return to order, the audience gets to enjoy the misrule Vice causes.

Falstaff is a direct descendent of Vice, as Prince Hal point out. In one of the play's central scenes, the prince and Falstaff playact Hal's return to court. At first Falstaff plays the king, scolding Hal for his behavior and the company he keeps. Falstaff-as-King does note his approval of one of Hal's cronies: "a good, portly man . . . of a cheerful look, a pleasing eye . . . his name is Falstaff." And then the roles are reversed. Hal-as-King remarks to Falstaff-as-Hal on the "devil [that] haunts thee in the likeness of an old fat man . . . that reverend Vice, that grey Iniquity, that father Ruffian, that Vanity in years." The language comes straight from a morality play.

But *Henry IV, Part One* is not a morality play, and Falstaff is not Vice but a three-dimensional human. Despite his many flaws, Falstaff is an attractive character. In contrast to the status-obsessed Hotspur, whose dying lament is for "those proud titles" Hal has stolen, Falstaff values life more than honor. Unlike the prince, Falstaff often makes fun of himself. And we would be hard-pressed to condemn his outsized appetite for food, liquor, and love. Because Falstaff, unlike Vice, is not an entirely unappealing character, his ultimate rejection is deeply disturbing. Falstaff-as-Hal argues that to "banish plump Jack," Hal-as-King would have to "banish all the world." The prince replies, "I do; I will." The exchange leads us to question Hal's character as much as Falstaff's. By making Falstaff fully human, Shakespeare shows us that in his quest for greatness, Hal loses some of his love for humanity.

PRINCE HAL IS COMPLEX, CALCULATING, AND OFTEN COLD.

The two plays *Henry IV, Part One* and *Henry IV, Part Two* are not so much the story of King Henry IV as they are the story of the making of a new king: Prince Hal, who becomes Henry V. At the end of *Richard II*, the newly crowned Henry IV asks after his "unthrifty son," a "young wanton and effeminate boy" in whom he nonetheless sees "some sparks of better hope, which elder years / May happily bring forth"—a reference to Henry V that would have been caught by the members of Shakespeare's audience, all of whom were familiar with the legends of the rowdy prince who became England's most successful warrior king. The three plays that follow *Richard II* depict Shakespeare's take on the popular legend.

Shakespeare does not attribute Prince Hal's transformation to a personal struggle against temptation, a change in Hal's point of view, or a successful attempt to become a better person. Instead, he portrays Hal's so-called redemption as a carefully planned PR stunt. The first time Hal appears, he remains on stage after his companions have departed to assure us that his rebellion is calculated, that he recognizes the worthlessness of his friends, and that he hangs out with them only to make his later reformation that much more impressive. King Henry hears about his son's support for his "dissolute" friends and their robberies, but the Hal we see is fastidious about what he will and won't be involved with. Hal declines to participate in actual highway robbery but is happy to allow his friends to do so and then to mock them for their failures.

Hal is far more troubling, but also far more interesting, than the rebel-turned-prince we might expect to meet. It would be easy to admire a man who carelessly wastes his youth but then matures and earns his throne, but Hal is not that man. From the first, he knows what he is doing. His self-awareness, and his cold manipulation of everyone from his drunken friends to his royal father, make him hard to love. In contrast to a character like Falstaff, who is always purely himself, a collection of uncontrolled flaws and appetites, Hal is never quite what he seems. Even when he appears to be a dissolute prodigal or a loyal son, he is playing a role he has created for himself. His transformation is not genuine. Rather, it is a bit of inspired and convincing stagecraft.

SEVENTEEN

HENRY IV, PART TWO

Putting aside his former friends, Prince Harry becomes King Henry V.

Brief Synopsis

At the end of Henry IV, Part One, **King Henry** and **Prince Harry** (Hal) defeat part of the rebel forces at the battle of Shrewsbury, and Harry becomes a military hero. Now, in *Henry IV, Part Two*, they must face the rebel forces of the **Archbishop of York, Lord Mowbray,** and **Lord Hastings.**

Hal's younger brother, **Prince John**, tricks the rebels into dismissing their troops by promising to negotiate with them. He then has the rebel leaders executed for treason.

Hal's rascally friends, including **Falstaff,** who is now a captain, think they will have the run of the kingdom once Harry is king. King Henry, who worries about the rebels and his wayward son, falls ill. Hal repents of his former debauched behavior and vows to be a responsible king. King Henry forgives him before dying. Hal is crowned King Henry V. Falstaff comes to greet him in London, expecting a warm reception, but the new king banishes Falstaff from his presence and goes to court to plan an invasion of France.

What to Remember About
Henry IV, Part Two

THE CHARACTERS THINK A LOT ABOUT DEATH.

Henry IV, Part Two is a much darker play than its predecessor, *Henry IV, Part One*. Changes to the character list are partly responsible for the more somber tone. In *Part One*, the battlefield exploits of the proud and vigorous Hotspur contrasted with Prince Hal's pretended fecklessness. In *Part Two*, Hotspur has died, and his absence dampens the mood. Lady Percy, Hotspur's loving wife in *Part One*, is now a widow bitter about her young husband's untimely death and angry at her father-in-law, Northumberland. For his part, Northumberland is haunted by his failure to join the last rebellion, and by the deaths that resulted from that failure.

Characters are preoccupied with impending death and lost happiness. The old king falls ill and eventually dies. Justice Shallow fondly recalls the "mad days" of his youth, when he frequented well-dressed whores, and marvels at "how many of [his] old acquaintance are dead!" These reminiscences are melancholy enough on their own, but they become even more depressing when we learn from Falstaff that they are largely invented: Shallow was a meager, dull-witted student who had few "mad days," if any. Shallow is not fondly recalling his better years; he is falsely recalling a youth he squandered. This false nostalgia is somehow sadder than the real thing.

Even Falstaff, invincibly jolly in *Part One*, is forced to face his own mortality. The Lord Chief Justice reminds the wayward knight that he is "as a candle, the better part burnt out," an aging guy with "a moist eye, a dry hand, a yellow cheek, a white beard, a decreasing leg, and an increasing belly." Doll Tearsheet, Falstaff's favorite prostitute, asks him when he will stop fighting and whoring "and begin to patch up thine old body for heaven?" Falstaff tries to ignore the Chief Justice and Doll, but the topic of death keeps coming up. Hal, now King Henry V, emphasizes Falstaff's age as he rejects his former drinking buddy, saying, "I know thee not, old man." Although Henry V's ascension to the throne represents a rebirth, *Part Two* is a play marked by death.

IN THE WORLD OF THIS PLAY, HOPE IS LIKELY TO BE DISAPPOINTED.

Hope leads to great disappointment for many characters in *Henry IV, Part Two*. For a few moments, Northumberland falsely believes that his son survived the battle of Shrewsbury. When he learns that his son actually died, his pain is more bitter because hope existed in the first place, if just for a moment. Other characters explicitly reject hope, for fear that it will only lead to disappointment. When Lord Hastings suggests to the war council that it couldn't hurt to rely on the chance that Northumberland will appear, Lord Bardolph replies almost angrily that if they base their plans on any sort of hope, they are simply inviting despair. This observation carries great weight in both the council and the play. Still, although the rebels avoid putting their faith in Northumberland, they hold out far too much hope for amnesty from the king.

The greatest miscalculation, and therefore the greatest disappointment, is Falstaff's. For years, he has been playing "when you become king" with Hal, and he is foolish enough to expect Hal's rule to resemble their tavern game. So confident is Falstaff that he draws credit on his expected access, convincing Robert Shallow to prepare an enormous feast in his honor. Hal's rejection of Falstaff is a hard pill to swallow, and it sets up yet another doomed hope: Falstaff promises to repay Shallow, a promise that he seems unlikely to carry out.

EIGHTEEN

RICHARD II

Henry Bolingbroke takes the throne from King Richard II to become the first English king of the house of Lancaster.

Brief Synopsis

King Richard II of England makes himself unpopular by spending money irresponsibly and giving too much power to his close friends. He exiles his cousin, **Henry Bolingbroke,** for six years as a way of resolving a dispute between Bolingbroke and the **Duke of Norfolk.** When Bolingbroke is away, Bolingbroke's father, **John of Gaunt,** the Duke of Lancaster, dies, and Richard seizes his property to pay for a war in Ireland.

Bolingbroke returns from exile with an army, bent on reclaiming his inheritance. Outraged by Richard's abuses, the commoners and noblemen both flock to Bolingbroke's cause, and Richard loses the kingdom completely without even a battle. Bolingbroke is crowned King Henry IV. **Sir Piers Exton,** acting on King Henry's suggestion, assassinates the deposed King Richard. Henry repudiates the deed and vows to go on a pilgrimage to Jerusalem for penance.

What to Remember About *Richard II*

THE STAKES IN *RICHARD II* ARE EXTREMELY HIGH.

Far from being a play of merely historical interest, the story of Richard II was almost too hot for Shakespeare to handle. Everyone in Shakespeare's audience knew that there was much more to this story than whether Richard or Bolingbroke—figures who had lived and died almost two hundred years before the play was written—would get to be king. Shakespeare had to handle his material very carefully, because any position he took on the deposing of Richard would imply a position on the legitimacy of the kings who came after him and on the legitimacy of a nation's right to depose its monarch in general.

THE EVENTS OF *RICHARD II* HAD FAR-REACHING CONSEQUENCES.

Richard's ouster sets in motion a chain of events that would occupy Shakespeare for eight plays. Although *Richard II* may suggest that the King's overthrow by Bolingbroke was well deserved, Shakespeare's audience was well aware that it inaugurated a long period of political unrest culminating in the Wars of the Roses more than sixty years later. Shakespeare's *Richard III* brings this sequence to a close with the ascension of Henry VII. In *Richard II*, Shakespeare suggests that Richard was just as corrupt a ruler as his enemies claimed, over-taxing his subjects and over-relying on sycophantic counselors. But by devoting seven more plays to exploring the consequences of that action, and all of the violence and instability that ensued from it, Shakespeare prompts us to consider the possibility that England might have been better served by leaving an ineffectual, self-indulgent monarch in the throne.

RICHARD II WAS HIGHLY CONTROVERSIAL IN SHAKESPEARE'S TIME.

The play was first performed in the last decade of Elizabeth's reign, when England was ruled by an aging, childless monarch and therefore faced a great deal of uncertainty surrounding the royal succession. Elizabeth had resisted marriage for years, and by the time of *Richard II* (c.1595) it had become clear that she would never marry, leaving her without an obvious heir. This state of affairs was to the queen's political benefit, because either a husband or an heir would inevitably have become a rival power center. Still, the situation made the queen's advisors and subjects, who had to live with the consequences of her political positioning, understandably nervous. In a deeply religious kingdom whose national religion had been dramatically changed by the last two successions, going from Protestant to Catholic and back again, the uncertainty was almost unbearable. Although we know that James I succeeded Elizabeth with almost no upheaval, when *Richard II* was first performed, the English could only hope for a smooth transition.

Moreover, people had begun to worry that Elizabeth was being misled by her advisors, just as Richard II had been. As the queen aged, she came to rely more and more on the Privy Council, the circle of her closest advisors. The malcontents came from different ends of the religious, and therefore political, spectrum. Catholics complained of new and burdensome fines levied against them to compel attendance at the national Protestant church. Meanwhile, thoroughgoing Protestants complained of just how Catholic that church remained and how slow it was to move against the Catholics within it. Though the groups raised precisely opposite objections, the prevailing doctrine surrounding the monarchy forced them to put those objections into a similar form. One could not stand up in public and say that the queen had it wrong, but it was somewhat safer to claim that the queen was prevented from getting it right by evil counselors.

Elizabeth herself recognized the parallel. In 1601, two years before her death, she told an advisor, "I am Richard II. Know ye not that?" Several months before, one of her subjects had founded an ill-fated rebellion on just that analogy. In 1599, Elizabeth sent the Earl of Essex to Ireland to strengthen England's control there. He returned to accusations that while in Ireland he had conspired against the queen. Essex was closely watched thereafter and blamed Elizabeth's counselors for his mistreatment. Early in 1601, he decided to raise a rebellion, storm Westminster Palace, free the queen from her counselors, and settle the issue of succession. The night before he planned to ride the streets of London gathering a mob, Essex paid Shakespeare's company to stage *Richard II*. The portrait of a monarch beset by bad-willed advisors, and the suggestion that an ambitious earl might do something about this, were enough to earn Essex a traitor's death.

RICHARD'S VERBOSE INTROSPECTION CONTRASTS WITH BOLINGBROKE'S QUIET ACTION.

Although Bolingbroke clearly wins the political battle, Richard carries the day in the theater. The scene at Flint Castle represents the moment at which the balance of power between them shifts for good. In that scene, Bolingbroke says almost nothing while Richard rages, laments, and complains—not at Bolingbroke himself, but rather at Northumberland, his messenger. Richard holds nothing back, allowing us to see him struggling to make sense of who he is and what he must do, but in doing so providing everyone else with just that same view. Richard is guilty of the fault that Henry IV will later attribute to his son: exposing too much of himself to the public view. It is not an error that Bolingbroke would ever make. When Richard descends to him, Bolingbroke kneels and acknowledges that they are headed to London. And that is all. If Richard embodies many of the virtues of Shakespeare's art, they nonetheless fail him in certain ways, and we must think therefore about their limitations.

NINETEEN

ANTONY AND CLEOPATRA

Antony's love for Cleopatra leads to his defeat at the hands of Octavius Caesar.

Brief Synopsis

Mark Antony, one of the three rulers of the Roman Empire, finds himself torn between his identity and duty as a Roman and his love for the exotic Egyptian queen, **Cleopatra.** Antony draws criticism from his fellow rulers, **Octavius Caesar** and **Lepidus,** for leading a life of pleasure in Egypt and ignoring his duties. Antony returns to Rome when he hears of his wife **Fulvia**'s death and the threat of the rebel **Pompey.** Antony marries Caesar's sister, **Octavia,** to cement his relationship with Caesar. The leaders make peace with Pompey, and Antony and Octavia leave for Athens. When Antony is gone, Caesar moves to seize exclusive power, waging war against Pompey and betraying Lepidus. Antony sends Octavia to Rome to make peace but leaves for Egypt and Cleopatra, raising an army to fight Caesar.

Antony fights Caesar at sea, but when Cleopatra's ship flees the battle, Antony shames himself by fleeing after her. Antony scores a surprise victory in the next battle on land, but in the sea battle following, the Egyptian fleet once again deserts Antony and he suffers defeat. Cleopatra hides herself in a monument and broadcasts that she has committed suicide, so Antony tries to kill himself. He is taken wounded to Cleopatra, with whom he dies. Caesar takes Cleopatra prisoner, but she kills herself to prevent being made taken to Rome and put on display.

What to Remember About
Antony and Cleopatra

ANTONY IS A GREAT ROMAN WHO TURNS HIS BACK ON THE ROMAN LIFESTYLE.

Mark Antony—both the real historical figure and Shakespeare's character—is a man of intriguing contradictions. On the one hand, he truly does embody the Roman ideal, or at least has proven that he can embody it when he wants to. A proven military leader and fearless soldier, Antony is also capable of the impressive feats of stoicism and self-discipline that were so highly regarded by the Romans. Even his enemy, Octavius Caesar, can recall a time when Antony endured famine and drank horse urine and muddy water to survive a grueling military campaign. But throughout his career, Antony was equally well known for his other side. When he was not at war, he displayed the exact opposite traits: extreme indulgence in drink, sex, and pleasure of all kinds. Shakespeare juxtaposes Rome and Egypt as a way of dramatizing Antony's choice of one side of himself over another.

Caesar's Rome is a world of order, a masculine, militaristic society in which emotions are kept under control. The only Roman woman we meet is Octavia, Caesar's sister, who is credited with "wisdom" and "modesty"; Antony's soldier Enobarbus describes her as "holy, cold, and still." We hear of one other woman: Antony's first wife, Fulvia, who leads an army into battle. Every other Roman we see is a man and a soldier.

Cleopatra's Egypt, by contrast, is a site of feminine sensuality: a warm, fertile climate where excess is celebrated. Certainly Egypt is a more diverse place. Cleopatra is attended by playful waiting women, a fortuneteller, and several men, including a eunuch servant. Above all, Egypt is embodied by the queen herself. Cleopatra's passion and pride burst out again and again—when Antony bids her farewell, when a messenger brings word of his marriage, when the Romans attempt to capture her.

Antony does attempt to bridge the two worlds he inhabits, but he's ultimately forced to choose between his Roman discipline and his Egyptian appetites. Though the play dramatizes this choice, we get the sense that Antony has chosen before the events of the play begin. Our first view of Antony is of him dismissing the Roman messenger, and we never meet the stoic Antony who drank horse urine. Though he still has his pride, the Antony we see is a drastically changed man. Instead of using his famous sword, we find him lending it to Cleopatra while he puts on her robes in a game of cross-dressing.

ANTONY AND CLEOPATRA EXPLOITS THE FLEXIBILITY OF SHAKESPEARE'S STAGE.

The action shifts from Egypt to Rome and back again in moments, whisking the audience from one end of the Empire to another, while skipping right past the months of travel in between, a technique that is effective but unorthodox. In Shakespeare's day, many people believed that plays should observe the "dramatic unities," a set of principles derived from Greek and Roman drama. The basic idea was that there should be as little time discrepancy as possible between the fictional world of the play and the real world in which it was enacted. Usually, this meant that a play should be set in one place on one day, describing actions that could occur in the several hours in which the play was enacted. Ben Jonson, Shakespeare's great rival in the theater, was a particularly forceful proponent of the unities, and Shakespeare himself occasionally observed them, most notably in *The Tempest*. In *Antony and Cleopatra*, however, Shakespeare creates a very different drama.

The power of language—and the lack of set pieces—allows *Antony and Cleopatra* to move quickly over such great distances. Although today we speak of going to "see" a play, in Shakespeare's time people went to hear one. Shakespeare's theater was primarily a verbal, not a visual, experience. While the costumes could be lavish, the sets were minimal. Our movies about Rome are often elaborate productions involving temples and chariots, but Shakespeare invoked the city with little scenery of any kind—a limitation in a certain way, but also an advantage. Without pyramids or columns to be changed each time the scene moved across the Mediterranean, those scene shifts could come more often and more smoothly. When Caesar talks to Octavia, the setting is clearly Rome. When Enobarbus and Cleopatra debate moments later, they obviously do so in Egypt. Costumes can help audiences to maintain this distinction, but it is Shakespeare's language that does most of the work. Because its visual vocabulary was so limited, Shakespeare's theater could say "Here we are!"—and there they were.

TWENTY

MEASURE FOR MEASURE

Lord Angelo enforces a strict code of sexual morals in Vienna, but then he himself tries to force the chaste Isabella to have sex with him.

Brief Synopsis

Vincentio, the Duke of Vienna, decides that he has allowed his subjects to become too carefree when it comes to obeying the law, so he pretends to go on a journey and appoints the strict, rigidly straight-laced moralist **Lord Angelo** as his deputy, to be assisted by the wise old lord **Escalus.** Immediately, Angelo begins cracking down on vice and sex crimes, making **Pompey,** a servant in a brothel, and the lascivious **Lucio** very nervous. Angelo arrests a man named **Claudio** for impregnating his fiancée, **Juliet,** before the two are officially wed, and as an example to the rest of Vienna, he condemns Claudio to death.

Isabella, Claudio's extremely devout sister, is about to enter a nunnery when her brother is arrested. Isabella goes to Angelo to beg him for mercy. He refuses but suggests that there might be some way to change his mind. When he propositions her, saying that he will let Claudio live if she agrees to have sexual intercourse with him, she is shocked and immediately refuses. Her brother begs her to reconsider, and Isabella is left to contemplate a very important decision.

The duke, who remains in Vienna disguised as a friar, intervenes and tells Isabella to agree to Angelo's request. He tells her Angelo was once engaged to a woman, **Mariana,** but abandoned her when she lost her dowry in a shipwreck. The duke forms a plan by which Isabella will agree to have sex with Angelo but will instead send Mariana in her place. The next morning, Angelo will pardon Claudio and then, when the ruse is revealed, be forced to marry Mariana according to the law. Everything goes according to plan, except that Angelo does not pardon Claudio, fearing revenge. The prison provost and the duke send Angelo the head of a dead pirate, claiming that it belonged to Claudio, and Angelo believes that his orders were carried out. The duke, still in disguise as the friar, tells Isabella that her brother is dead and that she should submit a complaint to the duke, who is due to arrive shortly, accusing Angelo of immoral acts.

The duke returns in his royal clothes and announces that he will hear all grievances immediately. Isabella tells her story, and the duke pretends not to believe her. Eventually, the duke reveals his dual identity, and everyone is forced to be honest. Angelo confesses to his misdeeds, Lucio is forced to marry the prostitute he impregnated, Claudio is pardoned, and the duke asks Isabella to marry him—though she remains silent at the proposal.

What to Remember About
Measure for Measure

THE DUKE IS AN AWFUL PLAYWRIGHT.

By abruptly abandoning Vienna, leaving it in the hands of a burgeoning moral despot, and then returning to spy on his deputy while disguised as a humble friar, Duke Vincentio sets the events of *Measure for Measure* into play. However necessary it is dramatically, though, his enigmatic behavior lacks a credible motivation. What starts as a project to reinstate lapsed laws and test Angelo's capabilities as a ruler quickly turns into a series of sadistic experiments in how people will react under extreme pressure. The duke allows Angelo to pursue his corrupted crusade to its conclusion, deliberately keeps from Isabella the news that her brother has escaped execution, and in the last scene accuses Isabella of lying and declares her insane. His confidence implies that his actions are calculated elements of a master scheme, but his precise goals never become clear.

Because of the duke's inscrutable behavior, some readers prefer to see him not as a truly human character but as an allegorical figure: that is, a character that stands for an abstract idea or force. One particularly popular interpretation casts Vincentio as a representation of God. Throughout history, earthly rulers have often been considered anointed representatives of God. The transfer of power from the duke to Angelo could symbolize the transfer of power from God to his earthly deputies. Without God's controlling presence, human rulers may run amok, but God always returns to mete out justice and bestow divine mercy on sinners. This argument, though, proves fairly reductive—especially when interpreters try to expand the allegory, casting Lucio as Satan and Isabella as the Human Soul.

However, a better analogy might be drawn between the duke and Shakespeare himself. Like Prospero in *The Tempest*, Vincentio is a sort of playwright figure, who manipulates the people in his vicinity just as Shakespeare manipulated characters on a page. In this scenario, Vincentio doesn't merely leave Vienna out of some divine sense of delayed yet inevitable justice. Instead, the duke—bored, artistically frustrated, or perhaps just meddlesome—strives to orchestrate the most dramatic effects possible. However, if Prospero is the manipulator par excellence, Vincentio needs a remedial lesson in playwriting. He proves a rather unskilled scene crafter who can never quite achieve his desired effect. The play becomes a dark farce as he scrambles to make things go right, especially when Angelo persists in warranting

Claudio's death even after (he thinks) he gets to sleep with Isabella. The duke may have intended for the events of his absence to play out as a large-scale parable about morals and ethics, but by the end of the show it's all he can do to keep his actors from mutinying and running away with the play.

MARRIAGE FAILS TO PROVIDE ORDER IN *MEASURE FOR MEASURE*.

For all of its dark subject matter, *Measure for Measure* is consistently listed among Shakespeare's comedies. Renaissance comedies usually ended in one or more marriages, and Shakespeare had a particular tendency to pair off his characters very abruptly in the fifth act. *Measure for Measure* is no exception. At the end of the play, Angelo marries Mariana, Lucio must marry the bawd, and the duke proposes to Isabella.

Most comedies, though, tend to celebrate these mass weddings, as they bring order, harmony, and a sense of closure to a chaotic situation. In *Measure for Measure*, though, marriage is first and foremost a punishment. Angelo must marry Mariana as a result of his lecherous ways. Lucio must marry the prostitute he impregnated, which he declares equal to "pressing to death, whipping, and hanging." The proposed marriage between the duke and Isabella is less clearly a punishment, but it's hardly an occasion for overwhelming joy. The duke picks the most awkward moment possible to breach the subject: in front of a large crowd, just after he has revealed to her that he lied about Claudio's death. Add to this the fact that Isabella wants nothing more than to devote herself to the celibate life of a nun, and it's no wonder that she doesn't respond to his proposal. The one marriage that the audience would surely applaud, the reunion of Claudio and Juliet, is conspicuously absent in this final resolution. Juliet is nowhere to be seen, and the play's climactic moment focuses on the restitution of brother to sister rather than the institution of husband and wife.

Even if it's amusing to see the debauched Lucio yoked to the old ball and chain, and satisfying to see Angelo be forced to do right by the woman who inexplicably still loves him, Shakespeare generally seems pretty down on marriage in *Measure for Measure*. Perhaps he approves of the freer sensuality advocated by Pompey. Pompey's speeches on the irrepressible nature of human sexuality are some of the sanest in the play. Given that prostitutes were probably milling among the audiences at the Globe, Pompey's speeches might have even met with public approval too. *Measure* might also reflect Shakespeare's own souring notion of marriage. Biographers agree that Shakespeare had to rush into a marriage because of an unexpected pregnancy, and after he moved to London to start his theatrical career, he could only have seen his wife a few times per year when he returned to Stratford-upon-Avon. Finally, it's possible that Shakespeare abandons the joyful comic resolution in *Measure* because he's already moved onto a more tragic point of view. After all, *Measure for Measure* is Shakespeare's last comedy, and he immediately followed it with three of his darkest tragedies: *Othello*, *King Lear*, and *Macbeth*.

PLAYS WITH WHICH TO SERIOUSLY IMPRESS YOUR TEACHER

TWENTY ONE

THE WINTER'S TALE

Leontes' insane jealousy causes him to lose his friend, wife, son, and daughter, but when his daughter grows up and marries the friend's son, he is reconciled with his family.

Brief Synopsis

King Leontes of Sicilia becomes insanely jealous of his pregnant wife, **Hermione,** convinced that she is cheating on him with his visiting friend, **King Polixenes** of Bohemia, and that Polixenes is the baby's true father. Against the objections of his entire court, he throws Hermione into prison and sends a messenger to the Oracle of Delphi to confirm his suspicions. When Hermione gives birth to a girl, Leontes gives the baby to a lord named **Antigonus** to abandon her in some desolate place. The Oracle sends word that Hermione is innocent, and that Leontes will have no heir until his daughter is found. Word arrives that Leontes' son, **Mamillius,** has died as a result of Hermione's imprisonment, and Hermione dies from Leontes' mistreatment of her.

Antigonus, following the instructions given to him in a dream by Hermione, names the baby **Perdita** and leaves her on the coast of Bohemia, after which he is killed by a bear. Perdita is found by a **Shepherd,** who raises her with the help of his son (known simply as the **Clown** in the stage directions). Sixteen years later, Polixenes' son, **Florizel,** falls in love with Perdita, and when Polixenes refuses to let Florizel marry her, they elope and flee to Sicilia. The shepherd who raised Perdita reveals her story, and Leontes is reunited with his daughter and reconciled with Polixenes. **Paulina,** a lady in Leontes' court, brings a statue of Hermione to life, then reveals that Hermione was alive in Paulina's house the entire time.

What to Remember About
The Winter's Tale

THE WINTER'S TALE IS SHAKESPEARE'S MOST RADICAL EXPERIMENT IN COMBINING TRAGEDY AND COMEDY.

Shakespeare often enlivens his tragedies with comic subplots or deepens his comedies with hints of near tragedy. *The Winter's Tale,* however, swings schizophrenically between comedy and tragedy, never quite managing to integrate the two genres into a seamless whole. In the first three acts, which take place in Sicilia, Leontes' outsized jealousy makes a tragic outcome inevitable. In sharp contrast to these early scenes, however, the Bohemian scenes of Act 4 are pastoral and comic, concerned with Autolycus's pranks, the festive dances of the shepherds and shepherdesses, and music of all varieties. Though threats of violence are uttered, chiefly by the outraged Polixenes, they are the empty, exaggerated threats of comedy.

The transition from the tragic world of Sicilia to the bright, comic world of Bohemia is an awkward one, suggesting how incompatible these two worlds really are. In the final scene of Act 3, Antigonus arrives in Bohemia and, unaware of Leontes' repentance, completes his mission. The scene has all the trappings of tragedy: A good man is forced to abandon a helpless infant, his ship sinks in a storm, and he himself is devoured by a bear. In all of these events, though, Shakespeare finds an absurd humor. Antigonus's final stage direction—*Exit, pursued by a bear*—is perhaps one of the most famous in English theater history. The actor who played Antigonus at the Globe may have been chased offstage by a live, trained bear, but it seems more likely that his pursuer was a man wearing a bear costume. Plenty of productions since have mined the moment's slapstick potential. The horror of the remaining events is further downplayed because they're narrated by the Shepherd's son, known simply as "Clown." This designation indicates that the original actor would have employed a broadly comic acting style, and the metaphors he uses to describe the killing and the sinking are likewise humorous: He compares the plunging ship to a cork being flung in a barrel of liquor and to a "flap-dragon," a raisin floating on flaming brandy. Bohemia is a place incapable of tragedy. When presenting the infant Perdita to his son, the Shepherd declares, "Thou met'st with things dying, I with things new-born." All thought of tragedy melts away in the presence of the newborn girl.

When the Sicilian and Bohemiam worlds collide again in the final act, "things dying" are again replaced by "things new-born," but comedy doesn't exactly win the day this time. Hermione is resurrected, either literally or figuratively, depending on whether you believe she was truly dead or merely hiding for sixteen years. Leontes' daughter, Perdita, is restored to him. By marrying Perdita, Florizel becomes a son to Leontes, thus replacing Mamillius. As a crowning touch, Leontes attempts to replace the dead Antigonus by betrothing Paulina to Camillo. There is something bittersweet about this ending though. The specter of sixteen years irrevocably lost—in friendship, marriage, and parenthood—hovers over the scene. The play, after all, is called *The Winter's Tale*, and, as Mamillius claims in Act 1, "a sad tale's best for winter."

SHAKESPEARE DEFIES REALISM IN *THE WINTER'S TALE.*

Mamillius seems to explain the title of *The Winter's Tale* when he comments that "a sad tale's best for winter," but Shakespeare offers another interpretation. Like the fantastical stories told around the fireplace to ward off the boredom and claustrophobia of winter living, the plot of *The Winter's Tale* strays far beyond what is conventional or believable. In Act 5, scene 2, as the Sicilian gentlemen discuss the reappearance of Perdita after sixteen years and the reunion of Leontes and Polixenes, they compare the story to just this sort of tall tale. Speaking of Perdita's return, one says, "This news, which is call'd true, is so like an old tale, that the verity of it is in strong suspicion." Another, speaking of Antigonus's death at the jaws of a wild bear, says, "Like an old tale still, which will have matter to rehearse, though credit be asleep and not an ear open." In other words, the truth is like a peculiar old story that persists even though no one believes it.

If *The Winter's Tale* were meant as a tall tale, that would explain Shakespeare's whimsical attitude toward time and place. Not only does he allow the story to swing from Sicilia to Bohemia and back again, but he also casually lets sixteen years fly by in between Acts 3 and 4. In addition, he mixes details from vastly different cultures and historical periods in creating his fictitious versions of Sicilia and Bohemia. The characters have ancient Greek-sounding names, and

Leontes sends two noblemen to the oracle at Delphi, an important religious figure in ancient Greece. However, the sculpture of Hermione was allegedly accomplished by Julio Romano, a real Italian Renaissance artist of the sixteenth century, and the sheep-shearing festival of Act 4 suggests festivals held in rural England during Shakespeare's time. Like a mythological beast whose every body part resembles that of a different creature, the world of *The Winter's Tale* is a magical, mythical mixture of different times and places.

The mythical nature of the play also accounts for Leontes' inscrutable psychology. Unlike *Othello*, Shakespeare's more realistic play about the dangers of jealousy, *The Winter's Tale* does not satisfactorily explain the source of Leontes' jealousy. In *Othello*, the main character begins to distrust his wife only after a self-proclaimed villain takes it upon himself to trick him. Leontes, however, has no such excuse. His jealous rage is baseless, and like a malicious disease it infects every organ of his mind and body. Every mythic character comes complete with his defining characteristic, his uncontrollable, irrational tendencies, and Leontes' happens to be jealousy.

Some critics see Shakespeare's casual disregard for historical realities and human psychology as a symptom of the playwright's carelessness, but Shakespeare seems so self-conscious of the story's implausibility that we must see this play as a deliberate rebellion against the rules and conventions of dramatic storytelling.

TWENTY TWO

THE COMEDY OF ERRORS

Antipholus of Syracuse and his servant Dromio visit Ephesus, not knowing that their identical twins already live there.

Brief Synopsis

Egeon, a merchant of Syracuse, is condemned to death in Ephesus for violating the ban against travel between the two rival cities. He tells the Ephesian **Duke** that he has come to Ephesus to find his wife and one of his twin sons, who were separated from him twenty-five years earlier in a shipwreck. The other twin, who grew up with Egeon, is also traveling the world in search of the missing half of their family. (Both twins are named **Antipholus,** and both have servants named **Dromio,** themselves identical twins.) The Duke is so moved by this story that he grants Egeon one day to raise the ransom that would save his life.

Egeon's missing son has grown up to become a prosperous citizen of Ephesus. His traveling son, **Antipholus of Syracuse,** has just arrived in Ephesus as well. **Adriana, Antipholus of Ephesus**'s wife, mistakes Antipholus of Syracuse for her husband and drags him home for dinner, leaving

Dromio of Syracuse to stand guard at the door and admit no one. Shortly thereafter, Antipholus of Ephesus returns home and is refused entry to his own house.

Antipholus and Dromio of Syracuse, pursued by Adriana and others, take refuge in an abbey. An enraged Antipholus of Ephesus tries to bring charges against his wife. The Abbess, **Emilia,** resolves the situation by bringing out the two sets of twins and revealing herself to be Egeon's long-lost wife. Antipholus of Ephesus reconciles with Adriana; Egeon is pardoned by the Duke and reunited with his spouse; Antipholus of Syracuse resumes his romantic pursuit of Adriana's sister, **Luciana**; and all ends happily with the two Dromios embracing.

What to Remember About
The Comedy of Errors

THE PLAY *IS* A COMEDY, BUT IT'S TINGED WITH SADNESS AND SUSPENSE.

Just as Shakespeare's tragedies have generous helpings of comic relief, his comedies are often colored by tragedy. Though *The Comedy of Errors* is at heart a slapstick farce, it is suffused with real emotion. Egeon's imminent death, which we learn about at the beginning of the play, casts a shadow over the play's comic developments. Because a man's life is at stake, the misunderstandings and convoluted plot are more than just setups for punch lines (and punches). We in the audience know that if the characters don't sort out the tangled mess of confusions that make up the plot, Egeon will be executed. Even as we laugh at the onstage antics, we watch them in great suspense, wondering if the characters will realize what's happening in time to save the kindly old man.

TIME ONLY *APPEARS* TO BEND.

During the madcap events of the play, the characters believe that time is playing tricks on them. From their perspective, Ephesus is operating outside the rules of time. The Dromios' masters berate them for their lateness (which is usually caused by the completion of a different errand). Because they are mistaken for each other, the twins seem to have the ability to accomplish impossible tasks instantaneously. When Dromio of Syracuse returns to Adriana to get bail for Antipholus, the clocks in the square seem to chime the hours in reverse, as if time has begun to go backwards.

Despite this seeming temporal confusion, the play actually adheres to unity of place and unity of time, two principles from classical Greek drama. *Unity of place* means that the play occurs in a single location—in this case, a street in front of two houses and an abbey. *Unity of time* means that the events of the play occur during a single day, and that the time span of these events roughly equals the play's running time. The characters might be confused about time, but Shakespeare has a firm grasp on it. In fact, in terms of temporal matters, *The Comedy of Errors* is one of Shakespeare's more orderly efforts. Many of his works play with the passage of time, leaping decades into the future or cramming the events of years of warfare into a single battle. Despite its zany events, *The Comedy of Errors* contains none of those leaps of logic.

EPHESUS SEEMS MAGICAL, BUT IT'S JUST A NORMAL COASTAL TOWN.

In Shakespeare's time, Ephesus was known as a city filled with magicians and witches, a place where unsuspecting tourists could be bewitched, enchanted, robbed, enslaved, or driven mad. Shakespeare's portrayal of Ephesus plays on this reputation. His Syracusian arrivals experience everything that Elizabethans might have expected to encounter in scary, intriguing Ephesus. Antipholus of Syracuse starts to worry that he has been bewitched. He and Dromio doubt their very identities and wonder if the untrustworthy Ephesians have somehow magically transformed them. Surrendering to Ephesian enchantments sometimes seems alluring (life with Luciana would suit Antipholus well, if only he could win her) and at other times horrifying (life with the fat kitchenmaid Nell, who claims to be his wife, is more than Dromio can bear). Eventually the two out-of-towners decide that even Ephesus's delights must be some kind of trick and plot to escape with their sanity intact.

Despite the experiences of Antipholus and Dromio of Syracuse, Ephesus is not bewitched at all. Unlike, say, Prospero's island in *The Tempest* or the woods of Athens in *A Midsummer Night's Dream*, two enchanted places inhabited by thrilling creatures, Ephesus is not a magical place. Rather, it is a normal coastal town. Every seemingly impossible event in the play has a perfectly logical, if unlikely, explanation. The plot twists escalate not because of magic, but because of comic coincidences. Even the exorcism specialist, Dr. Pinch, the one town resident with a connection to the occult, turns out to be not much more than a local quack. Ephesus is not infested with "goblins, owls and sprites," and the only truly amazing event that takes place there is the miraculous family reunion that brings everyone to a happy end.

TWENTY THREE

CORIOLANUS

Coriolanus's pride prevents him from becoming consul,
so he attacks Rome.

Brief Synopsis

The common people of Rome gain the right to elect five
political representatives, or tribunes, despite the objections
of the proud, aristocratic **Caius Martius,** who has nothing but contempt for the commoners. When Martius heroically captures the city of Corioles from Rome's enemies,
he is renamed **Coriolanus,** and the Roman senate offers
him the position of consul. Coriolanus has to ask for the
vote of the common people to earn the position. The common people support him until two of their tribunes accuse
Coriolanus of being an enemy of the people. Furious, Coriolanus denounces the very idea of popular rule, and the
tribunes and the Roman citizens demand that he be exiled.
Allying himself with his former enemy, **Aufidius,** Coriolanus leads an army of the Volscians, a neighboring tribe,
against Rome. Coriolanus's mother, **Volumnia,** convinces
him to call off the attack, and Aufidius's men later assassinate Coriolanus.

What to Remember About
Coriolanus

VOLUMNIA ACTS AS HER SON'S WIFE AND FATHER, AS WELL AS MOTHER.

Like a combination of Hamlet's mother, Gertrude, whose love life obsesses her son, and Lady Macbeth, whose demands guide her husband's career, Coriolanus's mother, Volumnia, both romances her son and exhorts him to perform bold, masculine deeds. Coriolanus is married, but his wife, Virgilia, is nearly silent throughout the play. The strong bond between Coriolanus and his mother leaves no room for her. When the two women await Coriolanus's return from battle, Volumnia scolds Virgilia, saying that "if my son were my husband" she would not be fearful, as Virgilia is. In essence, Volumnia usurps the role of Coriolanus's wife. She, not Virgilia, is the one who exerts influence on Coriolanus; she is the one Coriolanus aims to please.

Coriolanus is a martial man by nature, but his mother pushes that martial nature to its limits. Her role in shaping her son is widely known. In the beginning of the play, a Roman citizen opines that Coriolanus has performed his great deeds in battle "to please his mother, and to be partly proud." As a boy, Coriolanus sought conflict of his own volition; Volumnia recalls that she "was pleased to let him seek danger where he was like to find fame." But Volumnia fanned the flames of his bravery. Letting him find danger "pleased" her, and she says she willingly sent him off "[t]o a cruel war." By winning glory in battle, Coriolanus both establishes his manliness and pleases his mother.

Shakespeare suggests that it is dangerous for women to teach masculine virtues. Volumnia has turned her son into a proud fighter, but her overbearing influence has robbed him of the ability to make wise choices independently of her. Like a scientist who has created a monster, Volumnia is the only one who can control her prideful son.

At two crucial moments, Coriolanus yields to her: first when he submits to public approval in order to get the consulship (although he does so grudgingly and condescendingly, leading to his ouster from Rome), and then when he makes peace with Rome rather than sack it. Coriolanus may be a war hero, but he is still attached to his mother's apron strings.

CORIOLANUS SUGGESTS THAT COMMON PEOPLE AREN'T FIT TO RULE THEMSELVES.

In *Julius Caesar*, Shakespeare shows popular rule in a mostly positive light. While the common people might be worrisomely easy to trick with powerful oratory, Shakespeare suggests that government by the people is preferable to government by one man, and that Brutus is right to want to prevent Caesar from establishing a monarchy. In *Coriolanus*, however, Shakespeare takes a darker view of commoners, whom he portrays as self-interested and short-sighted. At the beginning of the play, before they get a voice in government, the citizens form an angry mob. They behave no better after they win representation, turning against Coriolanus and casting him out of the city. The people show themselves to be incapable of acting in their own best interests—a fatal indictment of popular rule.

Though he faults the citizens for their lack of judgment, Shakespeare also condemns Coriolanus's self-absorption. He suggests that if the people cannot rule themselves, their rulers must protect them, even if that protection requires the rulers to exercise a little humility and self-abasement. In his famous parable, Menenius likens a harmonious government in which rulers distribute wealth to a harmonious human body in which the belly distributes food. If the common people fail to perform the belly's necessary role, Coriolanus fails too, by prizing his personal honor over the well-being of Rome.

TWENTY FOUR

THE TWO GENTLEMEN OF VERONA

In this early comedy, Proteus betrays his best friend, Valentine, and his lover, Julia, in order to gain Silvia's love, but he repents his actions when Valentine offers him Silvia.

Brief Synopsis

In Verona, two friends, **Valentine** and **Proteus,** bid farewell to one another. Valentine is off to see the world, while Proteus stays behind to woo **Julia,** the woman he loves. Proteus's father, **Antonio,** however, has different plans: He wants his son to go to Milan to seek his fortune. Proteus and Julia tearfully exchange rings and vows of love before Proteus leaves Verona.

In Milan, Valentine has fallen in love with the **Duke**'s daughter, **Silvia.** When Proteus arrives, he also falls in love with Silvia. Betraying his friend's confidence, Proteus warns the Duke of Silvia and Valentine's secret plan to elope. The Duke banishes Valentine, giving Proteus the opportunity to start wooing Silvia for himself.

Julia disguises herself as a young man, **Sebastian,** in order to follow Proteus to Milan. There, she is shocked to see her beloved wooing Silvia. Proteus, mistaking the heartbroken Julia for a page, sends her to deliver a ring to Silvia.

The banished Valentine, while traveling to Mantua, is apprehended by a group of outlaws. The outlaws, all of whom are banished gentlemen as well, demand Valentine to become their king, and since they threaten to kill him if he refuses, Valentine accepts. Meanwhile, to avoid marrying **Thurio,** her father's friend, Silvia runs away from home with the help of her friend, **Sir Eglamour.** Making their way through the forest, however, Silvia and Eglamour are apprehended by the outlaws. Eglamour flees; Silvia is captured. Proteus arrives and frees Silvia from the outlaws, but then he tries to rape her. Valentine intercedes, Proteus repents, and Valentine, as a token of their renewed friendship, offers Silvia to Proteus. At this point, Sebastian faints, and his true identity becomes clear. Proteus decides that he really does love Julia more than Silvia, and he takes her instead. The Duke realizes that Thurio is a thug and, deciding that Valentine is a far nobler man, allows Valentine to marry Silvia. Valentine asks for clemency for the outlaws and suggests that his marriage to Silvia and Proteus's marriage to Julia should take place on the same day.

What to Remember About
The Two Gentlemen of Verona

THE TWO GENTLEMEN OF VERONA SAYS, "YOUR BOYS ALWAYS COME FIRST."

In *The Two Gentlemen of Verona*, the duties of friendship are pitted against the demands of romance. When following friendship means remaining loyal to those who trust you, and following romance means betraying both friends and lovers, the moral choice seems obvious to everyone but Proteus. *Two Gentlemen of Verona*, however, *consistently* maintains the supremacy of friendship—even when said friends act dishonorably toward one another. The play's final act, in which Valentine forgives his old friend even after he has terrorized and nearly raped Valentine's beloved, is shocking in the way it cheapens romantic attachments in favor of male friendships.

The characters in *Two Gents* betray their individual preferences in the friendship-vs.-romance debate through the kind of language they use. The men in particular rely on conventional images of love as a kind of slavery. Valentine complains that "affection chains" Proteus to Verona and declares, "Love is your master." These images of bondage eventually give way to legal and economic metaphors, such as when Proteus rejoices over a letter from Julia by saying, "Here is her hand, the agent of her heart; / Here is her oath, her honor's pawn." Despite Proteus's elation, his metaphors seem cold: He compares her handwriting to an authorized representative, such as might sign a legal document or bill of sale, and her oath of love to a valuable object, which she offers as collateral for her equally valuable chastity. In contrast, Proteus uses religious terms to describe his friendship, such as when he promises to be Valentine's "beadsman" (someone who prays on the behalf of someone else).

The only character who consistently takes the opposing stance is Julia. Unlike Proteus, Julia reserves her religious language strictly for her beloved. When they trade rings upon Proteus's departure, the two speak in conflicting metaphors. Proteus treats the exchange like a business transaction, saying, "Why then we'll make exchange. Here, take you this." Julia transforms his economical language into divine covenant, responding that they will "seal the bargain with a holy kiss." When she decides to follow Proteus to Milan, Julia's spiritual language becomes even richer, describing herself as a "true-devoted pilgrim" who finds in Proteus her "soul's food."

And yet, even though Julia seems the most noble and sympathetic character in the play, *Two Gentlemen of Verona* does not celebrate her viewpoint. Once Julia has accepted Proteus's apology, Valentine takes their hands and claims, "'Twere pity two such friends should be long foes." Valentine joins the two not as lovers but as exceptional friends. In this play, casting their romance as a special class of friendship seems the ultimate validation of the relationship.

PROTEUS GETS OFF EASY.

Elizabethan plays, including Shakespeare's, usually conclude with a scene that brings all the major characters onstage in a last-ditch eleventh-hour attempt to tie up any loose ends. In a tragedy, the corpses pile up; in a comedy, the marriages accumulate. Even if a modern audience understands this convention, however, the rapid reintegration of Proteus in the final scene can be shocking. Proteus has betrayed Valentine, contrived to have him banished, openly wooed his fiancée, and, within a few lines of the play's hasty resolution, come within inches of raping her. Yet as soon as Proteus delivers a bland four-and-a-half-line apology, Valentine quickly forgives his old friend. Proteus has also betrayed Julia, making her deliver his engagement ring to her rival and openly wishing her dead. The offense here seems greater and therefore requires a full six lines of trite contrition in order to achieve its effect. Proteus's clean escape seems baffling, until we realize that neither Valentine nor Julia could ever match Proteus in deviancy or cunning.

Proteus takes his name from a powerful ancient god. In Greek mythology, Proteus, also known as The Old Man of the Sea, has the special ability to change into any shape he chooses. He defeats his enemies by taking monstrous forms and escapes them by taking miniature ones. For every situation, he makes an appropriate transformation. It takes an equally legendary hero, Odysseus, to pin him down long enough to stop the endless chain of transformations. If Shakespeare's Proteus is a truly "protean" figure, perhaps he succeeds because neither Valentine nor Julia proves strong enough (or willing) to wrestle him down to earth, to hold him truly accountable for his actions.

In fact, there is only one character who consistently proves herself equal to Proteus and willing to knock him down: Silvia. Only she can scheme and shape-shift more deftly than Proteus. Her letter trick, in which she retains her modesty by having Valentine write a love letter to himself, is flawlessly conceived and executed. As adept as Silvia proves at deception, though, blunt honesty serves her best when she attempts to fend off Proteus's advances. She cuts him down at every turn, coolly pointing out his faults, the flaws in his logic, and the impudence of his tactics. As the play resolves itself at the end of Act 5, though, Silvia remains curiously silent. She neither protests the way Valentine nonchalantly offers her to Proteus, nor takes the villain to task for his cruel treatment of his friends and lovers. It's unclear whether Silvia is unable to speak because she's still recovering from the trauma of her near-rape or whether she's reeling from the revelation that Valentine will not champion her honor. Whatever the case may be, it is Silvia's silence that purchases Proteus's otherwise impossible happy ending.

TWENTY FIVE

TITUS ANDRONICUS

When Titus Andronicus sees his sons executed unjustly and his daughter raped and mutilated, he takes revenge by feeding the empress's sons to her in a pie.

Brief Synopsis

Titus Andronicus, a Roman general, returns from ten years of war with only four of his twenty-five sons left. He has captured **Tamora,** the cruel and beautiful queen of the Goths, her three sons, and her servant **Aaron the Moor.** In obedience to Roman rituals, Titus sacrifices Tamora's eldest son to his own dead sons, which earns him her unending hatred and her promise of revenge. The new Roman emperor, **Saturninus,** promises to take Titus's daughter **Lavinia** as his bride, even though she is already betrothed to his younger brother, **Bassanius.** Riled by the blatant insult, Lavinia's brothers help Bassanius abduct her; Titus, enraged by what he sees as a treasonous and dishonorable act against the emperor, ends up slaying one of his own sons in a vain attempt to prevent the kidnapping. Titus watches his fortunes fall even further when Saturninus quickly decides to make Titus's enemy, Tamora, his empress in Lavinia's place.

To get back at Titus, Tamora schemes with her lover, Aaron, to have his sons **Martius** and **Quintus** framed for the murder of Bassanius. Thanks to Tamora's machinations, these two sons of Titus are executed. Unsatisfied, Tamora urges her sons **Chiron** and **Demetrius** to rape Lavinia, after which they cut off her hands and tongue so she cannot reveal their crime. Finally, even Titus's last surviving son, **Lucius,** is banished from Rome. The aging, battered Titus—who had earlier been tricked by one of Tamora's sons into chopping off his own hand in an attempt to save Martius and Quintus—begins to act oddly. Everyone assumes that he is slipping into insanity.

In his exile, Lucius acts in accordance with his father's secret wishes and raises an army of Goths. Tamora tries to capitalize on Titus's apparent madness by pretending to be the figure of Revenge, come to offer him justice in exchange for convincing Lucius to stop his attack on Rome. Titus, having feigned his lunacy all along, tricks her, captures her sons, kills them, and bakes them into a pie. He feeds this pie to Tamora in the final scene, after which he kills both the empress and, to relieve her of her shame, his own daughter Lavinia. Saturninus then kills Titus, and Lucius in turn kills Saturninus. Lucius has the unrepentant Aaron buried alive and Tamora's corpse thrown to the beasts before assuming the throne as the new emperor of Rome.

What to Remember About
Titus Andronicus

IN ELIZABETHAN ENTERTAINMENT, VIOLENCE WAS THE NAME OF THE GAME.

Although the population of Elizabethan England may have been sharply divided by class and religion, it was nevertheless united in an almost universal love of blood and gore. In the entertainment district, bearbaiting and cockfighting arenas flourished and competed with theatres for their audiences. During bearbaiting events, a fierce bear was tethered to the ground while vicious dogs taunted him and slowly tore him to shreds. In the adjacent cockfighting pits, roosters ripped each other apart while audiences cheered them on. All of this took place directly next to—and sometimes even inside of— England's most popular theatres.

Although they typically took place in different venues, public executions were also an ingrained part of Elizabethan entertainment. In these displays, thieves and murderers often met their end in front of a rapt audience. Pamphlets circulated advertising the villain's heinous crimes, and as the execution commenced the audience greedily consumed each detail of the condemned man's sordid life. Before he was hung or brutally drawn and quartered, the criminal traditionally repented, offering the crowd a sort of moral spectacle in addition to satisfying their love of gore.

Knowing that his audience was intoxicated by violence and aware of the intense competition for spectators, Shakespeare peppered many of his plays with gruesome deaths. The lurid *Titus*, which often seems driven by pure bloody spectacle alone, represents the most extreme example of this tendency. For this reason, many critics dismiss *Titus* as a ridiculous and implausible farce, written to simultaneously satisfy and mock the desires of a bloodthirsty public. However, with its strong moral narrative, Shakespeare's drama resembles the phenomenon of public execution much more than the simple blood sport of bearbaiting or cockfighting. *Titus* doesn't rely on violence for its own seductive sake; rather, the play explores and analyzes the appeal of murder and revenge. Since no character in *Titus* can claim to be wholly innocent (except, perhaps, Lavinia), to some extent each death offers the satisfying delivery of punishment well deserved. By leavening his gory extravaganza with elements of clear-eyed ethical analysis, Shakespeare offered every member of his audience something to enjoy.

TITUS BRIDGES EARLIER RENAISSANCE PLAYS AND WORKS LIKE *HAMLET* AND *KING LEAR*.

When the young Shakespeare arrived in London, Christopher Marlowe was the preeminent playwright in town. Capitalizing on the popularity of villains from revenge tragedies, Marlowe filled his plays with a series of increasingly complex and unrepentant evildoers who reveled in engineering new and ingenious ways to make their enemies suffer. These enemies, however, were often little better than the arch-villain, and so the audience could enjoy the characters' cruelty with few pangs of conscience, much as they would any other piece of violent entertainment.

Titus, perhaps Shakespeare's earliest tragedy, takes its cue from Marlowe's inventions. Although spectators may be tempted to sympathize with the title character in his misfortunes, it is difficult to forget Tamora's admonishment as she begs for her son's life: "Sweet mercy is nobility's true badge." If this is indeed the case, then no character in the drama possesses true nobility. Titus initiates the cycle of vengeance by cruelly disfiguring and burning Tamora's eldest son, and each of the empress's subsequent actions—extreme though they may be—are to some extent justified by that first act of callous cruelty. As a result, wrong is heaped upon wrong and the characters are all left swimming in a sea of sins, just as in many of Marlowe's dramas.

However, despite its Marlovian tendencies, *Titus* is not without its innovations. In this play, Shakespeare takes the fascinating psychological complexity and amorality of some of Marlowe's most famous characters and sets it within the structure of a traditional revenge tragedy, in which murder is countered by murder and violence by violence. Inserting these complicated and self-aware characters into a stock plot allows Shakespeare not only to capitalize on the popularity of revenge tragedy but also to analyze the genre itself. As a result, he begins to ask some of the deep questions that will preoccupy him for the rest of his career as a writer. As he will in *Hamlet,* Shakespeare begins to ponder what place madness has in revenge drama—is it an impediment to his characters or its own unique brand of truth? Like in *Lear*, he reflects on the place of gratitude in the functioning of kingdoms and families—to what extent are our elders entitled to expect our loyalty and support? By combining old forms to suit his new purpose, Shakespeare produced a tragedy that would act as a springboard for his future dramas and deeper philosophical inquiries.

IN *TITUS*, REVENGE DOES NOT LEAD TO JUSTICE.

Due to its tit-for-tat plot structure and liberal distribution of well-merited punishment, it may be tempting to assume that by the end of *Titus* justice has been served. After all, each wrongdoer meets his or her demise, and in the final act Rome falls into the hands of Lucius, a proven leader. Although Christian spectators might have argued that Titus should have waited patiently for God to avenge his wrongs, *Titus* is not enacted in a Christian universe. When Titus's brother Marcus implores, "Revenge the heavens for old Andronicus," he receives no reply, and later his son Publius jokes that heaven's powers are too busy to bother with the Andronicii—the family would be lucky if Pluto, ruler of the underworld, sent a minion to aid them in their pursuit of revenge.

Nevertheless, in his exploration of the intricacies of revenge, Shakespeare is careful to differentiate between the concepts of justice and vengeance. While vengeance—especially as enacted in revenge tragedies—involves exacting an eye for an eye and a tooth for a tooth, justice must consider fairness and righteousness when it metes out its consequences. Publius argues that justice is most often "employ'd . . . with Jove in heaven"; that is, human beings are not known for their fairness and moral decency. Instead of striving to do what is right, the Roman characters of *Titus Andronicus* adhere to rigid codes of honor and conduct that lead them to counter violence with violence and lean on revenge rather than justice. In fact, the most interesting aspect of *Titus* may be the extent to which it criticizes the inflexible rules of loyalty and duty that underpin the whole structure of revenge drama

and earthly notions of "justice." Almost all of Titus's wrongs are cat-
alyzed by the fact that he insists on remaining scrupulously loyal to
Rome, abiding by its rigid rules no matter how flawed they may be.
As Shakespeare will proceed to argue in later works like *Measure for
Measure* and *The Merchant of Venice,* true heavenly justice would be
more flexible, more inscrutable, and less formulaic.

TWENTY SIX

HENRY VI, PART ONE

Following the high point of Henry V's reign, England devolves into personal rivalries and factionalism that result in the loss of France and the bloody War of the Roses.

Brief Synopsis

Henry VI, Part One begins with the funeral of Henry V, the English king who conquered France. Under the new king, **Henry VI,** England's supremacy and civil order begin to unravel. In France, the English military hero **Lord Talbot** meets increasing opposition from forces led by **Joan la Pucelle (Joan of Arc),** a Frenchwoman claiming to be sent by God to free her people. In England, the **Duke of Gloucester,** who will rule the kingdom until Henry VI comes of age, clashes violently with the **Bishop of Winchester,** who suspects Gloucester of being too ambitious.

In a garden in England, a quarrel begins between **Richard Plantagenet** (who later becomes **Duke of York**) and the **Duke of Somerset.** The other English noblemen choose sides by plucking red or white roses. This quarrel develops into the War of the Roses, in which the Houses of Lancaster and York fight for the throne. Within this play the struggle between York and Somerset results in the death of Lord Talbot and the defeat of English forces in France, as York and Somerset cannot cooperate to support Talbot adequately. Finally, the **Earl of Suffolk** persuades the young King Henry to marry Margaret, a beautiful Frenchwoman with whom Suffolk has fallen in love but cannot have, since he already has a wife. Henry submits to Suffolk's manipulations, despite the fact that he is already betrothed to a relative of the French Dauphin Charles, a marriage that would soothe the troubled political waters. Begging Gloucester's pardon, Henry agrees to marry Margaret, thus leaving himself vulnerable to domination by Suffolk via his new wife.

What to Remember About *Henry VI, Part One*

WIDESPREAD CHAOS ARISES FROM A FAMILY DISPUTE.

Henry VI, Part One depicts the beginnings of a cycle of violence and deception known as the War of the Roses, a thirty-year conflict that divided the royal family of medieval England. What begins as a rift between two branches of the same family tree eventually engulfs two entire nations, England and France. These familial conflicts have huge ramifications, as they consume the resources and lives of both nations as England embarks on a losing campaign to maintain its hold on its conquered territories.

The immediate conflict between England and France has its origins in the conquest of France that Shakespeare would later portray in *Henry V.* (Shakespeare wrote two sets of four English history plays. The first set includes the three Henry VI plays as well as a play about his successor, Richard III. The second set, written several years later, leaps back in time to cover the monarchs who preceded Henry VI:

Richard II, Henry IV, and Henry V.) Henry V argued that, according to a series of complicated ancient land laws, he was the rightful heir of the royal houses of England as well as France. The royal families of Europe had been intermarrying for a long time, making for extremely tangled family trees and complex succession laws, and because of this several nobles could make competing claims for an open (or easily vacated) throne. The Englishmen of *Henry VI* believe they rule France not solely because they defeated the French in battle but because the law supports their claim. The English did not simply conquer the throne: They made sure the rightful sovereign occupied it. Though the French, led by the Dauphin Charles, dispute the legitimacy of Henry's right to France, what is never in question is the fact that both Henry V and Charles are descendants of the same family.

On the domestic front, Henry VI's court is weakened by factionalism, and here too the disputes run roughshod over family alliances. Gloucester and Winchester are cousins, notwithstanding their bald-faced hatred of each other: Winchester's father, John of Gaunt, is Gloucester's grandfather. Likewise Richard Plantagenet, later Duke of York, and the Duke of Somerset are cousins, but that doesn't stop them from becoming bitter archenemies. Indeed, every English nobleman in the play can trace his roots to a common ancestor, Edward III, whose seven sons gave birth to all the complex and conflicting dynastic struggles that will plague the English court. In *Henry VI, Part One* Shakespeare presents a world in which family is not a source of support but a source of conflict; where only close relatives stand between a nobleman and his dreams of power.

SHAKESPEARE PRESENTS AN ENGLISH VIEW OF JOAN OF ARC.

Perhaps the most surprising and interesting aspect of *Henry VI, Part One* is the portrayal of Joan of Arc, whom Shakespeare calls Joan la Pucelle. Shakespeare presents Joan in a way that is at odds with our twenty-first-century assumptions about her but that was consistent with the Elizabethan view of Joan as an upstart French girl who defeated them so decisively and embarrassingly just a few centuries before. By portraying Joan as a scheming witch, Shakespeare asserts the superiority of Protestant thinking about Joan over the outlawed and suspect Catholic theology that esteemed her as a saint.

Modern legend depicts Joan as a brave and stalwart soldier who, at the behest of God, took arms up against the English and ran them out of France. This view has been confirmed by centuries of ennobling portrayals by the Catholic Church as well as secular works such as George Bernard Shaw's *Saint Joan*. For Shakespeare's audience, though, it was impossible to accept Joan as a heroic figure. She had humiliated England on the battlefield, acting upon what she claimed were orders from God—a claim confirmed by the Catholic Church. Given England's anti-Catholic bias, however, Joan couldn't have gotten a fair shake on its stages. Shakespeare's depiction, then, presents a point of view that is completely in line with the English orthodoxy of the time: Joan was, in fact, a witch, in league with the devil, who was only able to defeat the English using diabolical tactics.

Resentment against Joan, however, went beyond the religious: She dealt the English a stunning military defeat, and even more galling, she did it while being a woman. By portraying Joan as a witch, Shakespeare reassures the English that the loss of France was beyond their control. After all, it may be embarrassing to lose to a woman, but who can succeed against someone with satanic powers at their command? Shakespeare offers his audience a clear villain while simultaneously reinforcing the nobility of the English heroes by implying that they were beaten in an underhanded way: No man could beat Talbot in a fair fight, and by portraying Joan as the infernal force behind the French victory, it can be said that none ever did. Joan becomes a formidable antagonist and the Renaissance audience receives a reassuring narrative: God supports the English, and defeating them requires the intervention of no less than Satan himself.

TWENTY SEVEN

HENRY VI, PART TWO

King Henry VI's weakness makes England vulnerable to ambitious nobles, a manipulative queen, and rebellious commoners.

Brief Synopsis

King Henry VI of England finds his power dwindling. Infighting between the nobles has weakened Henry's support, as has disagreement over Henry's proposed marriage to **Margaret** of France, a politically dubious match. Likewise, many lords are angry that England has lost control of the French territories won by Henry's father, King Henry V. In light of Henry's lack of authority, support is growing for the **Duke of Gloucester,** the lord protector, who has ruled the kingdom since Henry was a child.

Gloucester's wife, the **Duchess,** perceives the king's weakness and decides that she wants to be queen. When her ambition finally becomes too blatant to ignore, she is arrested for having hired a witch and a conjurer and is forced to parade through the streets in shame. Gloucester is framed for treason by his fellow lords. Despite Henry's belief in his innocence, the king cannot save Gloucester because his opposition has become too powerful. Gloucester is imprisoned and assassinated by **Cardinal Beaufort** and Queen Margaret's lover **Suffolk.** Henry banishes Suffolk, though not before Suffolk and Queen Margaret can declare their love for one another. Aboard a ship bound for France, Suffolk is beheaded by pirates. Overcome with grief, Margaret carries the head around with her as she laments his death.

The **Duke of York** takes an army to Ireland to put down a rebellion there. While he is fighting the Irish abroad, York hires an English commoner, **Jack Cade,** to lead a people's rebellion against the king. York hopes that by further destabilizing Henry's power in England, he might return victorious from Ireland and lay claim to Henry's throne. Cade reaches London, where he creates havoc until he is defeated by the Lords **Buckingham** and **Clifford.** York returns from Ireland with his army, accuses **Somerset**—a supporter of Henry and York's long-time enemy—of treason, and demands his imprisonment. When King Henry fails to punish Somerset, York denounces the king and declares himself the rightful heir to the throne. With the help of his sons, York defeats Henry's army at the Battle of St. Albans, but Henry has already fled back to London at Margaret's urging. York prepares to enter London.

What to Remember About
Henry VI, Part Two

JACK CADE IS A MAN OF THE PEOPLE, SORT OF.

In Act 4 of *Henry VI, Part Two*, Shakespeare finally gives the English commoners a voice in the current problems of the kings. However, his depiction lacks a clear judgment of their role in the turbulence that surrounds England. Both comical and scary, justifiably angry and wildly anarchical, Jack Cade and his rabble give voice to the legitimate frustrations of the English citizenry with its rulers. However, they also embody a frightening element of violent chaos that reminds the audience of the brutality threatening the kingdom.

Introduced as a political pawn, Jake Cade is a commoner paid by York to stir up trouble. York also uses Cade to gauge how the public will react to York's planned coup. Once Cade launches his rebellion, though, he quickly becomes a law unto himself, marauding with his band through the towns and fields of England. Cade and his followers are fed up with the rulers of England, who remain obsessed with their own petty arguments and ignore the needs of the people. The citizens' grievances are justifiable, even though Cade himself often seems to be more concerned with his own power. In fact, Cade's response to the erring aristocracy is to claim the throne for himself while following a terrifying agenda of violence, rape, and plunder directed at women, the nobility, and anyone with an education. By the time Cade begins executing people for the crime of basic literacy, he and his band's knockabout buffoonery has taken on a decidedly nasty edge.

Despite the violent end, Cade and his revolutionaries initially provide a welcome change from the infighting of Henry VI's court. Their grievances are legitimate, and the audience—commoners themselves—may be tempted to side with them. Shakespeare may have sympathized with Cade and his men, but he also makes them vicious and stupid, murderous and actively opposed to learning. At the same time, Cade's rebellion is more than just Shakespeare's condemnation of the peasantry as thick-headed brutes who need to be controlled by more refined, better-born aristocrats. Shakespeare doesn't draw the lines so clearly. Those aristocrats, after all, have proven themselves to be just as brutal as the commoners. Shakespeare draws parallels between the two classes that suggest that the nobles are themselves a violent mob, though better dressed and with a veneer of civility. In trying to form an opinion about Jack Cade's rebellion, we end up feeling a bit like Cade's followers themselves, wooed by both a royal ambassador and a plainspoken anarchist, trying to decide whose side we are on.

WITH NO ENEMIES LEFT, ENGLAND BEGINS TO DESTROY ITSELF.

Having no threat from France to occupy them, as they did in *Henry VI, Part One*, the lords of *Henry VI, Part Two* focus their energies entirely on their own plans to acquire and consolidate power. Their conflicts tear at the nation's social fabric in a way that the war in France never did. Setting in motion a chain of events that will touch off civil wars throughout the kingdom, the feuding noblemen set about destroying the very country they are struggling to control. Shakespeare's vision of a chaotic and disordered society carefully balances the stories and perspectives of an enormous cast of characters, shifting between rival court factions, rebellious citizens, and endless casualties of war to paint a mosaic-like portrait of a country in a state of implosion.

As nobles and commoners jockey for power, and rivalries and grudges begin to give way to savagery, Shakespeare ratchets the violence and death to a level not seen in *Henry VI, Part One*. In *Part One*, characters either die of natural causes, fall nobly in battle, or, in Joan's case, are executed for war crimes. No one is murdered, and no one is dealt a deathblow on stage. In *Part Two*, violence is everywhere: Good people are brutally murdered, innocent citizens are beaten to death, and children are slaughtered. Death becomes unavoidable in a play full of horrifying images, such as Gloucester's corpse being dragged onstage. Revenge takes on a random quality as even messengers are killed when their news displeases the recipient. No one is safe. Henry himself becomes particularly vulnerable as many of his advisors revolt against him, and others who remain faithful to him are killed. His allies, including his wife, prefer to defend their own lives and honor than protect his. Henry is relegated to the role of a spectator in the drama, forced to watch as his kingdom comes apart but unable to stop it.

England's degeneration into civil war is a theme Shakespeare continues to develop in *Henry VI, Part Three*. By portraying a kingdom brought to the brink of ruin through political infighting, Shakespeare demonstrates how internal struggles can wound a nation more grievously than any threatening force from without. Shakespeare leaves few vestiges of order left intact by the end of *Henry VI, Part Two*, and what remains will be eradicated in *Part Three*.

TWENTY EIGHT

HENRY VI, PART THREE

With King Henry VI powerless, the Duke of York's family takes the crown, but the Duke of York's sons begin to struggle with one another.

Brief Synopsis

The play picks up where *Henry VI, Part Two* ended. The **Duke of York** enters the throne room in London and, finding it empty, sits in the king's throne. **King Henry VI** enters with his supporters and argues with York about who has the more rightful claim to the kingdom. York and Henry reach an agreement that Henry will remain king but that the kingdom will pass to York and York's heirs after Henry's death. **Queen Margaret** bitterly rebukes Henry for disinheriting his own son.

York's sons convince York to try to seize the throne from Henry without waiting for him to die. Angered by Henry's weakness, Margaret leads an army against York. Margaret captures York and gives him a handkerchief dipped in the blood of his dead son **Rutland** to wipe his face with. Margaret and her ally **Clifford** then stab York to death. York's remaining sons, **Richard, Edward,** and **George,** unite and continue their father's war against Margaret. Margaret and Clifford meet King Henry at the town of York, where they unsuccessfully try to convince him to reverse his decision about the throne's inheritance. Edward bursts in with his men and confronts them, demanding the throne. Arguments ensue, which Henry is powerless to stop, and Margaret and Edward agree to settle the matter on the battlefield.

Edward's and Margaret's armies battle again, with Henry watching from afar. Edward wins the battle and heads to London to be crowned king. Meanwhile, the fleeing Henry is apprehended and arrested by Edward's supporters. The **Earl of Warwick** hastens to France to negotiate a politically advantageous marriage between the newly crowned King Edward and the French king's daughter. When Warwick discovers that Edward has married **Lady Grey,** a woman beneath his rank, Warwick is furious at having been sent to France on a futile mission. Edward's brother, George, is also aggravated by Edward's marriage. In retaliation, George and Warwick join forces with Margaret and march against Edward. Richard, meanwhile, begins plotting secretly to seize the crown for himself.

Edward regains his brother George's allegiance and finally defeats Henry's forces for good. Warwick dies in battle, as does Margaret's son (also named Edward). King Edward imprisons the mourning Margaret. Richard secretly slips off to the Tower of London to murder Henry, who prophesies that thousands will suffer from Richard's deeds. Richard kills the deposed king before declaring himself separated from the ties of family and brotherhood. Since he was punished by the heavens with such unfortunate physical attributes—Richard is a hunchback—hereafter he will fight for himself alone.

Lady Grey, now queen, bears Edward a son. His kingship seems secure at last, though his brother Richard continues to plot his downfall.

What to Remember About
Henry VI, Part Three

RICHARD OF GLOUCESTER EMBODIES A LAWLESS KINGDOM.

Richard, the Duke of York's third son and namesake, dominates *Henry VI, Part Three*. During the play, Richard is named Duke of Gloucester, and he relentlessly plots to advance even higher by seizing the throne. Deformed, relentless, and unapologetically evil, Richard personifies the twisted, ruined state of England depicted in *Part Three*.

Though first introduced in *Henry VI, Part Two*, Richard only becomes a central character here in *Part Three*. At the outset, England has collapsed into a blood-soaked battlefield where loyalty, honor, and family ties are sacrificed in lethal battles for control of the kingdom. In a society already plagued by unscrupulous power struggles, Richard's amoral behavior and unrelenting pursuit of the crown seems par for the course. The England of *Henry VI, Part Three* lacks loyalty and honor; instead, ambition and avarice have replaced the country's traditional ideals. Richard is born to his time both literally and figuratively: He is a creature who embodies the warped values of a bloody-minded state. His murder of Henry VI brings Henry's tragedy to its logical conclusion: Henry is not simply murdered by his worst enemy's namesake but symbolically by a kingdom he is not fit to rule because he lacks the ruthlessness to control it.

Shakespeare's audiences would have recognized Richard's physical deformities as evidence of his inner evil. Elizabethans commonly believed that there was a strong correlation between a person's external appearance and their private selves. A person's face and body offered clues to many aspects of their personality, including their disposition, intelligence, trustworthiness, and moral character. A beautiful person was often assumed to possess an equally sterling character, while ugliness on the outside was seen as a harbinger of unattractive qualities on the inside. Deformities were considered signs of particularly grave deficiencies, and in this way Shakespeare alerted his first audiences to Richard's true nature before the villain ever speaks a word or seizes a weapon. In many ways, Richard is England: brutal, violent, twisted out of shape, and amoral.

FAMILIES DISINTEGRATE AS THE KINGDOM DOES.

In *Henry VI, Part Two*, the nation and its government descended into civil war. In *Henry VI, Part Three*, Shakespeare depicts the final collapse of that society. The chaos that stems from the breakdown of the British aristocracy also emphasizes the self-destruction of the family. At the end of this play, England has become a land of individuals, disconnected people with no ties or loyalty to anyone but themselves. The most obvious perpetrator is the ruthless Richard of Gloucester, but most characters in *Henry VI, Part Three* are guilty of having warred against either their country or their family. The entire *Henry VI* trilogy focuses on the destruction of the British royal family, but in *Part Three* the ties of blood become even more strained than before.

At each turn, family members slight each other for their own gain. Henry attempts to disinherit his son and pass the crown to York to guarantee himself a peaceful reign. His capitulation enrages Margaret and she and Prince Edward break off from Henry to engage in battle against York. From that point on, Margaret fights for herself and for her son's claim to the throne, concerning herself little with Henry, whom she only speaks to in one other scene. George, later the Duke of Clarence, turns on his own father and brothers. Betting that the Lancastrian forces can defeat the Yorkists, George exchanges family loyalty for personal safety and political expediency. Later, he returns to the Yorks when he realizes that he has picked the losing side. Richard of Gloucester confesses that he has no fraternal feelings at all for his brothers; his only loyalty is to himself and his determination to gain the crown. In fact, to reach his goal, Richard will not only have to step over his brothers and their children, he will

actually have to obliterate them. For these new rulers of England, the family as a source of loyalty and support no longer exists: In its place lies a treacherous collection of murderers and political obstacles.

During one of the bloody battles between Edward's and Margaret's armies, Henry watches as two soldiers survey the damage on the battlefield and realize, to their horror, that one has killed his own son and the other his own father. With this tragic image, Shakespeare offers a chilling symbol of the family violence that animates this play, condensing the costs and effects of civil war into a single scene in which the weeping soldiers represent the entire nation. The scene is even more starkly effective when we recall that the Lancasters and Yorks are indeed a single family, settling their domestic disputes through warfare and murdering scores of English citizens in the process.

TWENTY NINE

LOVE'S LABOR'S LOST

A king and his lords swear to avoid women but can't keep their oaths.

Brief Synopsis

The **King of Navarre** and his three lords, **Berowne, Longaville,** and **Dumaine,** swear an oath to study, fast, and avoid contact with women for three years. Their vows are soon tested when the king is visited by the **Princess of France** and her ladies, **Rosaline, Katherine,** and **Maria.** The men fall in love with the women, and although they try to conceal their feelings, their love poems and letters give them away. After agreeing to court the ladies, the men play a prank, disguising themselves as Russians before visiting the women. The ladies learn of the prank before it happens and dress in one another's clothing so that the men court the wrong ladies.

The jokes and games are cut short when a messenger arrives bearing the news that the princess's father has died. The ladies tell the men that they must wait a year before seeking them out again.

What to Remember About
Love's Labor's Lost

THE WOMEN IN *LOVE'S LABOR'S LOST* WIN THE BATTLE OF THE WITS.

In terms of action, not much happens in *Love's Labor's Lost*. But the wealth of wordplay counteracts the relatively thin plot. The women repeatedly best the men in verbal sparring matches. The princess mocks the king's oath to give up the company of women, a conversation that sets the tone for the subsequent courtships, during which the women ridicule the men's flattery and love poems. The princess also argues with the king over an old debt between their fathers. She deploys words with care and forethought, as if they are weapons. She enjoys listening to her attendants banter back and forth, but she considers such conversation a waste of their verbal skills and encourages them to save their fighting words for the king and his men.

The men fail to use words successfully or waste them on futile endeavors. Berowne quibbles over the terms of the oath he winds up signing. The king and his lords argue over whose beloved is more beautiful, with no resulting changes to their viewpoints. Costard's clever arguments about the language of the law do not save him from punishment. Nathaniel and Holofernes's contest to see who can deliver the more learned speech makes them both look ridiculous.

And at the play's end, the king tells the princess that she should remain in romantic spirits, rather than mourn the death of her father, a confusing and callous argument that does not persuade the princess to stay, as it was meant to do. *Love's Labor's Lost* is the only one of Shakespeare's romantic comedies that does not end with marriage, in part because of the men's underwhelming language skills.

THE MEN'S TALK IS A LOT OF HOT AIR; THE WOMEN'S TALK RESULTS IN ACTION.

The actions of the king and his noblemen continually conflict with their words. The men decide to form an all-male academy in the style of the ancient Greeks but cannot put this plan into practice. They swear to forgo the company of women but break their vows as soon as the princess and her entourage arrive in Navarre. Because these broken oaths begin the play, they cause us—and the princess and her ladies—to regard the men's subsequent statements with suspicion. If weakness doesn't cause the men's plans to fail, ineptitude does. For example, Berowne's and Armado's letters to their respective beloveds end up in the wrong hands, a comic emblem for men's inability to get their words in line with their goals.

Unlike the men, the women are able to convert their spoken desires into action. They not only talk in a sharply witty way, but they also prove themselves in the real world. When they desire a deer, they pursue it and kill it. When they decide to trick the men into wooing the wrong person, they carry out the prank successfully. They also recognize the difference between their words, which translate into action, and the men's words, which don't. The princess knows she can't rely on the king's word, so she refuses to accept his marriage proposal. Instead of trusting his oaths, she demands that he prove his love by living as a hermit for an entire year. The other women require similar actions from their loves. In essence, the women want the men to become more womanly by narrowing the gap between word and deed.

THIRTY

THE MERRY WIVES OF WINDSOR

Falstaff tries to seduce two wives, but they turn the tables on him and shame him.

Brief Synopsis

Sir John Falstaff attempts to seduce **Mistress Ford** and **Mistress Page,** two wealthy married women, in an effort to get money from them. Offended, the women decide to get revenge on Falstaff by pretending to desire him and playing tricks on him. They use the jealous nature of **Ford,** Mistress Ford's husband, to their advantage. After interrupting a meeting between Falstaff and Mistress Ford, Ford beats Falstaff and dunks him in a river. To pacify the jealous Ford, the wives tell him about their game. They agree to meet Falstaff in the woods and arrange to have children dress as fairies to terrify and pester Falstaff while he is exposed in front of the whole town.

Meanwhile, the unmarried men of Windsor compete for the chance to marry the Pages' daughter, **Anne Page.** Anne's mother wants her daughter to marry **Caius,** a French doctor, while her father wants her to marry a fool named **Slender.** Each parent tries to persuade Anne to disguise herself and elope with one of these men during the confusion with the children in the woods, but instead Anne elopes with **Fenton,** the impoverished gentleman whom she loves.

What to Remember About
The Merry Wives of Windsor

UNLIKE MOST OF SHAKESPEARE'S PLAYS, *THE MERRY WIVES OF WINDSOR* FOCUSES ON THE MIDDLE CLASS.

Most of Shakespeare's tragedies feature royalty or aristocracy, with an occasional country bumpkin or fool appearing for comic relief. His comedies usually depict lovers from the upper classes. In contrast, *The Merry Wives of Windsor* dramatizes the everyday lives of the emerging English middle class. Shakespeare investigates the tension between the middle class and the upper class with the story of Anne Page and her suitors. Because he is impoverished, Fenton's upper-class rank makes him seem dangerous, rather than desirable: Anne's parents worry that he only wants to marry their daughter for her wealth. Indeed, Fenton admits that he did covet Anne's money before he got to know her. The situation reverses the traditional hierarchy, suggesting that the gentleman is not good enough for the middle-class girl.

Still, elements of *The Merry Wives of Windsor* reinforce the traditional notion that the nobility are inherently superior. In the end, Fenton proves to be the most intelligent and charming of Anne's suitors. Master Slender and Doctor Caius, Anne's other suitors, are more financially stable than the gentleman Fenton, but their middle-class status makes them figures of fun. Slender is comically paralyzed with shyness when Anne appears, for example. Caius's French background makes him doubly suspicious: He is not only middle class but also a foreigner. Like the comic speech of the Welsh parson, Evans, Caius's humorous mispronunciations and malapropisms underline his position as an outsider.

If Shakespeare does not overturn conventional ideas about the superiority of the upper class, neither does he allow the aristocracy to escape unscathed. Fenton might be a smart and honorable member of the upper class, but he is counteracted by the bumbling, unethical Falstaff. A knight who reveled with Prince Harry at the royal court (see parts one and two of *Henry IV*), Falstaff represents the lingering presence of the aristocracy in Windsor. His mockery and abuse at the hands of the townspeople demonstrate the middle class's willingness to ridicule members of the upper class. Mistresses Page and Ford are offended, rather than flattered, by the advances of the fat, drunken knight and outsmart him continually. Even Falstaff's own followers, when asked to help the knight seduce the ladies, reject the request as unprincipled and insulting to their honor.

FALSTAFF IS THE CENTER OF THE PLAY'S SLAPSTICK COMEDY.

Falstaff is an amusing yet noble and moving character in the Henry plays. In *The Merry Wives of Windsor*, however, he is a slapstick physical comedian. As punishment for his attempted seduction, Falstaff is made the butt of crude jokes: beaten up while dressed as an old woman, for example, and pinched and burned by children dressed as fairies. According to an unverified legend, Queen Elizabeth I enjoyed Falstaff so much in the Henry plays that she asked Shakespeare to write a romantic comedy for him, a request Shakespeare fulfilled by penning *The Merry Wives of Windsor*. Whether or not this story is true, its existence tells us how popular Falstaff was during Shakespeare's day.

THE PROSPECT OF ADULTERY CAN BE COMIC—
BUT ONLY IF IT REMAINS A PROSPECT.

While *The Merry Wives of Windsor* finds comedy in female marital fidelity, a serious subject in early modern England, that comedy has a dark edge. The play overflows with the fear of being cuckolded (cheated on by one's wife). Horns, the traditional symbol of the cuckold, appear often, from the deer Falstaff has stolen to the horns he is made to wear in the final scene. And Ford, an obsessively jealous husband, is characteristic of a society fixated on female propriety. The play's comedy is sustained because adultery remains a threat, rather than becoming a reality. The women are faithful to their husbands and heap scorn on the man trying to tempt them. While Ford's jealousy and Falstaff's attempts at seduction become objects of ridicule, we can imagine Ford reacting violently if Falstaff had made any headway with the women.

PLAYS FOR HARDCORE SHAKESPEAREANS

THIRTY ONE

KING JOHN

King John's reign is challenged from all sides, but after he dies, England unites around his son.

Brief Synopsis

King John's right to rule is under attack. His nephew, **Arthur,** is only a child, but he has a stronger claim on the throne than John does, and **King Philip** of France supports that claim. The English and French battle to a stalemate over the French town of Angers. The townspeople propose that the two countries end their quarrel by having **Blanche,** John's niece, marry **Louis,** King Philip's son. After the marriage takes place, **Cardinal Pandolf** arrives and excommunicates John for disobeying the pope, convincing Philip to make war on John once again. John captures Arthur and returns to England, where he orders his follower **Hubert** to assassinate Arthur. Hubert can't do it, but Arthur dies trying to escape prison. The English nobles turn against King John and welcome the French invaders. John promises Pandolf that he will obey the pope, but Pandolf cannot persuade Philip to call off his armies. The English nobles come back to John's side and defeat the French. A monk poisons John, killing him. The English swear loyalty to John's son **Prince Henry.**

What to Remember About *King John*

IN *KING JOHN*, GOD DOES NOT TAKE SIDES.

While both kings claim that God inspires their actions, it becomes clear as the play progresses that they are more concerned with power than they are with piety. At the outset of the play, each monarch tries to prove that God is on his side. King John introduces himself as an agent of God, who has sent him to uphold his own right to the English throne and punish all would-be usurpers. King Philip also claims that he has come in the name of God and repeatedly defends primogeniture (the practice of allowing the oldest son to succeed the father) on religious grounds. When John asks him where he got the authority to interfere in England's affairs, Philip says "that supernal judge" gave it to him and will help him to win the war, to boot.

But God seems to have little interest in siding with one faction or the other. Every battle ends in a draw, which suggests to the citizens and kings that God is not watching them or controlling events. As time passes and both kings suffer multiple losses, they lose faith in God and become increasingly concerned with personal gain. Even the pope's legate is less interested in keeping the peace than in making the church more powerful. Eventually, people stop even paying lip service to God. When the legate demands that the Dauphin put an end to the war he started in the church's name, the Dauphin replies that he is not Rome's slave and that he will fight until he receives his fair share of power and wealth from England. Shakespeare portrays war as chaotic and purposeless, a conflict governed not by God but by men's hunger for personal gain.

FALCONBRIDGE, AN OUTSIDER, VOICES THE PLAY'S KEY IDEAS.

In a drama filled with rigid decorum, Falconbridge provides a wild, honest outsider's perspective. While the kings must maintain consistent, morally defensible political positions, Falconbridge is not obliged to be diplomatic. He can speak candidly and mock even the most powerful personalities. Falconbridge's status as a bastard child reflects his character. Both literally and figuratively, he exists in a territory between the royal, legitimate world and the common, debased one. Noting that the kings' inflexible, black-and-white positions often force them to contradict themselves, Falconbridge resolves to do what is most practical for himself and his country. His insightful opinions, interjections, and asides to the audience often express this utilitarian ethic.

Despite his habit of insulting his superiors and voicing brutal truths, Falconbridge is deeply loyal. When King John falters, Falconbridge stands by him. When John doubts himself, Falconbridge urges him to fight to keep his crown. Falconbridge is also a moral man. He says that if Hubert killed Arthur, his soul must be darker than Lucifer's. Falconbridge understands the English psyche in a way that John and the lords do not. His idea that life, justice, and truth must have fled the earth when Arthur's soul fled his body out turns out to be a surprisingly accurate prediction of the chaos that follows Arthur's death. Falconbridge's parting words provide an important insight into British history: The country will never crumble unless it undermines itself. Perhaps because of his outsider's view, Falconbridge's thoughts are some of the most truthful and enduring in all of *King John*.

THIRTY TWO

TROILUS AND CRESSIDA

Troilus persuades Cressida to be his lover, but she betrays him after being traded to the Greek camp.

Brief Synopsis

During the Trojan War, a Trojan prince named **Troilus** falls in love with **Cressida,** the daughter of a Trojan priest who has defected to the Greek side. **Pandarus,** Cressida's uncle, assists Troilus in his pursuit of Cressida. In the Greek camp, the general, **Agamemnon,** wonders why morale is low. The crafty **Ulysses** informs him that the fault lies with **Achilles,** whose lack of respect for authority has infected everyone. Achilles, the greatest Greek warrior, refuses to fight and instead spends his time sitting in his tent with his comrade and lover **Patroclus,** mocking his superiors. A challenge to single combat arrives from **Prince Hector,** the greatest Trojan warrior. Ulysses decides to have **Ajax,** a headstrong fool, fight Hector. He hopes that being passed over will hurt Achilles' pride and draw him back into the war.

Pandarus brings Troilus and Cressida together to consummate their love. The next morning, the Trojans agree to trade Cressida to the Greeks in exchange for a prisoner. She is led away by the Greek lord **Diomedes.** That afternoon, Ajax and Hector fight to a draw. After Hector and Achilles exchange insults, Hector and Troilus feast with the Greeks under a truce flag. As the camp goes to bed, Ulysses leads Troilus to the tent of Cressida's father, **Calchas,** where the Trojan prince watches from hiding as Cressida agrees to become Diomedes' lover.

The next day, Hector and Troilus return to the battlefield and drive the Greeks back, but Patroclus is killed, which brings a vengeful Achilles back into the war. Unarmed, Achilles catches Hector, orders his followers to kill him, and then drags Hector's body around the walls of Troy.

What to Remember About
Troilus and Cressida

THE EVENTS ARE SIMILAR TO THOSE IN *THE ILIAD*, BUT THE TONE IS COMPLETELY DIFFERENT.

Shakespeare's play deals with the same basic events of the Trojan War covered in Homer's *The Iliad*. In Shakespeare's hands, though, Homer's epic poem of heroes and lovers becomes a cynical tale. Battles are not frequent, bloody, and noble. Rather, on the rare occasions when battles do occur, they are lackluster affairs. Achilles, the greatest Greek warrior, repeatedly refuses to fight. When he finally does take up arms, he continues to act dishonorably, killing the defenseless Hector rather than chivalrously sparing his life, as Hector has just spared his. The highly anticipated duel between Hector and Ajax unfolds like a sparring match, with both warriors refusing to do the other harm. Finally, Diomedes' and Troilus' rivalry never progresses beyond stealing horses. The anticlimactic nature of the fighting suggests a world-weary refusal to idealize warfare.

Shakespeare casts the major figures of the Trojan War in a decidedly negative light. Greek and Trojan characters alike disparage Helen of Troy, the famed beauty whose abduction launched the war and "a thousand ships," calling her an adulteress and a whore. Most people, regardless of their nationality, think she is not worth fighting over. Homer suggests that Achilles' rage inspires his refusal to fight, but Shakespeare blames his cowardice and his homosexual relationship with Patroclus. Ulysses, the cunning Greek warrior and the hero of Homer's *The Odyssey*, is portrayed as a manipulative statesman and a spy. Even Hector, the most honorable of the bunch, quickly submits to his younger brother Troilus as he advocates returning Helen to make peace. And after Achilles and his men brutally slay him, Hector's decision to spare the life of Achilles appears foolish, rather than charitable.

Shakespeare treats love just as skeptically as he treats war. In the play's opening scenes, the comically lovesick Troilus resembles an immature Romeo. Cressida, in contrast, appears to have a sophisticated knowledge of courtship. She understands that men make promises that they break once they get what they want. Despite this knowledge, she submits to Troilus the first time we see them meet. Pandarus' constant sexual jibes make it appear that Troilus and Cressida's relationship is founded on lust, rather than on love. Cynicism pervades the scene in which Troilus and Cressida exchange vows of fidelity. An Elizabethan audience would have been familiar with Cressida's story and would have known that she was going to betray Pandarus.

CRESSIDA IS CUNNING, BUT THAT ISN'T NECESSARILY A BAD THING.

In his fourteenth-century poem *Troilus and Criseyde*, Chaucer depicts Criseyde as a pawn of forces beyond her control. While Shakespeare drew on Chaucer's poem for his play, his depiction of Cressida seems harsh in comparison to Chaucer's sympathetic portrait. Shakespeare's Cressida responds to Troilus's overtures in an intelligent, controlled way. She recognizes the value of playing hard to get. At the Greek tents, she seems to be a willing participant, rather than a helpless victim of a rapacious enemy army. She kisses the generals one by one, bragging about her skill. Later, as Troilus looks on, Cressida entertains Diomedes in her tent, flirtatiously leading him on and pushing him away. She crowns her treachery by giving Diomedes the sleeve Troilus presented her with as a token of his love.

Shakespeare's portrait of Cressida is not entirely negative, however. She may not be a model of womanly virtue and modesty, Shakespeare suggests, but that is in part because her situation forces her to be cunning. In the play, women are described as "pearls." Like pearls, they are objects of value, which also makes them objects of exchange. The Trojans literally trade Cressida for a Greek prisoner, like jewelers bartering one gem for another. Cressida is not in control of her own fate. She resembles a Greek prisoner or a trophy more than she does a free agent steering her own romantic destiny. When she flirts, withholds affection, greets her captors in a shockingly affectionate way, or seems to betray her lover, she is not necessarily acting on licentious whims; she is more likely acting in a calculated manner and using her sex appeal to gain some measure of control.

THIRTY THREE

ALL'S WELL THAT ENDS WELL

Bertram tries to avoid marrying Helena, but she tricks him into sleeping with her.

Brief Synopsis

Helena, the orphan daughter of a famous physician, cures the **King of France,** who in return allows her to marry the man she loves, **Count Bertram.** Bertram is appalled by the match and, after the wedding, flees with his scoundrel friend **Paroles** to fight in the army of the **Duke of Florence.** He sends Helena a letter stating that he will never be a husband to her until she can get his family ring from off his finger and become pregnant with his child. Helena travels to Florence and discovers that her husband is trying to seduce a widow's daughter named **Diana.** Bertram gives Diana the ring, but Diana gives it to Helena and trades places with Helena when Bertram comes to sleep with her. Back in France, Helena reveals that she is pregnant with Bertram's child, and he agrees to be a good husband.

What to Remember About
All's Well That Ends Well

ALL'S WELL THAT ENDS WELL IS NOT A TYPICAL COMEDY.

All's Well That Ends Well upends our expectations at every turn. Shakespeare takes a very familiar story pattern, in which a young man undertakes a quest and gets to marry a princess as a reward, and reverses the gender roles so that the woman undertakes the quest and gets to marry a nobleman—against his will—as her reward. This twist is surprising and unsettling, even to the characters involved. What's more, Bertram is a conspicuously unattractive character, making him an unexpected choice for a romantic lead. Shakespearean audiences are used to seeing admirable women picking men who are unworthy of them (e.g., Portia and the fortune-hunter Bassanio in *The Merchant of Venice*; Hero and the feckless Claudio in *Much Ado About Nothing*, and many others), but it seems especially difficult to reconcile ourselves to a romantic lead as odious as Bertram, who abandons Helena, tries to seduce and then abandon another innocent woman, and only repents in the play's final scene. We may be meant to perceive him as salvageable in some way, and to expect that he will mature in marriage, but the play gives us only a few hints of this, preferring to focus on his obvious flaws.

All's Well That Ends Well is often described as a "dark" or "problem" play, distinguished from the earlier, more cheerful comedies by unpleasant characters and a sophisticated bitterness toward human relations, all capped off with a "happy ending" (the marriage of Bertram and Helena) that is nothing of the sort. Nonetheless, apart from Bertram, the characters in general are a pleasant group, distinguished either by the wisdom of experience (the King of France, Lafew, the countess) or by basic decency and good intentions (Diana and the First Lord and Second Lord Dumaine). The only truly unsympathetic figure in the supporting cast is Parolles, who is less a villain than a comically value-free rogue. The ending, while controversial, is far from tragic.

The resourceful Helena, meanwhile, loved by everyone except Bertram, cuts a far more appealing figure than he does. However, her relentless pursuit of a man who is obviously unworthy of her has the unfortunate effect of diminishing her appeal as the play goes on. Nothing stands in Helena's way as she determinedly pursues the man she loves, and while we may admire her, by the time she appears to triumphantly show Bertram how he has been tricked, we no longer like her as much as we did—and our opinion of her good taste, after so long watching her chase a cad, is all but gone. The final scene demands that we celebrate the triumph of love, but it seems less a fairy-tale ending than a cynically contrived close to a cynical comedy, in which true love plays little part.

ALL'S WELL THAT ENDS WELL TAKES A PESSIMISTIC VIEW OF LOVE.

For a play ostensibly concerned with romance, *All's Well* takes a harshly cynical view of sexual love. We would expect coarse humor from characters like the clown, who exist to provide smutty comic relief, and cynics like Parolles, but surprisingly even the romantic heroine, Helena, indulges in sexual banter and has a low opinion of male sexual behavior in general. This view is justified, the play suggests, since the successful central deception, the bedroom switch that enables Helena to become pregnant by her husband, Bertram, and thus force him to stay by her side, hinges on the fact that in the dark, all women are alike to men.

Like all of Shakespeare's comedies, the plot of *All's Well That Ends Well* is primarily concerned with bringing young people together in marriage. It is not, however, a romantic play, in that it portrays men and women as fundamentally at odds. The good characters, like Helena and Diana, are moral, defending female virtue and monogamy against the lechery of Parolles and the adulterous advances of Bertram, but they are cynical about the opposite sex nevertheless. Helena is "in love" with Bertram, but she seems unconcerned by the fact that he does not love her back, busying herself instead with trapping him into marrying—first through the king's command and then by tricking him into sleeping with her. "But, O strange men!" she says, anticipating her night with Bertram. "That can such sweet use make of what they hate, / When saucy trusting of the cozen'd thoughts / Defiles the pitchy night; so lust doth play / With what it loathes for that which is away." (IV.i.21–25) In other words, men will sleep with anyone and cannot tell one woman from another. Helena takes advantage of this animal-like trait, and we applaud her practicality, but we cannot say that her ultimate union with Bertram has anything to do with romance. Marriage in this play is the result of determination on one side and lust and foolishness on the other.

THIRTY FOUR

TIMON OF ATHENS

When Timon goes broke and discovers that his friends are false, he turns against Athens, his homeland.

Brief Synopsis

Timon, a rich citizen of Athens, displays amazing generosity to his fellow citizens. When he runs out of money and into debt, his so-called friends turn on him and demand repayment. He throws a final banquet at which he serves stones and water, and then he leaves Athens. Accompanied by his faithful servant **Flavius,** he goes to live in the woods, only to discover a hidden supply of gold. Timon gives some of this gold to **Alcibiades,** an Athenian who was exiled from Athens and who plans to lead an army to destroy it. Two **senators** of Athens apologize to Timon and urge him to return, hoping his presence will stop Alcibiades, but Timon refuses. Alcibiades only punishes those Athenians who injured Timon or himself, and on hearing of Timon's death, he honors Timon, who was more admired in Athens than he believed.

What to Remember About
Timon of Athens

TIMON OFFERS SHAKESPEARE'S MOST PESSIMISTIC VIEW OF HUMANITY.

In the play's opening scenes, a philosopher named Apemantus mocks Timon for his generosity. The "churlish philosopher," as the list of characters calls him, tells Timon that his many friends are merely fools and flatterers who will abandon him after they have drained him dry. Apemantus refuses all of Timon's extravagant hospitality, sulking in a corner and scorning the lavish banquet Timon has prepared. Apemantus is a familiar type in Shakespeare. In different ways, both Jaques in *As You Like It* and the fool in *King Lear* perform a similar function, standing apart from the action of the play to comment upon it, exposing truths that the participants in that action either ignore or cannot see. These voices of realism and melancholy are usually balanced by figures of optimism and trust: the young couples who marry, the daughter who keeps faith with her father. Shakespeare generally allows for a wide range of human experience, accommodating both the lover and the cynic. But not this time.

Timon of Athens is constructed as one long vindication of Apemantus's dark view of mankind. The play is divided roughly into thirds. The first portion presents Timon as an overly generous lord, trusting of all and careless of his own limited means. He pays the artists of Athens handsomely for their work in praise of him, clears the debts of a friend who has been jailed for them, and bestows upon his servant enough money to allow the man to marry. Timon sums up his attitude toward those he loves when he tells them, "More welcome are ye to my fortunes, / Than my fortunes to me." Apemantus, of course, sees the disaster to which such a posture must lead, and from the outset the audience can see it coming too. As two lords enter Timon's banquet, they comment upon his habit of giving thanks for a gift with another gift seven times the value of the original. While the guests speak in praise of their host, we see an element of calculation to their remarks. Every friend of Timon's knows that a kindness done to the lord is an investment as much as a gift.

TIMON BECOMES THE ARCHETYPAL MISANTHROPE.

Timon outdoes even the misanthropic Apemantus by exiling himself entirely from human society. Alone in the woods, Timon curses mankind and digs for root vegetables, the most basic form of sustenance. He finds gold instead. Calling himself "Misanthropos," which means "hater of man," he lavishes that gold upon a series of visitors. His gift, however, springs from malice rather than generosity. He gives money to a general making war upon Athens so that he may have better success, and to a band of thieves hoping that the gold will ruin them. When Apemantus visits Timon in the woods, he accuses Timon of copying his act.

The conversation that follows drives home just how similar the two men have become. They begin by disagreeing, with Apemantus claiming that Timon's disaffection is illegitimate because it has been forced upon him by a change in fortune, rather than chosen freely. Timon retorts that having had so much taken from him, he now has all the more reason to hate society. The two continue back and forth in this vein until they achieve an almost comic rhythm, each playing off the other's latest jibe and taking it one step further. Though their game is a series of insults and distinctions, with Timon proclaiming that he "had rather be a beggar's dog than Apemantus" and Apemantus returning that Timon is "the cap of all the fools alive," the overwhelming effect of the scene is to demonstrate how little separates the two. Where Timon once disdained to speak with Apemantus when he put on his cynical manner, the fallen lord now competes with him to see who can be the more biting pessimist.

Timon of Athens ends with Timon dead and Athens overthrown. Only at this very end does some hope seep into the play. Though Timon is buried under an epitaph that reads, in part, "Here lie I, Timon, who all living men did hate," his hatred is buried with him. Alcibiades, the general to whom Timon had given gold in the hopes that he would lay waste to Athens, instead negotiates the peaceful conquest of the city. The play ends, as so many of Shakespeare's do, with a promise of renewal. Like *Hamlet* or *Macbeth*, *Timon* suggests that the next regime may correct the failings of the prior one. Unlike those plays, however, the ending of Timon feels almost forced—somewhat like a Hollywood movie in which the romantic happy ending is included because it is required, not because it is the natural endpoint of what precedes it. *Timon's* unique bleakness, deriving as it does from an unrelentingly dark view of human nature, cannot readily be erased by the hope of better times to come.

THIRTY FIVE

PERICLES

Pericles undergoes a long series of trials before being reunited with his wife and daughter.

Brief Synopsis

In the kingdom of Antioch, **King Antiochus** has created a riddle. Anyone who solves it correctly will win his daughter; anyone who guesses wrong will be put to death. **Pericles,** the Prince of Tyre, solves the riddle, but the answer reveals that Antiochus is having an incestuous relationship with his daughter. Worried that Antiochus will want him dead for knowing his secret, Pericles flees home to Tyre. Once there, however, he becomes fearful that Antiochus will wage war against Tyre in order to kill him, so Pericles leaves home once again. His journey brings him first to the starving nation of Tarsus, which he supplies with corn, earning the gratitude of **King Cleon** and **Queen Dionyza.** Later he is shipwrecked in Pentapolis, where he is helped by a group of fishermen. In Pentapolis, his victory in a jousting contest and his virtuous behavior win him **King Simonides'** daughter, **Thaisa.**

On the way back to Tyre, Pericles and Thaisa are caught in a storm. Thaisa dies in childbirth, and her body is thrown overboard to save the ship. Thaisa washes up in Ephesus, where **Cerimon,** a doctor, discovers she is alive and revives her. She becomes a priestess of Diana.

Concerned that she won't survive the ship voyage, Pericles leaves his daughter, **Marina,** with the king and queen of Tarsus. When Marina is grown, the jealous queen tries to murder her, but before she can commit the deed Marina is captured by pirates and sold into prostitution in Myteline, on Lesbos. Marina protects her virginity by converting the men who come to her, and eventually she finds work in a respectable house. Meanwhile, Pericles returns to Tarsus to claim Marina but is told by the king and queen that his daughter has died. Distraught, Pericles stops speaking for three months. On the way back to Tyre, Pericles and his crew land at Myteline, where they are told that a certain woman on the isle can surely cure Pericles' muteness. The woman is none other than Marina, and father and daughter are happily reunited. Later, a dream leads Pericles to Diana's temple in Ephesus, where he joyfully finds his wife, Thaisa, to be alive and well.

What to Remember About *Pericles*

THE PLAY IS A HODGEPODGE.

Pericles is a jumble of intentions, styles, times, and tones. Ben Jonson, one of Shakespeare's contemporaries, attributed the play's curious success to its use of "scraps out of every dish." This haphazard mixture may be due to the play's collaborative authorship: Most scholars believe that playwright George Wilkins wrote the initial nine scenes of *Pericles*, with Shakespeare writing the final thirteen. In *Pericles*, we get every kind of dialogue, from lowly whorehouse banter to the anguished, lofty conversations of kings and lords. We also get mixed media: Gower, the chorus figure, presents dumb shows (silent pantomimes of the ensuing action), Pericles sings to himself, and the celestial spheres themselves play heavenly music.

Pericles also mixes various sources. Many elements of the play seem to draw from classical myth and literature. The character of Pericles, for example, resembles Oedipus when he solves Antiochus's riddle and relieves the famine-plagued Tarsus. Like Odysseus, he weathers storms at sea while usurpers threaten to take his throne in his absence. The appearance of the Roman goddess Diana in the final scene strengthens the feeling that *Pericles* is a classical play. Yet other elements of the play seem to place it in Christian times. The pristine virgin Marina beatifically converts her would-be clients to virtuousness, and the fishermen who find Pericles suggest St. Peter, who was told by Jesus that he would be a "fisher of men." Pericles himself sometimes resembles Job, the biblical figure who endures an endless parade of misfortunes but remains steadfast in his belief in God, except for the fact that Pericles' endurance doesn't seem motivated by any particular faith but rather a vague commitment to staying the course.

The tournament of knights on Pentapolis, in turn, resembles the chivalric tales of King Arthur, a decidedly English and medieval source. The use of John Gower—a fourteenth-century writer whose *Confessio Amantis* was a major source for *Pericles*—as the play's narrator further emphasizes the play's medieval heritage. Finally, the alternately legendary, Christian, and medieval aspects of *Pericles* conflict with the contemporary, bawdy slang the pimps and clients use in the Lesbos brothel scenes.

PERICLES WAS A CROWD-PLEASER.

Pericles was enormously popular in Shakespeare's time and continues to be performed with success today. It contains most of the elements that give modern movies mass appeal and turn them into blockbusters: a mix of comedy and pathos, scenes packed with surprising and thrilling action, and heavy-handed moralizing. The play features plenty of sensational plot elements—some might even say too many. The imagery alone is instantly compelling, as the audience is treated to rows of skulls, stormy seascapes, and parades of knights. The plot twists are frequent, fantastic, and entertaining: A king has an incestuous relationship with his daughter; the gods strike people down with fire; pirates save a virtuous woman from death; would-be rapists are deterred by a seemingly helpless young woman; a man survives a shipwreck that kills everyone else on board; a woman buried at sea turns up alive; goddesses visit in dreams; against all odds, families are reunited.

In addition to the fantastic, occasionally absurd spectacle, *Pericles* also shows us a morally comforting vision of a world in which bad people are punished and good people are saved—eventually. The good characters suffer greatly, but they are also rescued from storms and the sea, saved from murder attempts, freed from fates worse than death, happily reunited with their long-lost loved ones, and finally given the power they deserve. The bad characters, on the other hand, suffer in due time. Antiochus and his daughter are burnt to a crisp for their sins in a magical fire from heaven. When the people of Tarsus discover Cleon and Dionyza's evil, they revolt, burning the king and queen to death in their palace. The characters in *Pericles*, however, act without any sense that a divine plan is in operation. The biblical Job knew he was being tested, but Pericles seems to have no such knowledge: He just keeps on, resigned to the power of fate, and as fortune would have it he lucks out in the end. God (in the form of his pagan stand-in, Diana) makes a brief, eleventh-hour appearance, but other than that the machinations of fortune seem entirely impersonal and mostly random. Pericles has no particular faith and learns no specific lesson from his sufferings. His tale resembles the testing of Job by God and Satan but lacks the trial aspect, which can make his eventual triumph—though deserved—seem arbitrary and unsatisfying.

THIRTY SIX

CYMBELINE

Believing that his wife Innogen is unfaithful, Posthumus tries to have her killed, but she saves herself by disguising herself as a boy.

Brief Synopsis

Innogen, the daughter of the British **King Cymbeline,** goes against her father's wishes and marries **Posthumus,** a low-born gentleman, instead of Cymbeline's oafish stepson, **Cloten.** Cymbeline sends Posthumus into exile in Italy. There, Posthumus makes a bet with **Iachimo,** a smooth-tongued Italian, that Iachimo cannot seduce Innogen. Iachimo goes to Britain, fails to seduce Innogen, hides in her bedroom to observe her as she sleeps, and steals her bracelet. He convinces Posthumus that he won the wager by showing the bracelet and accurately describing a mole on her breast. Posthumus orders his servant **Pisanio** to murder Innogen, but Pisanio convinces Innogen to disguise herself as a boy and search for Posthumus.

Innogen gets lost in the wilderness in Wales and discovers a cave wherein lives a banished nobleman named **Belarius,** who had kidnapped Cymbeline's two sons, **Guiderius** and **Arviragus,** and raised them as his own. Cloten appears, searching for Innogen. Feeling ill, Innogen drinks a potion given to her by an unsuspecting Pisanio, who was told by Cymbeline's evil wife that it was medicine. The potion makes Innogen fall into a deathlike sleep. Guiderius then kills Cloten. While she sleeps, a Roman army invades England. When Innogen awakens, she hires herself to the Roman army as a page. Posthumus and Iachimo arrive with the Romans, but Posthumus, regretting having killed Innogen, fights for the Britons, then lets himself be taken prisoner as a Roman when the Britons win. Cymbeline calls the prisoners before him, and the confusion resolves. Iachimo confesses, and Posthumus and Innogen reunite.

What to Remember About *Cymbeline*

JUPITER COMES TO THE RESCUE.

Cymbeline presents a world watched over by benevolent gods capable of sorting out the most complicated dilemmas. However, the gods' benign influence isn't felt directly until the play is close to becoming a full-fledged tragedy. In *Cymbeline*, Shakespeare piles on banishment, attempted rape, exile, kidnapping, duels, alleged poisons, various disguises, beheading, imprisonment, and warfare with such alarming speed that simply keeping track of it all becomes difficult. In fact, the play opens and closes with scenes in which characters try to untangle the story: Two gentlemen in Act 1 fill us in on the convoluted back story, and by Act 5 nearly the entire cast of characters comes onstage to help explain to the king what's been happening in the play that bears his name. The mounting complications don't just provide the play with an exciting plot: They also create a situation so dire, so complex, that only with divine help can order be happily resolved. The appearance of Jupiter and the oracle he leaves for Posthumus encourages us to see the various plot twists in *Cymbeline* as trials presided over by a higher power to some purpose, rather than a series of random close calls and bizarre coincidences.

Shakespeare wasn't the first dramatist to bring a god onstage to sort things out in the end. The device can be traced back to the ancient Greek convention known as *deus ex machina*, or "god from the machine." In many Greek plays, particularly comedies, an actor playing one of the gods in the Greek pantheon would appear in the final scene to put things right, often using elaborate stage machinery and special effects to make a dramatic entrance. By borrowing this device in a Roman context and allowing Jupiter a benevolent role in the story, Shakespeare presents a world in which the gods are firmly in charge and can be expected to reward deserving individuals, even in the midst of seeming calamity. This is ultimately a much more reassuring worldview than the one Shakespeare presents in *King Lear*, a play in which no amount of pleading seems to persuade the gods to relieve human suffering.

SHAKESPEARE REASSEMBLES HIS GREATEST HITS INTO A NEW KIND OF DRAMA.

Anyone familiar with Shakespeare's more popular plays may be forgiven for feeling a strange sense of déjà vu while reading or watching *Cymbeline*. Nearly every plot development seems to have been borrowed from another play: From *Romeo and Juliet*, there is the poison that turns out to be a sleeping potion and an exiled young man separated from his beloved; from *The Comedy of Errors*, a pair of lost twins; from *As You Like It*, a forest that seems a pastoral paradise; from *Antony and Cleopatra*, an invasion by the Roman army; from *All's Well That Ends Well*, a plot about a swindled ring; and from *Othello*, a loving husband who gives into jealous rage due to the plottings of a villainous Italian. (Even the villain's name in *Cymbeline*, Iachimo, means "little Iago.") On top of all that, Shakespeare throws in the girl-disguised-as-a-boy trick he had already used in no less than four previous plays. It's enough to suggest that Shakespeare— either bored or simply fresh out of ideas—slapped together a bunch of devices that had worked for him in the past, wrote a few scenes to connect it all, and called it a day.

The writing process probably wasn't quite so slapdash, however. Toward the end of his writing career, Shakespeare began to experiment with plays that borrowed elements of comedy and tragedy but didn't fit easily into either category. In the late nineteenth century, critics noted that four of the late plays, with their many adventures, swashbuckling heroes, and virtuous maidens, were quite similar to a certain kind of romantic adventure story popular in the Middle Ages. Because of this similarity, and in an effort to find a new name for these plays that were neither comedies nor tragedies, they began to call these set of plays—*Cymbeline, Pericles, The Winter's Tale*, and *The Tempest*—the *romances*. Prior to that distinction, there was no clear consensus about what genre these four plays fell into: In the First Folio, the first collected volume of Shakespeare's plays, *The Tempest* and *The Winter's Tale* are placed with the comedies, *Cymbeline* with the tragedies, and *Pericles* was not included at all.

These four plays share certain common thematic features, but they are united mainly by plots that center on characters who achieve happiness and redemption through extreme trial and suffering. In *Cymbeline*, both Imogen and Posthumus find happiness only after enduring tremendous pain, and we sympathize with them in part because of the sheer number of obstacles they must overcome, particularly Imogen, who seems to encounter every setback Shakespeare ever devised for one of his heroines in nonstop, rapid succession. By making the journey to happiness as arduous as possible, Shakespeare highlights the relief and joy at the end of the play, creating a resolution that seems not just happy but miraculous. In *Cymbeline*, one of his very last plays, Shakespeare creates a fantasy world where people are faced with nearly every dilemma imaginable and then shows us how courage, faith, diligence, and an occasional assist from the gods can transcend them all.

THIRTY SEVEN

THE TWO NOBLE KINSMEN

Arcite and Palamon, two equally worthy cousins, compete for Emilia's hand. Arcite beats Palamon in battle, but Palamon wins Emilia anyway.

Brief Synopsis

As **Theseus,** the Duke of Athens, returns to Athens to celebrate his wedding to **Hippolyta,** the Amazonian queen whose tribe of warrior women he has recently conquered, he is accosted by three **widowed queens** who beg for his help. Creon, the ruler of Thebes, has killed the queens' husbands and left their bodies to rot, denying them burial. Theseus goes to Thebes, conquers Creon, and restores the dead kings' remains to their spouses. He imprisons two of Creon's noblemen, **Palamon** and **Arcite,** cousins who performed nobly in the battle. From jail, Palamon and Arcite see Hippolyta's sister **Emilia** in a garden and both men fall in love with her. Because Theseus's friend **Pirithous** advocates for him, Arcite is freed on the condition that he stay away from Athens forever.

Arcite returns in disguise and wins a wrestling and running competition, gaining the attention of Theseus and Emilia. Theseus makes Arcite Emilia's servant, and the Athenians treat him as a gentleman. Meanwhile, the **Jailer's Daughter** has fallen in love with Palamon and helps him escape into the woods, where he goes into hiding. Later, when she looks for Palamon in the woods and doesn't find him, she assumes he has been devoured by wild animals and goes insane. Later, a **Doctor** tells her former **Wooer** that he can cure her by making love to her while pretending to be Palamon.

Arcite encounters Palamon in the woods, and the two agree to fight each other after Arcite brings Palamon food, armor, and files for his shackles. As they begin to fight, Theseus finds them. He is about to have them executed, but Hippolyta, Emilia, and Pirithous intervene. Theseus decrees that Palamon and Arcite will return in a month and fight a tournament for Emilia. Before the tournament, Arcite prays to Mars, the god of war, and Palamon prays to Venus, the goddess of love. Arcite wins the tournament, but before he can marry Emilia, his horse falls on him, mortally wounding him. Before he dies, he gives Emilia to Palamon.

What to Remember About
The Two Noble Kinsmen

CHIVALRY IS DEAD.

In *The Two Noble Kinsmen*, Shakespeare and his co-author, John Fletcher, criticize the knightly code of chivalry. Adherents to the chivalric code were expected to be loyal to their superiors, kind to their inferiors, and gallant to women. The rules of chivalry are not ridiculous in themselves, but Shakespeare suggests that rigid obedience to them results in absurd behavior. Arcite and Palamon sincerely love each other, but in their rush to play the traditional chivalric role of the knight who fights for glory and the hand of a beautiful woman, they poison their cousinly affection for each other. Even after their friendship dissolves, they treat each other with the gallant courtesy chivalry demands. When Arcite finds Palamon in the forest, for example, he behaves very properly, feeding him, clothing him, and allowing him to rest. His behavior is by the book, but it is also ridiculous, for both men know that their ultimate aim is to kill each other.

The chivalric code is meant to inspire noble behavior, but Shakespeare argues that it actually marginalizes women and oversimplifies complex emotions. Emilia, perhaps the most sensible character in the play, laments that Arcite or Palamon will have to die simply because the code requires men to fight over women. Her inability to stop the duel reflects the code's objectification of women. The knights speak of Emilia's power over them, but she is actually a prize to be won, rather than a wielder of power or a maker of rules. The manslaughter-committing horse puts the final nail in chivalry's coffin. The accidental slaying of Arcite shows that we can't make the world a just place simply by following a set of rules. Men might imagine that living by a code will give them control over events, but in the end, Shakespeare suggests, a bad-tempered horse will squash their rulebook.

THIS ISN'T JUST THE "KNIGHT'S TALE."

Shakespeare and Fletcher adapted the main plot of *The Two Noble Kinsmen* from "The Knight's Tale" in Geoffrey Chaucer's *The Canterbury Tales*. Like Chaucer, they focus on the conflict between the aristocratic cousins Arcite and Palamon. Unlike Chaucer, they add a prominent subplot with compelling lower-class characters. This subplot looks forward to the drama of the Restoration, the period that directly followed the English Renaissance and whose theater was characterized by bawdy language and tragicomic marriage plots. As in Restoration comedies, the lower-class characters in *Kinsmen* are known only by generic names such as the Jailer, the Jailer's Daughter, and the Wooer.

The Jailer's Daughter is at the center of the subplot. At first, it appears that her humble social status, which places her well below most of society's radar, gives her more freedom than the noble Emilia enjoys. She is not given away, like a prize; her father insists that the Wooer gain his daughter's consent before he will agree to a marriage proposal. Her love for Palamon challenges social norms: It is a product of genuine sexual attraction, and it blatantly crosses class boundaries. She further flouts society's rules by helping Palamon escape, disobeying Athenian law and threatening her father with execution. But once Palamon spurns her advances, the power of the Jailer's Daughter dissipates. In a development typical of seventeenth-century female characters, she goes mad with lovesickness, singing and raving wildly as the Doctor and the Wooer conspire to cure her hysteria by taking her virginity. Just as Emilia is forced to accept a spouse based on Theseus's rules, the Jailer's Daughter must accept her father's choice in the end.

THIRTY EIGHT

HENRY VIII

During Henry VIII's reign, a series of powerful men
and women of the kingdom fall from grace so that
history can bring about the birth of Henry's daughter,
Elizabeth.

Brief Synopsis

The powerful **Duke of Buckingham** publicly criticizes
the influence that the church leader, **Cardinal Wolsey,** has
on **King Henry,** and he promptly ends up in prison. After
Wolsey produces a witness accusing Buckingham of disloy-
alty, Henry has Buckingham executed, despite Buckingham's
eloquent defense. Henry falls in love with **Anne Boleyn** and
petitions the pope for a divorce from his wife, **Katherine.**
Katherine beseeches Henry not to divorce her after her years
of faithful devotion, but Henry is not convinced. Henry discovers that Wolsey has betrayed him by urging the pope not
to grant the divorce and by enriching himself with possessions
seized from fallen lords. Henry strips Wolsey of his title and
possessions and has him killed. Henry marries Anne Boleyn,
who soon becomes pregnant with **Elizabeth.** Henry's friend
Cranmer, the Archbishop of Canterbury, is falsely accused
by Henry's council and almost executed, but Henry rescues
him. Cranmer is godparent at Elizabeth's christening.

What to Remember About *Henry VIII*

THE PLAY COMMENTS ON CONTEMPORARY POLITICAL ISSUES WHILE DENYING THAT IT IS DOING SO.

Stories about a nation's history are often viewed as commentary on its present. *Richard II*, the first in Shakespeare's sequence of English history plays, is set in the Middle Ages, but audiences saw parallels between the ill-advised and ultimately deposed Richard and their own Queen Elizabeth. All of Shakespeare's histories are relevant to the issues of his day, but *Henry VIII* is unique in the starkness of its political relevance: The play concludes with the onstage presentation of the infant who will become Queen Elizabeth, whose reign was only ten years past when *Henry VIII* was first performed.

The same questions about succession and religion that animated the reign of Henry VIII were alive in Shakespeare's England. When *Henry VIII* debuted, uncertainty abounded. Queen Elizabeth had died childless and heirless, and people questioned the legitimacy of her successor, King James. King James's son, Prince Henry, had recently died. His death worried critics of James's pacific response to Europe's religious wars, as they had hoped that Henry would prove more bellicose. The English Reformation had begun under Henry VIII, but many felt that neither he nor his successors had completed it. Some wanted further religious reform. (Disagreements about the beliefs and practices of the Church of England would contribute to the outbreak of a civil war within thirty years.)

Shakespeare (and John Fletcher, his collaborator on this play) did not enjoy freedom of political speech, so they had to exercise caution. Their handling of Archbishop Cranmer's prophecy illustrates their method of dealing with politically sensitive subject matter. At the play's end, Cranmer predicts that the infant Elizabeth will die a virgin and therefore reproduce like the mythological phoenix, which emerges reborn from its own ashes. In Cranmer's metaphor, the reborn phoenix is Elizabeth's successor, King James I, who will inherit the queen's "peace, plenty, love, truth, terror." Cranmer's assertion that no political tensions will exist in the future—for surely there can be no dissent in a land that knows "peace, plenty, love, truth, terror"—denies that any parallels exist between past tensions and the present. The speech offers the play a neat conclusion and the playwrights a chance to deny that theirs is a politically provocative work.

THE PLAY DOESN'T GIVE ALL THE JUICY DETAILS OF HENRY'S REIGN, BUT IT DOES PROVIDE A HEALTHY DOSE OF POLITICAL INTRIGUE.

While Shakespeare and Fletcher tackle many politically tricky issues, they avoid just as many as they address. They ignore Henry's colorful religious and personal background, for example. Before he initiated the English Reformation, Henry VIII had been named a Defender of the Faith by the pope for his vigorous opposition to Protestantism. His passion for reform was motivated less by a commitment to doctrinal reform than by a desire to remarry. Henry was an adulterer who would renounce and execute the future queen's mother before marrying four more women.

The most curious omission may be that of the future Queen Mary, Henry's daughter by the Catholic Queen Katherine. Mary was an inflammatory figure who reversed the English Reformation and returned the country to Catholicism. When, in the play, Henry says that he has never fathered a child before Elizabeth, the strength of the statement derives from its blatant contradiction of widely known facts. Just as Anne Boleyn is redeemed because she mothers Elizabeth, so Katherine, an attractive character opposed throughout the play to the conniving Wolsey, would have been undermined by an emphasis on her daughter Mary.

Henry VIII refuses to satisfy its audience's desire for political dissension and lurid personal details, probably because Shakespeare and Fletcher were eager to avoid subjects that might offend the royals.

The play does, however, provide an insider's view of the king's council. We get intrigue among Henry's advisors, false charges of treason, unjust executions, secret correspondences with Rome, double-crossings, and falls from power. As the play's events unfold, two unnamed gentlemen repeatedly gossip and exchange the news. They, like us, are titillated by the inner workings of a royal court. *Henry VIII* was originally performed under the title *All Is True*. Though Shakespeare and Fletcher withhold a great deal, they bring us into the most private spaces of the monarchy and promise the truth about what they depict.

BONUS: POETRY!

THIRTY NINE

THE SONNETS

In a series of 154 sonnets, Shakespeare explores themes of love, desire, and jealousy.

Brief Synopsis

In the early sonnets, the speaker tries to persuade a young man to marry. In the later sonnets, the speaker describes his desire for a dark woman, about whom he has ambivalent feelings. The middle sonnets are addressed to the speaker's beloved, whose gender is not usually specified.

What to Remember About the Sonnets

THE SONNETS ARE FILLED WITH MYSTERIES.

Shakespeare's sonnets raise many questions that we cannot answer conclusively. The dedication sets the mysterious tone. It is not entirely who wrote it, although the printer seems to be the author. Neither is it clear whether the "begetter" mentioned is the author of the poems or the person or persons who inspired them. Likewise, the initials "W. H." could be a misprint of "W. S." (William Shakespeare) or a reference to the addressee of the sequence. The poems themselves are chock-full of interpretive mysteries. The relentless punning gives single words multiple meanings, and most lines support several interpretations. Because each poem functions on different levels, it is impossible to decide whether the poems mean what they say on the surface or whether their underlying implications are more important. The sequence provides nearly endless opportunities for analysis and interpretation.

Perhaps the most intriguing question is whether the speaker of the poems is a character created by Shakespeare or a mouthpiece for Shakespeare himself. The poems feel not like abstract meditations, but rather like deeply personal declarations of love to particular lovers and meditations on the poet's specific concerns. The qualities of the male and female addressees don't change. Throughout the sequence, the man is young, beautiful, and unfaithful to the poet, and the woman is dark-haired, possibly dark-complexioned, and also unfaithful. The speaker of the sequence worries about aging, hopes that his poetry will live for generations, and compares his verses to those of other poets. Still, there are no true markers of identity that suggest Shakespeare is writing in his own voice. No names, places, or specific events appear in the sequence. The only possible exception comes in Sonnet 135, which puns repeatedly on the word "will."

THE SONNETS ARE EROTIC.

Shakespeare's sonnets are often thought of as love poetry, and they certainly are that, but they are also *lust* poetry. They include lots of sexually suggestive language. Bawdy puns often deflate lofty meditations on love and mortality. Shakespeare frequently uses Elizabethan slang for genitalia, semen, and sexually transmitted diseases. In addition to this sexual wordplay, the poems take sex as a serious theme, investigating lust and the guilt that accompanies it, promiscuity and its effect on reputation, and the emotional suffering that comes with sexual jealousy. They deal with love's carnal elements as much as they do with its spiritual elements.

The sonnets' eroticism is both heterosexual and homosexual. The poems describe extramarital affairs between the speaker and his male and female lovers. By playing with gendered pronouns, the speaker draws attention to his love for both men and women and reveals his self-consciousness about it. The first 126 poems clearly address a young man, and though there is no conclusive evidence that the addressee is the same man throughout, consistent thematic concerns and the series of betrayals and counter-betrayals seem to point to one particular relationship. The later poems refer to a mistress who takes other lovers. One of these lovers is a friend of the poet's, perhaps the young man addressed in the earlier poems. The love affairs are tangled, but the speaker's erotic and jealous feelings toward the man and the woman are clear.

THE SONNETS ARE POEMS ABOUT POEMS.

The sonnet form, modeled after Italian love poetry, was extremely popular in Renaissance England, and Shakespeare seeks to differentiate himself from the emerging mass of sonnet writers. He does this most obviously by writing brilliant poetry. The speaker takes the unusual step of criticizing his addressees. He refuses to compare his lover to traditional objects such as precious jewels or the sun, moon, and stars. He employs familiar tropes in unexpected ways, comparing, for example, his lover to a worm-infested flower. Like a swaggering emcee, the speaker also explicitly points out his own unique style and the lasting power of his words. In addition to using surprising metaphors, he discusses his own use of surprising metaphors. He points out his frank criticism of his beloved and notes his own refusal to trade in the exaggerated flattery most poets rely on.

He might refrain from exaggerating his lovers' good qualities, but the poet doesn't mind boasting about his own poetic prowess. He says that his poetry is more honest than his rivals'. He also claims that it will survive to show his lover to successive generations. Time is the great antagonist in the sequence, the inevitable destroyer of life and beauty. The speaker of the sonnets offers poetry as the best defense against time. His poetry, he says, will immortalize both his beloved and his own words. He compares his verses to monuments that might outlast even the pyramids. These claims are bold, but we know them to be entirely accurate: In the sonnets, Shakespeare's speaker, his addressees, and his words have survived to this day.

FORTY

VENUS AND ADONIS

In this long narrative poem, the goddess of love fails to make Adonis love her.

Brief Synopsis

Venus, the goddess of love, falls in love with a beautiful youth named Adonis. He is more interested in hunting boar with his friends than he is in spending time with her. Afraid for his safety, Venus urges him not to hunt, but he does anyway, and a boar kills him. Adonis turns into a purple flower, which Venus plucks and keeps between her breasts.

What to Remember About *Venus and Adonis*

VENUS AND ADONIS URGES YOUNG MEN TO TAKE ADVANTAGE OF THEIR YOUTH AND BEAUTY.

Shakespeare patterns *Venus and Adonis* after many of the tales in Ovid's *Metamophoses*. Like Ovid's stories, the poem features gods, goddesses, and mortals and ends with a human being transformed into something inhuman. Unlike Ovid's stories (and unlike the poetry of Shakespeare's day), the poem does not offer clear moral instruction. There is a moral, but at times it is hard to discern. The two main characters, Venus and Adonis, represent two warring moral viewpoints, and for much of the poem, we are not sure which opinion we are meant to support. Venus believes in seizing the day and enjoying love while you can, while Adonis differentiates between love and lust and says that young men can be corrupted if they submit to lust too early.

For the first three quarters of the poem, it seems possible that Adonis's point of view will triumph. Sensual, whimsical Venus defends her philosophy at greater length, but the grave and wise Adonis holds the more traditional viewpoint. In addition, Shakespeare's Venus often comes across as pitiful. She makes desperate arguments, and when she cannot persuade Adonis with logic, she resorts to retaining him physically. However, at the poem's end, Adonis is punished for not taking advantage of his youth. Shakespeare may have intended this lesson to sink in with the eighteen-year-old Earl of Southampton, to whom the poem is dedicated. Whatever the Earl thought, other youths approved: Shakespeare's entertaining, sensual romp became very popular among young men.

VENUS AND ADONIS CRITICIZES FEMININE LUST.

Shakespeare's Venus is opaque. At times she seems as coy, fair, and rosy-cheeked as the traditional Roman characterization of the goddess; at other times, she appears grossly physical and almost human in her needs and desires. Her moods change rapidly. One moment she is discoursing eloquently, and the next she is fainting or weeping like a child. She comes across as proud but frequently acts desperate. This Venus is particularly feminine and peculiarly fickle. Although her philosophy wins the day, Venus herself is not held up as a model of womanly behavior. With his unflattering portrayal of the goddess, Shakespeare may be criticizing feminine carnality. As Adonis notes,

Venus seems to represent Lust more faithfully than she does Love. Shakespeare suggests that other forms of love, such as friendship or intellectual attraction, may be more enduring and rewarding than the lust that motivates Venus.

FORTY ONE

THE RAPE
OF LUCRECE

**Shakespeare's second narrative poem describes the rape
that led to the creation of the Roman republic.**

Brief Synopsis

At the Roman siege of Ardea, a group of Roman noblemen
compete to see who has the best wife. Collatine's wife, Lucrece, wins. Tarquin, the son of the Roman king, goes to Collatine's house and rapes Lucrece. She sends for her husband
and kinsmen, reveals Tarquin's crime, and makes them swear
to avenge her. She then stabs herself to death. Junius Brutus,
a Roman nobleman, avenges her rape by driving the Tarquins
out of Rome and founding the Roman republic.

What to Remember About
The Rape of Lucrece

IT'S LUCRECE'S STORY, BUT SHAKESPEARE
FOCUSES ON TARQUIN.

If *The Rape of Lucrece* adhered to the genre conventions of
the heroine's lament, it would present events from Lucrece's

point of view and ask us to sympathize exclusively with her. But Shakespeare breaks with genre conventions. He doesn't introduce Lucrece, the title character, heroine, and victim of the story, until midway through the poem. His interest in her seems perfunctory. She is moral and unimpeachable and therefore not nearly as fascinating as Tarquin, the rapist, who knows that he is making a bad choice but lets his lust overwhelm his judgment. Shakespeare places the drama primarily in Tarquin's head, capturing his intriguing thoughts and philosophy. As in *Venus and Adonis*, the lustful, imperfect sinner is far more complex than the victimized character and therefore far more worthy of Shakespeare's attention.

THE RAPE OF LUCRECE IS PEPPERED WITH PARADOX.

Tarquin is a contradictory character. A thoughtful, moral man, he nevertheless commits a thoughtless, immoral act. The results of his actions are as paradoxical as the man himself, which Shakespeare conveys using paradoxical language. He notes that Tarquin loses by gaining: He has his fun but loses his honor. Lucrece finds herself in a similar situation. She is her own friend, because she must support herself, and her own foe, because she hates anyone who has been unfaithful, as she has been against her will. She wants both to defend herself and to harm herself. Her body has been defiled, but her intentions are pure. The relationship between Tarquin and Lucrece is also paradoxical. Lucrece's beauty and chastity elicit sinful behavior from an intelligent man. The fact that virtue inspires vice may be illogical, or at least unfair, but Shakespeare suggests that it is an inescapable fact of human existence.

Notes

Notes

Notes

Notes

Notes

Notes

Notes

Notes